READING MYSTICAL LYRIC

The Case of Jalal al-Din Rumi

STUDIES IN
COMPARATIVE RELIGION

Frederick M. Denny, Series Editor

READING MYSTICAL LYRIC

The Case of Jalal al-Din Rumi

Fatemeh Keshavarz

UNIVERSITY OF SOUTH CAROLINA PRESS

Published in Columbia, South Carolina, by the
University of South Carolina Press

Manufactured in the United States of America

Published 1998
Paperback edition 2004

08 07 06 05 04 5 4 3 2 1

The Library of Congress has cataloged the cloth edition as follows:

Keshavarz, Fatemeh, 1952–
Reading mystical lyric : the case of Jalal al-Din Rumi / Fatemeh Keshavarz.
p. cm.—(Studies in comparative religion)
Includes bibliographical references and index.
ISBN 1–57003–180–0
1. Jalal al-Din Rumi, Maulana, 1207–1273—Criticism and interpretation. I. Title. II. Series: Studies in comparative religion (Columbia, S.C.)
PK6482.K46 1998
891′.5511—dc21 97–21236

ISBN 1-57003-584-9 (pbk.)

For Ahmet
with unceasing love
"ān chinān kaz sharq rūyad āftāb"

CONTENTS

EDITOR'S PREFACE

In this day of global fundamentalisms and stress between Islam and the West, people on all sides nevertheless find common ground in the poems of Jalāl al-Dīn Rumi, increasingly known and admired by poetry lovers of all religions, cultures, and nations. Indeed, Rumi is one of the best-selling poets in English!

People who study Islam, and particularly Sufism, usually discover Rumi to represent one of the deepest springs of Islamic sensibility and values, accessible to ordinary readers as well as scholars, to pious Muslims as well as seekers from other faiths. Rumi's lyric poetry is treasured for its incisiveness, wit, playfulness, paradoxes, imagery, music, and beauty. Although Islamic themes and ideas are part of this art, Fatemeh Keshavarz goes well beyond such reductions to an engagement with a Rumi heretofore unknown to outsiders, who often think of his poetry merely in terms of correspondences between artistic imagery and spiritual/doctrinal meaning, however fresh and arresting. But a dimension of Rumi that is not well known is his thoroughly realized identity as a creative artist. That is, his poetry is not inspired by "mysticism" so much as his vision is achieved through the medium of poetic art. Keshavarz has given us a new way of reading, appreciating, and understanding Rumi through a masterful analysis of his development of the Persian lyric (*ghazal*) in relation to his life and times.

Frederick Mathewson Denny

PREFACE

This book is a first step toward a new critical engagement with the poetry of Jalāl al-Dīn Rumi and by extension all medieval Near Eastern lyric. It is time that this vast and dynamic body of poetry be appreciated for its lively presence in all arenas of human struggle and change. I describe this critical approach, in chapter five, as "observing the poems in action."

In my own attempt to observe the colorful but turbulent lyrics of Rumi in action, I do not depend on single *ghazals* but on the entire *Dīvān-i Shams* as an embodiment of a world view. In the first chapter, I look at Rumi's life and personality to highlight factors besides the presence of Shams that are relevant in the orientation, coloring, and dynamics of his poetry. In chapter 2, I target the two general misconceptions that he wrote poetry reluctantly and that his poetic experience was other than his mystical yearning. Chapter 3 is devoted to Rumi's use of paradox, a literary device he employed abundantly to articulate the unresolved duality in love. Rumi's constant, loud comments on silence have often been taken as proof of his reluctance to write poetry. However, in chapter 4, I attempt to demonstrate that, far from a sign of reluctance, in the *Dīvān* silence is an effective poetic tool. The process of image-making is one in which the dynamic and interactive nature of Rumi's lyrics can be examined effectively. It is mostly through this technique that the "wondrous birds grown from the palm of [his] hand" are given, through the fictive force of poetry, the momentum to remain airborne. To capture the playfulness of these images is the key to decoding their symbolic enactment. Chapters 6 and 7 explore Rumi's use of rhythm in the *Dīvān*. The former focuses on rhythm at the sonic surface of the poems, the audible music that they make, and the latter on a more deeply ingrained rhythm, the organizing impulse within the work. In chapter 7, I attempt to show that although Rumi was devoted to dancing and music, his fundamental poetic impulse was inspired by a more rudimentary circumstance: the experiences of childhood. Chapter 8 is a summation of the previous chapters intended to underscore Rumi's contribution to remapping the horizons of the Persian *ghazal*.

I have received unceasing support from many friends and colleagues in completing this project. Above all, I am grateful to the Department of Asian and Near Eastern Languages and Literatures at Washington University, a fine environment for work and growth. I am particularly indebted to Peter Heath and the late William H. Matheson of Washington University and John Renard of St. Louis University for their in-depth critical comments and to Beata Grant of Washington University for her patience in smoothing the stylistic rough edges in the unruly first draft. Engin Akarli of Brown University and Marvin Marcus and Mohamed-Salah Omri, both of Washington University, read the entire manuscript and made pertinent suggestions. Ahmad Karimi-Hakkak, of the University of Washington in Seattle, provided constructive criticism for the revision of the first draft.

Finally, it is to my husband, Ahmet T. Karamustafa, that I am fully and happily indebted for the beginning, growth, and completion of this project. Without his inspiration, support, criticism, and love, this venture might not have happened at all and certainly would have been a lot less fun.

A NOTE ON TRANSLITERATION AND DATING

I have used the Library of Congress Transliteration system throughout, except in the case of the Persian originals quoted in chapters 6 and 7 for the study of their sonic rhythm. In the Library of Congress system the emphasis is on accurate transcription of the alphabet, whereas in these chapters I wish to foreground the accent, intonation, and generally the sound. Minor modifications adopted for this purpose include the substitution of *e* for *i* in the case of the short vowel *kasrah* and the omission of the silent *h*.

In dating, I have used the Christian calendar alone to avoid cluttering a text that contains Persian terms and numerical references to the *Dīvān*. The process for conversion to the Islamic calendar is widely known and available to the interested scholar.

READING MYSTICAL LYRIC

The Case of Jalal al-Din Rumi

CHAPTER 1

Rumi
The Person and the Poet

The Problem of Defining Rumi's Identify

I Wonder Which Me Is Me?

Rumi's persona is prominent in his didactic work, the *Masnavī*.[1] In that chain of colorful stories interspersed with ringlets of lyric moments, his personality is defined and palpable. His voice remains distinct in the midst of the numerous narrative lines that fade into one another, personalities that merge and separate, and parables that are revived long after they were thought to have been abandoned by the author. At times, his voice acquires an admonishing tone, a biting humor with an almost postmodern hint. Despite his general devotion to lyricism, here he is the "sober mystic," the "master," the "mace-bearer." When the need arises, he reaches within to resurrect the jurist, the logician, the prosodist, the grammarian, or the philosopher. Yet readers know the one voice that is his, the voice that contains the others and still remains distinct. One soon realizes that this distinctiveness is intentional, designed to serve a very special purpose. He intends to remain visible as does a lighthouse in a stormy sea, so that travelers will not lose their way. In the *Masnavī*, nothing obscures this ultimate homiletic purpose.

When he preaches from the pulpit of *al-Asrār al-Jalālīyah*, today known as the *Fīhi mā fīh*, it is a different story. These anecdotes, comprising a fragmented mirror that was pieced together by his disciples after his death, reflect a different accessible presence.[2] In them, Rumi preaches as he interacts with the congregation. The purpose of his utterances is clearly to be more immediate and to evoke everyday matters to which his audience can readily relate. The language is accordingly simpler, the stories shorter, and the concepts easier to disentangle. Rumi's own personality finds a diverse reflection in the work: at times he admonishes an amir as powerful as Muʿīn al-Dīn Parvānah, at others he remains permissive enough for some members of the congregation to fall asleep as he speaks.[3] Indeed, he takes pride in this latter event, because it is an indication of the extent to which his words instill a sense of safety in his audience. He likens these words to the barking of the dog and crowing of the rooster in a village which fill the travelers on a dangerous road with relief as they realize that a safe destination is within reach.[4] This metaphor is a good example of how personal and intimate his relationship with his audience in this work is, despite the fact that he is preaching to them from a pulpit. As a result of the relative informality of this oral genre and the presence of a familiar audience, the *Fīhi mā fīh* gives readers glimpses of Rumi's own personal experience, too. His remarks frequently come close to being autobiographical, often in the form of little allegorical tales. The intoxicated, he thus reminds us, do not look for an attentive audience. They are so full that their words overflow irrespective of the merits of those who hear them. Then, in compensation for portraying his audience as possibly undeserving, Rumi transforms them into *sag'bachigān-i maḥallih* (little puppies in the neighborhood) and assigns himself the motherly role of feeding them. Such intoxicated wayfarers, he says, are like a woman whose breasts are so full of milk that she offers it to the little puppies in the neighborhood so as to be relieved of her own pain and pressure.[5] Here, not only is the audience assured of being fed regardless of who they are, but they encounter a vulnerable Rumi who confesses to the pain of concealing secrets in moments of intoxication. He has descended from the pulpit and offered his audience a mutual relationship in which caring is important and shortcomings are safe to be revealed. Refreshing as these anecdotes are, they create complications. It is hard, at least in a conventional sense, to reconcile the able master, the preacher, and the jurisprudent with the rooster of the village and the feeder of the puppies.

There is a rarely mentioned fact which adds to this complication: besides the *Masnavī* and the *Fīhi mā fīh*, Rumi is the author of the *Dīvān-i Shams*, a collection of over 35,000 verses of mystical lyric.[6] When Rumi's role as the author of the *Dīvān* is added to the picture, the enigma of his identity becomes even harder to resolve. In the *Dīvān*, Rumi presents an entirely new face. He abandons his narrative style and didactic tone in favor of visual articulation through imagery. Furthermore, he adopts a deeply paradoxical mode of expression that mocks verbal articulation as well as other conventional tools. In general, his engagement with the lyric genre leads to unpredictable results. The traditional *ghazal* was thoroughly selective concerning its themes and terminology. Its tight sonic surface encased sets of elusive concepts, juxtaposed with one another and shaped into poems of five to twelve or thirteen lines. In the *Dīvān*, there are new thematic concerns, a broader poetic vision, and *ghazals* that are often over twenty verses long.[7] In place of the usual love-stricken and tearful poet disappointed with his beloved and discouraged with destiny, we see flashes of a dynamic personality. The poet is not overheard as he whispers to himself. Instead, dramatic moments arise in which we are confronted with his fleeting but forceful personality. At times, he exhibits the persistence or playfulness of a child. The reader/audience is directly addressed, questioned, intrigued, and finally dragged into whirling scenes of images and ideas. The somber and melancholic tone, so common to the genre of *ghazal*, gives way to a lively musical beat. In this poetic universe, Rumi's unconventional, dramatic, and action-oriented self reveals to us a many-sided face that embodies the paradoxical coexistence of conflicting human desires. It brings together the restless child and the wise thinker, the spiritual guide and the earthly teacher, the champion of silence and the prolific poet. This facet of Rumi's artistic persona has remained neglected probably because by nature it eludes full comprehension.

It is the rainy season, I dig a canal;
In the hope of union I clap my hands.
The clouds are pregnant with drops from the sea of love;
I am pregnant with those clouds.
Don't say you are not a musician, clap your hands!
Come! I will teach you to become one.

So bright! will you tell me whose house is that?
I love bright houses so!
Alas! I hide my own water of life
As oil drops cover the surface of water.

(D, 1672)

"The master" who leads the way with certitude in the *Masnavī* and the preacher who feeds his audience in *Fīhi mā fīh* are wearing the garb of their age. They speak to us with the rhetoric of centuries passed. The poetic persona in the *Dīvān*, however, despite being rooted in the Middle Ages and despite his many faces, looks as familiar as a contemporary poet living in the neighborhood. In a poem as short as the above, for instance, he performs a task as "unpoetic" as digging a canal and combines it with the least-expected role a male Persian poet may play in the classical period: becoming pregnant with raindrops. In the rest of the *ghazal*, he poses as a music teacher, an ordinary person desiring a home, a drop of oil, and finally a philosopher searching for his "true" self.

The present monograph is dedicated to an exploration of this fascinating face of Rumi: that of the poet. The *Dīvān-i Shams* will constitute the source material for this study. To find Rumi the poet, we shall have to concentrate on the poems themselves and on the events in his life that are likely to have been formative for his poetic vision.

The Two Major Uprootings: A Fresh Reading of Biographical Facts

Rumi is one of the few figures in classical Persian literature whose life has been comprehensively documented by his contemporaries.[8] Modern scholars have also taken a keen interest in his biography.[9] Considering the sophistication of these scholarly biographical explorations, it is unlikely that entirely new facts of Rumi's life will be unearthed. Our purpose, however, is to devise fresh ways to read the existing information in search of clues that would lead to a better understanding of Rumi's lyric poetry. In Rumi's case, seeing the old facts in a new light is essential in constructing a fresh perspective on his life and his literary contribution.

As an illustration of this point, let us scrutinize the way the existing biographical literature on Rumi handles moments in his life in which our poet allowed the force of his individuality to transgress the boundaries of tradition. One frequently discussed example is his whirling in the marketplace, which must have been striking and probably disruptive to the commercial life of the market.[10] Similarly, he abandoned all ordinary activity and took to wearing black from head to foot. On another such occasion, he turned the funeral of his disciple Ṣalāḥ al-Dīn the Goldsmith into a whirling dance.[11] Such unconventional actions are often portrayed by Rumi's biographers as interesting isolated events. The inquiry is not extended to his literary output. In other words, there has been no effort to critically investigate parallel unconventional features in his lyric work. Even at the outset, nonconformist qualities of the *Dīvān* challenge us to find out if here, too, we are facing a whirling in the marketplace, a symbolic change of the outfit, or better still, a funeral transformed into a whirling dance.[12] It is my contention that this, in fact, is the case. In Rumi the lyricist, we have a poet whose whirling disrupted the ordinary generic life of the *ghazal*. In more technical terms, his response to the conventional challenges of the genre, in tandem with his reaction to social and intellectual conventions, altered its main features and expanded its generic horizons. Let us therefore sift the existing biographical data on Rumi in search of events that may help us find a fresh perspective in understanding his lyric poetry.

Jalāl al-Dīn Rumi was born in 1207 in the city of Balkh in present-day

Afghanistan. In the early decades of the thirteenth century, the area in which he lived was threatened by the imminent wide-scale invasion of the Mongols from Central Asia.[13] Although Rumi was fortunate not to witness this invasion personally, he nevertheless experienced being completely uprooted at the age of five when his family embarked on a westward migration that lasted at least two years. The events of the journey are shrouded in mystery: all we know is that the family finally settled in the city of Konya in the heart of Anatolia.[14] On the whole, the upheavals and the deep social and economic problems of the last years of the Khvārazmshāhid rule must have greatly affected the family.[15] On a different note, the hostilities between the well-known theologian Fakhr al-Dīn Rāzī (d. 1209–1210), who was influential at court, and Rumi's father Bahā᾽ al-Dīn Valad must have been another source of anxiety, though Rumi was too young to be directly exposed to it.[16]

The journey brought Rumi into contact with a variety of peoples and ways of life. In Konya, he must have learned to come to terms with yet more cultural differences. When he grew older, he must have realized that the journey had saved his life and that of the entire family. Whatever the change meant to him in terms of lifestyle, it seems to have led him to associate exploration and change with a better comprehension of objective and subjective realities. He later wrote:

> If the tree was able to move from place to place;
> It would not suffer from the saw and the harshly inflicted wounds.
> (D, 214:1)

The uprooting had been vital. The move had led him away from death and destruction to life and to a new home.

In Konya, Rumi spent what seems to have been a happy and uneventful adolescence. He must have been well-trained and well-liked among his father's circle of friends. Upon Bahā᾽ al-Dīn's death, and in response to popular demand, he took over his father's teaching and preaching duties at the age of twenty-four.[17] This event marked the beginning of a decade characterized by Rumi's own pursuit of knowledge more than by teaching or preaching. The sources tell us that this quest took him to such centers of learning as Aleppo and Damascus. His own works demonstrate that he received a rigorous education that rooted him firmly in the literary, legal, and theological sciences of the time. As his frequent allusions to Sanā᾽ī (d. 1130) and ʿAṭṭār (d. 1220) as well as his possible encounter with Ibn al-ʿArabī (d. 1240) indicate, his interest in and his knowledge of literary and speculative mysticism must have been equally profound.[18]

Rumi could have enjoyed a long life of peace and conformity as a teacher and preacher. As it happened, however, life had a second uprooting in store for him, this time from the age-old tradition of learning to which he had devoted his life. On a Tuesday morning in 1244, sixty-year-old Shams al-Dīn, a learned but little-known wandering dervish, arrived in the city of Konya. In an encounter so shrouded in legend that it would be impossible to reconstruct accurately, Shams awakened in Rumi the wayfarer who had to free himself of rational and speculative knowledge in order to seek new horizons. Rumi did not fight this change, not so much because of Shams's magical powers, but because the moment must have been ripe for him. Once again, just as when he was five years old, a decisive journey took him from the Balkh of learning, conformity, and convention to the Anatolia of freedom, anonymity, devotion, learned ignorance, exploration, and ultimately transformation.[19]

Opting for Poetic Utterance

After three years, Shams disappeared as mysteriously as he had appeared. The process of change he had instigated continued, however, taking Rumi full circle from serenity and sobriety to frenzy and back to the inner peace he had once possessed. Yet things were never the same again. Before the encounter, solidity and certitude of knowledge were his guides; after, the confusion, uncertainty, and turmoil of love gave direction to his inner search. Almost every action became a symbolic idiom. Poetry embraced the life of intoxication, which itself came close to a poetic utterance. Rumi continued to wear black to mourn the loss of Shams, and since dancing was not enough to express his feelings, he whirled to be a step closer to the celestial dance of the heavens. He molded pain and pleasure, death and laughter, music and mourning together. Most of all, he unleashed an outburst of lyrical verse, flowing like a stream of water and covering everything in its path, from a grasshopper to the moon, with a brilliant poetic coat.[20]

The second uprooting was as vital as the first. Rumi became his own source of strength and returned to his life of serenity with the intention of assisting others to experience the same transformation. This he achieved through the medium of his poetry. When Rumi died in the year 1273 in Konya, the city that had once been furious with him for his intimacy with the mysterious Shams mourned his loss. He had been a source of vitality. He had sensed, better still experienced, the wisdom of change. He had seen the advantage of exploration, a discovery he visually declared through the practice of whirling.

Rumi was a poet of turmoil in the sense that he portrayed the beauty in the stormy experience of love. He did not try to smooth away the frenzy of the event by making it a pleasurable journey through the heavens. For him, love had a gentle and pleasurable side, but it worked its transformation on individuals mostly through its rougher and more chaotic aspects. Thus in Rumi's poetry warnings of the following kind from the beloved are common:

> You are in love with me, I shall make you perplexed.
> Do not build much, for I intend to have you in ruins.
> If you build two hundred houses in the manner that the bees do;
> I shall make you as homeless as a fly.
> If you are the mount *Qāf* [in stability];
> I shall make you whirl like a millstone.
>
> (D, 1665:1, 2, 4)

In other words, Rumi understood the constructive turmoil of love not in dreamy and unrealistic terms but like a long journey on a rugged road. Turmoil and long journeys were both familiar events in his early years.

When Rumi turned to poetic experience as a constituent of his mystical transformation as well as a vehicle for its expression, he was not attracted to the discourse of conformity but that of exploration and change. He needed a discourse equally at home with the confusion and pain of uprooting as with the joy of love, both of which had played a part in his growth. The poetic experience, which was part constitutive, part expressive of this reality, had to encompass both. He chose the medium of the *ghazal*, the genre characterized by lyrical brokenness, poetic ambiguity, and supreme flexibility.[21] In the twenty-nine years that he lived after his encounter with Shams, Rumi produced more than 35,000 verses, the largest collection of mystical lyrics in the widest variety of metrical patterns ever used by any single Persian poet.[22] It was as if he had said: "Everything I wish to say is in these verses." To those who required more than hints he offered the following advice:

> I am not the physical presence you observe but the pleasure and the happiness you sense inside as you hear my name and my words. If you feel such a pleasure, treasure the moment and express gratitude, for that is me.[23]

How to Read Mystical Lyric?

Mystical consciousness has usually been understood as a form of withdrawal of the mind from the sensory-intellectual domain in favor of a nonintellectual and therefore ineffable mode of awareness.[24] It has been assumed that the poetry produced in this mode of consciousness will not be intellectually accessible unless it is "translated" back into the language the sensory-intellectual medium, the mind, can grasp. This process, which sums up critical efforts to deal with Persian mystical poetry, has been called interpreting, elucidating, and paraphrasing, among other things. This search for a corresponding concept in the sensory realm leaves an essential question unanswered: if the poet despairs of putting his mystical experiences into intelligible terms (because of which inability he/she has to resort to allegorical expression), how are we who are further removed from the experience going to achieve the interpretive task? As suggested by Hollander's allegory of cooking the trope, poetry works through a complex interplay of its various elements. No word or image, extracted from a poem, expresses what it is able to express in relation to the various elements of the poem.[25] How do we propose to interpret an isolated allegorical construction when it can produce a dozen different effects in a dozen different poems? This would be attempting to determine the taste in the raw ingredient when it could acquire distinctly different tastes in different dishes. In other words, hermeneutical attempts to decode words, images, and ideas as rigid literary signs run the risk of assigning a fixed meaning to them thereby bringing to an end a potentially endless process of new readings.[26] The assigning of fixed meaning to literary signs, however, should not be confused with providing contextual basis for a poem through the use of extra textual information.

If hermeneutical interpretation of isolated elements of a poem is not a viable approach to mystical poetry, then what kind of a critical process should replace it? The first step would be to re-examine the textualization of the mystical experience. We need to reconsider the notion that since mystical experience occurs in a mode of awareness inaccessible to our senses, its poetic product is incomprehensible to us in our sensory-intellectual mode of awareness.

The main problem is the reduction of poetic utterance, particularly that of the medieval period, to an ornamented version of referential language. Scholars have often studied various elements of this poetry in isolation as if they were in a fixed posture, ignoring the changing mood and attitude of their constituent parts from verse to verse. Consequently, they have not acknowledged that what empowers these poems is not their exotic ornamentation (or other isolated characteristics) but the extent to which they are able to create the fictive poetic game. This leads them to miss the engaging power of make-believe within the *ghazal*, a dimension that enables the verses to exceed the level of expression attained in referential language.

True, one may never be able to demonstrate the extent to which a poem has successfully captured a mystical experience (an inability for which one should be thankful). It is, however, not hard to see that the ambiguity inherent in poetry corresponds to the ambiguous nature of indescribable experiences. It is not a coincidence that mystics have turned to poetry more than any other medium to give expression, through its matching reluctance to be articulated, to their inner explorations.[27] The explanation for this lies in the same "magic making quality" we have already touched upon. This "magical" effect, a result of the interplay between the poem's constituent elements, exhorts the reader to see the invisible and believe the unbelievable. Thus the ineffability of an experience (mystical or otherwise) may be overcome in poetic articulation. Those who argue for the validity of psychology in literary criticism have this particular phenomenon in mind.

Thus the mystics resorted to writing poetry just as they continued to mourn the inadequacy of words. They did not do so, I maintain, in the hope of someday finding an empty shell of words which could be filled with lofty mystical meaning. They did so because the linguistic game of creating poetic magic, of sending an inexplicable message, came close to the inexpressible they experienced in the confusing and paradoxical maze of love. Like any poet, they struggled furiously with the concept of language as a pre-existing system of rules, expressing themselves as best as they could.[28] There is no reason to treat the images or ideas they employ as singularly interpretable units which may be deciphered and reassembled for their "true" *meaning* to emerge.

The present work argues that this poetry should be seen in the active (and interactive) performing posture that it has long displayed.[29] In this posture, the poetry is an active part of the experience, the incomprehensible rendered comprehensible through poetic transformation. In this respect, poetry with all its elements, is not the key to a mystical truth, it *is* the mystical truth in the guise of a linguistic message. The effect of this new approach is to foreground the poetry and not the "hidden message." When the poems are thrown into sharp relief, it is easy to see that they are complex fictive games that the readers need to play to the full, joining the whirling dance, to realize what they entail.

The *Dīvān*: A Mere Collection of *Ghazals* or a Unified Body of Mystical Literature?

The *Dīvān* contains 3,229 *ghazals*.[30] These vary in length from under five to more than sixty lines. It is easy to consider them completely independent poems with common thematic concerns. A closer look at this literary corpus, however, reveals that they are connected more than first appears.

This intratextual resonance draws attention to the unified nature of the *Dīvān*. As is demonstrated in chapter 6, individual *ghazals* exhibit an awareness of one another. For instance, familiar repetitive patterns emerge randomly in rhymes and refrains. Among the *ghazals* that end in letter *alif*, to give an example, the words *mā* (us), and *biyā* (come) appear as refrains in twenty-nine and seven instances respectively. In the same brief section, the two hemistitches *Ay khvājah namībīnī īn rūz-i qiyāmat-rā?* (O wise man! do you not see this day of apocalypse?) and *zahī ʿishq, zahī ʿishq kih mā-rā-st Khudāyā!* (glory to love! glory to love which is ours, O Lord!) each appear in full twice. The repetition of interior patterns and the reappearance of larger portions of *ghazals* in one another provide the *Dīvān* with further intratextual resonance. Although each *ghazal* functions independently, many acquire additional potency through the fact that their constituent parts evoke portions of other *ghazals*. This gives rise to a continuous memory for the entire *Dīvān*.

Another unifying element in the *Dīvān* is the adoption throughout the work of a paradoxical mode of expression. Naturally, different emotional dispositions may be detected in individual *ghazals*. However, paradox is chosen to expose the fragility of conventional boundaries of experience. Through the inversion of common tropes, use of oxymora, frequent praise of silence, and juxtaposition of contrasting images and ideas, Rumi emphasizes the tendency to bend reason and mock verbal expression. Chapter 3 discusses this unifying feature in the *Dīvān* in detail.

The underlying rhythm, the natural organizing impulse in the *Dīvān*, which I compare to the rhythm of childhood in chapter 7, is another element which suggests the work should be criticized in whole instead of a collection of disparate *ghazals*. The mimetic patterns, the sense of discovery, the playfulness, the naturalness of syntax, and many more qualities are reminders of the familiar rhythm of childhood. These features are frequently present in the majority of *ghazals*, weaving together these variously patterned poems in the fabric of the *Dīvān*.

The perspective described here encourages the adoption of a critical methodology that tackles the entire *Dīvān* in search of significant features that may enrich our understanding of Rumi's poetry. When one utilizes such a methodology, three prominent features emerge, which I explore in independent chapters. The adoption of silence not to allude to emptiness (as in twentieth-century literature) but as a positive concept and a tool for expression is the subject of chapter 4. The unconventionality of the utilized imagery and the dynamic ways in which they perform in complex visual settings is dealt with in chapter 5. The intricacies of the sonic surface and Rumi's constant grappling with sound and rhythm are other characteristics of the *Dīvān* investigated in chapters 6 and 7. Finally, the concluding remarks in chapter 8 tie together the previous findings to shed light on the contribution Rumi made to the genre of *ghazal* and to Persian poetry as a whole.

The Comparative Perspective

The work adopts a broad comparative perspective. Where the comparison involves medieval critics, poets, and philosophers of the East the approach seems natural. However, the question might arise as to the relevance of contemporary Western figures such as Wittgenstein, Kierkegaard, and Heidegger whose views are frequently evoked to shed light on Rumi's poetry. Beckett's use of silence, for instance, is dealt with in some detail in chapter 4. Can Beckett's work enrich a critical understanding of Rumi? The answer is yes, providing the critic remains aware that the poets are rooted in different times and traditions. Certain philosophical and literary concepts remain unexplored in Contemporary Middle Eastern debate. Why deprive ourselves of the Western perspective on the experiential nature of the linguistic discourse when Rumi uses the same tool for expression albeit from within a different cultural and historical context? An even more compelling argument for applying some of the Western critical views to Rumi's work is that as twentieth-century readers and critics we are influenced by such critical views. When dealing with the concept of silence, for instance, it is impossible for us to ignore what Beckett's allegorical use of this concept has done to our contemporary perception of the term. For most of us, silence will automatically evoke the "emptiness" that *Waiting for Godot* or *Krapp's Last Tape* have brought to the concept. It is, therefore, not only useful but necessary to compare our understanding of silence to that of Rumi, regardless of whether similarity or contrast will result from the comparison.

How Does the Present Work Use the *Dīvān*?

The vastness of the *Dīvān* has placed exceptional demands on the present study. Although a pleasurable exploration, choosing an adequate number of representative samples from the work was laborious and time consuming. Furthermore, providing a sufficient number of examples to document credibly the existence of major features common to the entire work, particularly if each referenced *ghazal* is quoted in full, would take inordinate space. The present work has utilized the method of providing a large number of excerpts from across the entire *Dīvān*. In a deliberate attempt to demonstrate that the features under investigation do not appear in selective and unrepresentative examples, no specific section of the *Dīvān* has been privileged. For considerations of space, full poems have been quoted only when absolutely necessary. As it is, more than five hundred verses have been quoted to illustrate the points.[31]

Examples from the *Dīvān* are given in English.[32] It would have been ideal to add an analysis of the poetics of these verses in the original Persian in each instance. This, however, has been done only in chapters 6 and 7, in which the phonetic features of the poetry are under investigation. Elsewhere I cite translation for the critical inquiry into the poetics of the *Dīvān*. It may be questioned whether citing the poetry only in translation provides enough transparency for an in-depth study such as this. The answer to that depends exclusively on the nature and objective of the inquiry. The present study aims at investigating certain broad and fundamental features of the *Dīvān*, such as its use of paradox and utilization of silence, which may be fully appreciated in translation. An analysis of linguistic detail in more than five hundred Persian verses would divert attention from the larger picture to finer nuances. Furthermore, it would leave the present study accessible to a very small readership.

As these introductory remarks end and the analysis of the poems begin, it should be clear that this study attempts to shed light on the unacknowledged contribution of Rumi to Persian literature. It will demonstrate how he worked against a sense of inevitable defeat to transcend language. With the aid of his poetic vision, he frequently departed from tradition to dismantle the serious-looking edifice of the *ghazal* and to reshape it into the fairyland he wished it to be. This is the same transformation I have earlier described as turning the funeral of words into a whirling dance. How this transformation came about is the focal point of this study.

CHAPTER 2

Rumi's Lyrical Output
Historiography and Analysis

For centuries Rumi has remained one of the most widely read poets in the Persian-speaking parts of the world. Although no surveys have been conducted, the size of this readership makes it safe to assume that it represents a variety of backgrounds, from lay to highly educated. The expert critic, on the other hand, has not yet come to terms with Rumi the poet. Rumi's poetry has been considered second-rate, a mere vehicle necessary to convey his mystical thought. The poet whose vision revolutionized the Persian lyric has been portrayed as clumsy with poetry and disrespectful of it. The critical literature on Rumi has left out the fun, the vigor, and the artistic excellence in his lyrics. It has overlooked the role that this poetry played in the life of the poet and in the formation of later Persian poetry. Literary historians and critics have been confused by the presence of such a progressive seeker of change in premodern Persian literature. They have felt equally ill-at-ease with accepting the existence of an intoxicated mystic and poetic craftsman in one person. These misconceptions about Rumi need to be dispersed before we turn to his poetry in the following chapters.

Rumi's Disapproval of Poetry: The First Misconception

The critical misunderstanding of the message embedded in Rumi's lyric is due in part to the paradoxical nature of the message. The fact that he, side by side with praising poetry, so often vehemently denied its value and condemned attraction to it has played a part in our judgment of his literary achievements. Bemoaning the inadequacy of poetic expression is a recurring theme in these lyrics. Indeed, next to love, hardly any subject receives as much attention in the *Dīvān* as poetry itself. In a vast and complex array of observations on poetics, Rumi commented on almost every aspect of the topic. An independent volume could be devoted to Rumi's contribution to a literary critical analysis of the verbal discourse and its ramifications for mystical development. I shall here deal with a number of commonly held misconceptions concerning Rumi's cynical approach to the credibility and relevance of poetry.

Rumi's remarks on poetic discourse range from considering it a "heavenly" phenomenon (D, 328:3) to viewing it as a complete failure in telling the tale of inner turmoil. He often bemoaned the human need for verbalization, longing instead for a flight into the expanse of silence, where things are not told but manifested.[1] The critical literature on Rumi has tried to resolve the love/hate paradox by opting for a simple solution: he must have loved the inner meaning but detested the outer form. As the present study will demonstrate, however, Rumi's understanding of poetry was considerably deeper and more complex. We will limit our discussion here to specific remarks concerning Rumi's own poetry as well as those referring to poetry in general.

During the past two decades, there has been much attention to the intricacy of the process of literary creation. As we have become aware of the variety and complexity of the mechanisms at work, we have come to regard with suspicion much of what we used to consider the author's domain of authority and control.[2] Using this vantage point, we might consider Rumi's criticism of his own poetry as a view like any other and not as the premise for our investigation of his work. This does not underestimate the value of the author's self-critical remarks insofar as they provide us with clues to his understanding of poetry and poetic creativity. However, it does indicate that such remarks should not serve as replacements for independent critical analysis of his work. For instance, the fact that Rumi did not consider sonics his area of strength, or a significant aspect of poetry in general, should not discourage the critic from carrying out an analysis of the sonic surface in the *Dīvān*. On the other hand, we are free to incorporate the poet's self-critical assertions, as well as his general comments on poetics, into the conceptual core of our study. There should be no cause for hindrance if his point of view does not replace ours and become the only prism through which we find our rainbows.

Any attempt at characterizing Rumi's view of poetic discourse must acknowledge the whole range of the poet's comments. An analysis based on a small nonrepresentative selection of poems runs the risk of being seriously misleading. Sadly, this is the case with the samples from Rumi's comments that are commonly used in support of the idea that he had an acute distaste for poetry. The following is a frequently quoted example:

> [At last] I am freed from verse and versification
> O my eternal king!
> *Mufta'ilun, mufta'ilun, mufta'ilun* killed me.
> (D, 38:2)

Mufta'ilun is a basic prosodic pattern in the Persian metrical system that here represents the conventional restrictions imposed on poetic creativity. As the chapters to come will make clear, Rumi was constantly attempting to stretch the limits of poetic convention; hence his dislike for *mufta'ilun.* His observations on poetics, however, pertain to a much larger array of intellectual concerns that transcend objection to formal restriction. Indeed, the frequency of such remarks alone is reason to believe in the magnitude, in Rumi's view, of the intellectual, emotional, and spiritual place of poetry. The comments themselves fall into at least three separate categories, each highlighting a distinct area of emphasis.

Many of his disapproving comments concerning poetry are directed at the notion of *shā'irī* (literally, being a poet). This had little to do with the act of poetic expression and was instead directed at the social implications of the particular profession. Most probably, the often-quoted passage from the *Fīhi mā Fīh* beginning with the phrase *dar valāyat va qaum-i mā az shā'irī nang'tar kārī nabūd* (in my homeland and among my people there was no occupation more contemptible than *shā'irī*) alludes to this attitude.[3] As De Bruijn's meticulous study of the life and works of Sanā'ī demonstrates, in order to remain in favor and carry out his job a poet had virtually to perform the part of a clown in the social circles in which there was hope of finding patronage. No wonder the occupation was seen in certain circles as less than socially acceptable, for apparently it often involved "drinking and gambling with the patron and his boon companions, and amusing them," among other things.[4] That such activities were not in line with Rumi's convictions is clear. To decode this social criticism as an antipoetic statement, however, is to misread the situation.

A second group of Rumi's critical statements about poetry involves his familiar declaration of dissatisfaction with the inadequacy of the linguistic medium (incidentally, a complaint common to the world's greatest poets throughout history). As a poet who dealt in mystical love, Rumi was aware of the ultimate inexpressibility of that which inspired his poetry. If such confessions to frustration with the artistic medium were to be taken as signs of hostility to poetry or disrespect for it, then many writers would have to be considered hostile to the craft to which they contributed most. If anything, such remarks should testify to a sensitivity to the limitations of the medium, concern for poetry, and artistic conviction in the face of the challenge. Rumi was aware of the limited and limiting nature of verbal discourse but not overwhelmed by it. The entire *Dīvān* attests to his continuous struggle to transcend linguistic limits and free himself from the prisonhouse of language. Whether through utilizing the power of illogical tropes, turning silence into a literary tool, or producing wondrous birds of unconventional imagery from the palm of his hand (D, 328:4), Rumi always sought to expand the horizons of verbal expression.

One might even argue that the general message of such critical remarks is that of hope. They remind the reader that the point at which speech falls into despair often signifies not the end of communication but the beginning. Pointing to these limits is itself a form of bridge-building, a new strategy for communication. Note how sympathetically the following protestations depict the perplexity of the poet who is challenged by the multiplicity that surrounds him. Only one who has tried to catch the swift "birds" of images and ideas in his net of poetry knows how hard it is to find the rare bird that wears "the ring of Solomon's secrets" around her neck. But another major thrust of this poem is a plea for ears "suited to understand the speech of the rare birds":

> There is no edge to my vast desert;
> There is no peace for my heart and my soul.
> The world is taken, from end to end, by image and form;
> Which of these images is mine?
> If you see a severed head on the way
> Rolling in the direction of the battlefield;
> Ask him, ask him concerning my secrets
> For, from him you hear my hidden mysteries.
> What if one ear could be found;
> Suited to understand the speech of my birds.
> What if one bird could fly,
> Who wore my ring of Solomon's secrets [around her neck].
> What am I saying? when I know telling this tale
> Is beyond my limits and my abilities.
> How can I utter one word when each moment
> My perplexity is more perplexing.
>
> (D, 239:1–8)

Far from a protest tainted with contempt and hatred, these verses reveal a heartfelt affinity with the rare birds of poetic expression and with those able to understand their speech.

However, Rumi was aware of another vulnerability of poetic expression, namely its helplessness in the face of time. This forms a third category in his accusation of the imperfection of poetic utterance. Like any poet of vision, he was aware of the shortness of poetry's effective life if it failed to extend itself beyond its immediate context. By the same token, of course, he was conscious of the concept of universality of poetic insights whose relevance defies a change of context. In the stream of his creative moments there are instances of distress where this susceptibility to time is deeply felt. These moments, however, are not ones of complete despair, for they are often presented in a humorous tone. The analogy of fresh bread in the following poem, for instance, creates a warm and witty atmosphere. Furthermore, it evokes the nourishing aspect as much as it does the shortness of the useful life in poetry:

> My poetry is like Egyptian bread;
> You cannot eat it, if it is a night old.
> Eat it when it is still fresh—
> Before the dust [of time] settles on it!
> The warm land of the mind is its abode
> In this world, it dies of cold.
> Like fish, it can live on land but for a moment;
> The next, you will see it devoid of life's warmth.
> (D, 981:1-4)

As a reader of the works of earlier poets, Rumi knew that there were rare brands of fish who were able to adapt to new climates and live a long life. He could not, however, resist the playfulness of the analogy between poetry and a lively little fish dashing about in the ocean. The warm and bouncy tone of the poem affirms its sense of optimism. "Be quick!" Rumi tells us, "spread your nets, for there is many a wondrous fish you may catch in these waters."

This is precisely what the present volume will do, spread its nets as wide as possible and catch as many fish as possible. Before that, however, we have to deal with another major misconception, the commonly held view that Rumi's mystical and poetic experiences are two unrelated phenomena. This view has long maintained that the mystical experience was of an exalted nature and bore no relevance to poetic activity. The subscribers to this view argue that Rumi engaged in writing poetry because he was left with no other expressive outlets. He was not dedicated to literature nor did his work possess "true" literary merit.[5] In what follows, I shall discuss the flaws in this view and argue for the inseparability, indeed the unity, of his poetic and mystical experience. As for the literary merit in Rumi's lyric poetry, the present volume should provide the necessary evidence.

Rumi's Experience: Poetic or Mystical? The Second Misconception

The scholarship on Rumi has accepted the premise that the concerns of a mystic devoted to the "inner meaning" of things were far removed from the concerns of a poet who adored the beauty of the "outer shell" (i.e., elegant speech). Based on this superficial division of labor, the biographers of Rumi have felt compelled to opt for one of the two possibilities: true mystic or skillful poet.[6] They have attempted to salvage his mystical dignity by placing him solidly in the first category. The literary biographers have not been able to ignore the force of Rumi's poetry, which they included in their anthologies. However, they have told the reader far more about his religious training, his interaction with other Sufis, his mystical doctrine, and his mysterious encounter with his master Shams than about his poetic artistry.[7] The fact that, though thoroughly devoted to its "inner meaning," Rumi's poetic experience was permeated with energy and enthusiasm and could not be reduced to a reluctant venture of secondary significance posed a problem. How did this enormous body of inspired poetry come into existence if Rumi was not a poet? Here, the mysterious encounter with Shams was turned into a useful tool in dealing with the inexplicable. Shams was assigned the role of the magician who robbed Rumi of any concern for conventions and transformed him alchemically from a sober preacher and jurisprudent into an intoxicated poet.[8] There is no denial that Shams brought fundamental change into Rumi's life and outlook. These accounts, however, overlook the clear evidence that Rumi enjoyed poetry and was accustomed to reading it long before he met Shams. Indeed, such was the extent of his literary interest that Shams admonished him more than once for studying the *Dīvān* of the Arab poet al-Mutanabbī.[9] Furthermore, as we have seen, there is no doubt that Rumi wrote some of his poetry prior to his encounter with his influential master.[10] Textual evidence strongly supports an acknowledgement of Rumi's long-standing interest in poetry: his works reveal traces from a wide range of masters of classical Persian poetry, including Anvarī Abīvardī and others (d. ca.1190), who did not have any particularly mystical inclinations.

The consequences of accepting the encounter with Shams as responsible for a complete change of personality and of interest in Rumi have been considerable. While the mystical transformation theory solved some immediate problems, it also created a detrimental bifocality which still persists despite the lessening of the significance of the original theory. On the one hand, as rational observers of history, we are no longer satisfied with a miraculous event as the sole explanation for Rumi's poetic creativity. On the other hand, we still maintain that it was under the pressure of this overwhelming experience that Rumi took to writing poetry. Particularly harmful is the erection of an imaginary barrier that divides our understanding of his experience into two separate compartments, mystical and poetic. The former is seen as the core of his experience and the latter as a necessary shell whose sole purpose is to encase this mystical event. In this scheme of things, Rumi's poetry is not seen as related to the inner experience in any other way.

No doubt Rumi's own subscription to the common mystical vision of the universe as the material manifestation of an inner, and more sublime, reality has played a part in the above critical understanding of his poetry. He does tell us frequently that outer shells are insignificant compared to the inner truths they conceal. That, however, we must remember, is an all-encompassing view of the universe in which poetic utterance is also included. This means that Rumi did not single out poetry as particularly devoid of spiritual value unless, of course, it was used for unworthy purposes.[11] Furthermore, this cosmic view rests on a much more subtle and complex understanding of division than that of a literal separation of mystical from poetic. Even if such an arbitrary and artificial division were to be applied, accepting that no interaction takes place between the two parts requires a fairly narrow vision not only of poetry but of mysticism as well. Turning the poet into a suitcase maker who provides the bag (words) in which to transport valuables (thoughts) has had profound implications for the criticism of Rumi's contribution to Persian literature and for our understanding of mystical poetry in general.

The first major problem with this view is that it is based on an erroneous and outdated understanding of poetry, namely that poetry consists of pre-existing meaning placed into form. The view that there is no center of meaning or informing power preceding a given structure of signs and that meaning is generated by the interplay of elements rather than by the copying of some pre-existing signification is now well established.[12] In this sense, the poems themselves are the mystical experience and the meaning, not a container holding them. They, therefore, require a critical attention cognizant of this unitary nature.

The second negative impact of the "suitcase" theory has been to divert our attention from the lyrics as poems in their own right. This oversight explains the reaction of many biographers and critics of Rumi who have expressed doubts about the literary merit of his poetry. They have turned their backs on some of the finest examples of mystical lyricism in Persian language in the mistaken belief that they do not offer much in the way of poetry.[13]

As a direct consequence of the suitcase theory, most critics have been content with compiling catalogues of images in dealing with Rumi's poetry. This is usually part of a larger attempt to unravel the "mystical purpose" buried deep beneath the insignificant facade of words. In this way, even when the poems have been studied their poetics has remained unexplored and Rumi's artistry and poetic vision unappreciated.

If pursued closely, the view that the poetic and the mystical are separate leads to yet larger complications. It rests on obscure and unexamined premises that need serious reformulation if we wish to work toward a rigorous critical tradition capable of tackling the vast and largely unexplored body of classical Persian literature.

It is alarming that we can feel comfortable with vague and undefined notions that lead to unwarranted results such as the above compartmentalization. We have no reason to isolate two particular moments of activity in Rumi's emotional and intellectual life and to suggest that they had no relation to each other. Neither do we have any evidence for maintaining a general division between what we vaguely term literary creation and, even more vaguely, mystical experience. This two-tiered observation is based purely on our own unscrutinized understanding of what this process must have been like. For instance, how do we explain the irony of dismissing the poems that form our only clue to the experience as unrelated to its formation? Secondly, for a mystic the entire universe is the site of God's presence and the arena for spiritual development. Why, then, should poems that encourage such a development, coincide with it, and preserve its aura for centuries to come be passive carriers and not formative for the event?[14]

The analysis of the poems in the pages that follow is based on the premise of their affinity with the inexpressible, the baffling, and the mystical. In this approach the poems are seen as textualizations of an experience which included confusion, disorderliness, and change. They reflect the pains, the pleasures, and the many stumbling blocks on the journey of transformation. It is assumed that an examination of these poems would provide examples of the linguistic transformation of the dirge of referential language into the whirling dance of poetry. As the mode of expression, images, and complex rhythm are analyzed it will be demonstrated that these poems are nothing if not textualizations of the mystical changes within. They are the experience itself.

The present discussion was not part of the philosophical debate or concern during Rumi's time. Even the exact verbal tools for a full articulation of these points were not available to him. Yet, interestingly, he came fairly close to arguing for the inseparability of the poetic and the mystical self. As we have already observed, Rumi located as the source of his identity "not the physical presence you observe but the pleasure and the happiness you sense inside as you hear my name and my words. If you feel such a pleasure," he continues, "treasure the moment and express gratitude, for *that is me*."[15]

Ghazals that Bleed: Poetry as Experience

In separating poetry from experience one defines human intellectual endeavor as a collection of separate compartments unrelated to one another. This approach endorses a conception of poetry divorced from life and reduced to a luxury one can do without, and thus marginalizes one of the most effective cultural products of human civilization. Conversely, if poetry is seen as an act, and as pertinent to experience, its full relevance to life can be appreciated.

In a *ghazal* that refers to Ṣalāḥ al-Dīn's departure, perhaps his death, Rumi compares his sadness to a wound. As the poet suffers the injury, the poems emerge stained with blood:

> He cut me, I bled;
> The *ghazals* emerged covered in blood.
> Ṣalāḥ al-Dīn separated from me and came to that land.
> (D, 588:9)[16]

Is Rumi explicitly commenting on the intimate connection between poetry and human experiences? It is possible to see this and many similar examples in the *Dīvān* in this light.

Before exploring further examples, however, it is imperative first to deal with a number of specific philosophical questions. It is necessary to ascertain the explicit premises that ground Rumi's poetry in his mystical experience. This will lead to a clearer perception of the problem and a more concrete response to it. In addition, it will place our discussion within the current intellectual debate that has attempted to tackle these and related issues.

The debate on the relation between experience and linguistic expression not only enhances understanding of Rumi but also enriches critical analysis of Persian classical literature, connecting it to modern criticism and to the philosophy in which it is grounded. Where criticism has ceased to be a regional effort, an intellectually isolated position of loyalty to unexamined notions is no longer justifiable. Neither is the fact that Rumi lived in the Middle Ages an adequate justification for applying archaic methodology to the critical analysis of his poetry.

Outside the domain of the criticism of premodern Persian literature, much has taken place. The idealist elimination of the world as a source of knowledge and its empiricist counterpart, which stressed the passivity of consciousness, have been discarded. Phenomenological insights have had much to do with this state of affairs. The late nineteenth and early twentieth centuries witnessed efforts to create a space between idealism and empiricism and to ground knowledge in experience.[17] According to the phenomenological school of thought that subsequently developed and penetrated a wide range of disciplines, consciousness was not a passive state but a unified intentional act. It was not a submission to knowledge but a real intercourse with exterior reality.[18] Martin Heidegger further radicalized the Husserlian definition of consciousness by emphasizing its dynamism. Indeed, he defined consciousness, the essence of human being, as existence or, in his own terms, as "being-in-the-world."[19] For the phenomenologist critic, literature came to be defined as the embodiment in recorded language of the *act* of consciousness.[20] It would be misleading to reduce the significance of the phenomenologist contribution to criticism to the above statement. Husserl's and Heidegger's philosophical insights, along with their modified versions, gave rise to a wide range of new approaches to the understanding and analysis of the literary text. These approaches were not always consistent; indeed, at times they violently clashed on fundamental critical issues. Rene Wellek, a promoter of the Geneva School, considered the Heideggerian approach to be a metaphysical one. Similarly, Herbert Spiegelberg, a historian of the phenomenological movement, declared that Heidegger's *Being and Time* was a kind of "bastard phenomenology." He considered Heidegger's later works as not phenomenological at all.[21]

Differences notwithstanding, the contributions of the above thinkers gave impetus to a continuous struggle to redefine the concept of meaning and with it the entire process embodied in literary discourse. What allows us to see them as parts of a single current is, as Magliola puts it, the fact that they all incorporated an epistemology of mutual implication (that is, of the interpreter and the interpreted). In addition, they all saw the essence of Being as rooted concretely in experience.[22] Furthermore, their notion of discourse as a disclosure of the experiential state of being-in-the-world situated the literary text at the heart of experience and rendered the two inseparable.

Heidegger and Literary Text

We shall follow Heidegger's views both in his early and later phases of development, for several reasons. To begin with, Heidegger's long-term interest in the works of the eminent medieval mystic Meister Eckhart (1260—1327/9) endows his thought with an awareness of the mystical dimensions of experience, a characteristic not prominent in the works of other phenomenologists. Secondly, as we shall see, toward the end of his career he came to acknowledge explicitly a deep affinity between mysticism and philosophy. And last, but not least, his ideas have had a distinct normative influence among literary critics.[23]

Heidegger's Being is essentially revelation, bound intrinsically with the revelation of beings in human awareness. The acts by which beings become revealed in human awareness are hermeneutic acts. These acts are in large part linguistic.[24] Heidegger insists that "thinking" about language and poetry is central to existence and should transcend the traditional limits set by philosophy. Heidegger finds poetry to be particularly significant and defines it as "pure speaking." This purity has to do with the so-called power of "unconcealment" intrinsic to poetic utterance.[25]

Also significant to our concern about Rumi's poetry being understood in relation to the mystical experience embodied in it (and generated from it) is the phenomenological approach to meaning. For the phenomenologist, meaning in and through language arises from the *action,* or more precisely the *interaction,* between self and the world.[26] Heidegger emphasizes that meaning is not content placed into form but rather an existential phenomenon in which "the formal framework of what can be disclosed in understanding and articulated in interpretation becomes visible."[27] Elsewhere he emphasizes the same concept through a slight reformulation. Meaning, he tells us, must be conceived as the formal-existential framework of the disclosure which belongs to understanding, not a property attaching to entities, lying "behind" them or floating somewhere as an "intermediate domain."[28]

Heidegger expresses his deep appreciation of what poetic discourse can achieve in a variety of ways, not the least of which is his description of all great philosophy as "thoughtful-poetic."[29] More significantly, where in *Being and Time* linguistic discourse is described as an existential state in which Dasein or "being-in-the-world" is disclosed, the nature of the disclosure makes it *constitutive* for Dasein's existence.[30] In poetic discourse, where the communication of the existential possibilities of one's state of mind becomes an aim in itself, the process of disclosure, in Heideggerian terms equal with constituting existence, reaches its pinnacle.[31] In his later works, Heidegger insisted on the "originative" quality in literary work and on the fact that it does not point to Being as a sign would. He maintained instead that within the text's own unique realm, the literary work "brings forth" Being as a symbol does.[32]

The phenomenological view contends that a text is neither an absolute nor a purely aesthetic object. Rather, a text is a "thoroughly contingent linguistic precipitation of the styles of being in the world."[33] This approach may imply a marginalization of the text compared to the formalist practice of considering it as the sole focus of criticism. On the other hand, it may be seen as highlighting the text's centrality by emphasizing its oneness with experience. Indeed, this repositioning, which shed new light on textual analysis and its functions, made literary texts relevant in all kinds of unlikely places. Ludwig Binswanger, the psychiatrist who, inspired by Heidegger's *Being and Time,* postulated a state of consciousness that he called an "experiential circle," applied his theory to clinical patients and literary texts simultaneously. The experiential circle, he declared, regards selfhood and the outside as participating in the same unified ontological field. It locks body and spirit together in an encompassing circle of experience and brings past and future together to contribute to the shaping of the present. Regardless of what it actually achieved in the way of curing mental patients or enriching our understanding of literary discourse, Binswanger's experiential circle points to an acute awareness of the complexity of the relationship between literature and experience.[34]

Interestingly, as perhaps should be the case, the above debates have not brought us any closer to definite answers to any major critical questions. For instance, we may accept that consciousness is an intentional act in the form of "being-in-the-world" and linguistic discourse is a disclosure of, and constitutive for, this being. However, we are still at a loss as to the degree of autonomy, or subjugation to textual signals, in the generated meaning. We are similarly quite unclear concerning the handling of conflicting interpretations. Is there such a thing as a valid interpretation? How do we structurally define the concept of validity to begin with? Considering these and other such questions, our minds tend to "wander in estrangement" rather than "establish itself in the comprehensible," to use Heidegger's terms.[35] The debate, nevertheless, has focused attention on the unitary nature of experience and literary discourse, in itself an outstanding achievement.[36] This shift, rightly described by Frank as being "from an overriding concern with literary art's end product, understood as form, to an interest in the form-generating modes of poetic impulse," has indeed resulted in fruitful explorations. A good example is Emil Staiger's attempt to penetrate the artistic consciousness in order to understand and describe the pretextual experience that an author undergoes.[37] His explorations led to a new perception of the various genres as textual renderings of basic human experiences. In his work, Heideggerian temporalities are perceived as the long-missing link between existence and literary form. As far as Staiger is concerned, with these temporalities genres are no longer suspended in the air but are rooted instead in history. Not only do Staiger's insights reveal the close link between literary genres and concrete historical existence, they completely revolutionize the study of genres.[38] Staiger's work is by no means the only insightful critical analysis sparked by the phenomenological debate over literary creation and experience. The scope of the present discussion, however, does not warrant a more detailed treatment of the topic.

Heidegger and Mysticism

Instead, we will here address a question that arises from the wide range of what fits in the semantic field of the umbrella term "experience." The question arises as to the possible peculiarities of the unknown entity we loosely define as *mystical experience*. To what extent, we may ask ourselves, can this experience be treated as experience in its general sense? In other words, to what extent may we apply the above views on the unity of poetry and experience to a poet such as Rumi, who deals chiefly with experiences of a mystical nature? The question acquires special prominence due to the fact that our entire discussion of poetry and experience here has been based on rational philosophical insight. Indeed, it might be assumed that the concept of experience to which Heidegger and his fellow phenomenologists refer must be limited to concrete experience that is subject to verification. Philosophy, it may be argued, comes from the realm of rationality, whereas mystical experience is rooted in the personal, the subjective, and the inexpressible. The dominant historical view confirms this dichotomy and tells us that in the East and the West the philosopher and the mystic have always been and continue to be diametrically opposed.

Interestingly, once again it is Heidegger who offers a solution. This solution is in line with his general principle of the necessity for constant redefinition of basic concepts and ideas. In one of his early writings, *Frühe Schriften* (1972), he challenges "the conception of the Christian philosophy of the Middle Ages as Scholasticism which stands in opposition to the contemporaneous mysticism" as fundamentally wrong.[39] As far as he can see, the pairs of so-called "opposites"—rationalism/irrationalism and scholasticism/mysticism—do not coincide. Such categorization, in his view, can only rest upon an extreme rationalization of philosophy. Concluding in good philosophical tradition, he recapitulates the core of the argument in a brief statement of extreme significance. "Philosophy as a rationalist creation, detached from life is powerless; mysticism as an irrationalist experience is purposeless."[40] In a comprehensive and insightful study, John Caputo looks at the "mystical element" in Heidegger's own works by examining the affinity between the Heideggerian concept of "thinking" and mystical experience. He describes the "likeness of Heidegger to the mystic" as similar to the kinship between two main trends in his intellectual struggle, namely "overcoming metaphysics" and the desire for a "mystical leap."[41] On a textual level, Caputo finds some key parallel concepts between Heidegger's philosophy and the writings of the medieval German mystic Meister Eckhart of Hochheim. In his youth Heidegger developed a strong interest in the writings of this influential mystic which lasted throughout his life. He described Meister Eckhart as "genuine and great."[42] It is clear that when Heidegger talked of literary writing as the quintessential act of Being and regarded poets as "most dedicatedly occupied with being's creation," he did not exclude, in his mind, the mystic writers and their respective experience.[43]

The Long *Ghazal* that Was about a Camel: Rumi on Poetic Experience

It is not necessary to plunge any deeper into the philosophical debate to establish that the view of poetry as a container for a pre-existing meaning needs serious reconsideration. Similarly, the notion of poetic creation as external to experience is outmoded. It may be interesting at this point to examine some of Rumi's own observations on the matter. The purpose here is not to adopt his remarks as critical tools to evaluate his poetry. We have noted earlier that an author may have a special interest in criticizing his own work but he does not necessarily have a peculiar authority to do so.[44] However, it is useful to examine Rumi's complex perception of poetry, to illustrate the earlier reference to his interest in poetics, and to observe the curious affinities between his views and the modern debate discussed above.

Rumi often treated the question of poetic creativity. Usually, he did not attempt to explain the poetic event for the obvious reason that it was not supposed to be explicable and because the ambiguity was seen as enhancing its effectiveness. Yet there are clear indications that Rumi did not subscribe to the notion of poetry as simply a container for meaning. As far as he was concerned, the process was more complex and clearly involved a kind of linguistic transformation:

> A jar in hand, I ran to the stream of meanings;
> But my jar turned into water, when the water of life entered it!
> (D, 902:6)

The above passage is one of a wide range of verses in the *Dīvān* in which Rumi contemplates the source of the poetic event and its relation to experience. In many of these examples, he describes the process of inception in some detail. Often the incident is clearly connected to the Divine.

Rumi's critics are fully aware of this point; yet in their critical assertions, which promote the notion of the separateness of the mystical from the poetic, a significant point is overlooked. In Rumi's poems there is often no differentiation between the process of divine intervention which results in poetic creation and the process of writing the poems. As a result, the interaction with the Divine and the composition of poetry become one and the same. For instance, often the image of mother of pearl is used to refer to the poet and raindrops to the divine generosity that impregnates the poet with the pearls of words (D, 984:9). Here, the creation of poetry, far from being secondary, is the divine act itself. Elsewhere, Rumi compares himself to a bagpipe, swearing by the sweet lips that breathe into him that he has no control over his own singing (D, 227:10). Once more, the divine contact and the moment of singing must coincide for music to be created. In some instances, the language is not even metaphorical: the process of poetic creation is explicitly described as inseparable from the moments of ecstasy. For instance, in one poem, the heart "intoxicated with the primordial love" is singing a *ghazal*. The more the "wine of love" affects the heart, we are told, the "sweeter" the *ghazals* will be (D, 538:10). The *Dīvān* is filled with examples that testify to Rumi's view of the divine nature of the poetic experience.

Remarkably, the sanctified nature of the poetic event does not separate the poet from his ordinary readers. For Rumi, the experiential plane on which the poems are created is vast. It contains the parameters in which the poems operate. Though it can blend with the sacred, it is accessible to earthly humans. The readers, the hearers of the bagpipe or the users of the pearls, are assumed to be involved in the poetic process to the extent that they are often given the task of finishing an incomplete poem:

> I beseech you by the one whose heart
>   is a sweet and fermenting ocean—
> The ocean that has given the jewels
>   their precious nature;
> That you compose the rest of this *ghazal*;
> And hence cast the magician Sāmirī to the depths of envy!
> (D, 102:13, 14)

The decision to appoint the reader to finish the poem, a poetic device unknown in Persian classical *ghazal* in general, sets a number of processes in motion. On the one hand, it brings the poetic persona from the heights of mystical experience to a personal and reachable level. On the other, it reminds the reader of his/her interpretive autonomy by emphasizing that the matter is not finalized by the author. Furthermore, it makes clear that to share in the poems passive listening does not suffice. Poetic communication, Rumi tells the reader, is an act of participation that requires two sides. Finally, the poems and their creation are identified as mystical and transformational. If the reader accepts the challenge presented by the poet in the above poem, he/she may produce verses that would leave the magician Sāmirī in a state of envy. The option of producing wondrous poems with the aid of the Divine is, hence, offered to the reader as a way of discovering his own divine potential. Although the reader is usually trusted with completion of such poems, at times the finishing touch has to come from the divine itself:

> Two or three verses are left, you complete them!
> it is much sweeter when it comes from you;
> For it is the cloud of your speech that has left
> my heart and my breast all covered in green!
> (D, 772:11)

This insistence on maintaining a relationship with someone outside the poem is another acknowledgement of the importance of the experiential nature of poetry in the *Dīvān*. Many *ghazals* contain references to the audience present during the composition and to the poet's desire to take them along on the poetic/spiritual journey:

> Begin a *ghazal*! one that resembles those
> who are present here.
> O your face as bright as a candle!
> come to the center, [join the dance].
> (D, 2060:1)

At times the call is explicitly to the future readers of the text, reflecting Rumi's vision of an audience broader than his immediate circle. In the following example, the call is unexpected and comes at the end of a relatively long *ghazal*. As the reader is absorbed in the rhythm of the poem, his attention focused on things external to himself, he is unexpectedly made self-conscious by a voice that calls out to him, saying:

> We have been describing two kinds of birds;
> Find out, O the reader of this *ghazal*!,
> of which kind are you.
> (D, 1920:9)

This kind of dramatic confrontation with the reader makes the presence of the poet hard to ignore. It is, perhaps, Rumi's most effective way of encouraging observers to join the dance. It is also part of a larger scheme to prevent the reader from plunging so deeply into poetry as to lose touch completely with external reality. The campaign to stress the existence of the experiential dimension at times takes on exaggerated and humorous proportions. It does, however, fit with the rhythm and the overall ambience of the poems. Thus, a *ghazal* which has used a camel as a metaphor for a journeying lover in its first line concludes as follows:

A camel was the opening verse to this *ghazal*!
look how long the poem has become!
But do not expect a camel to be short, O my
intelligent king!
(D, 1828:12)

A prominent theme in the *Dīvān* is that of the pervasiveness of poetry. In Rumi's expansive poetic vision, there are *ghazals* which have not been captured in verbal expression; in fact, *ghazals* are everywhere and in all forms (D, 1028:11). This is one of Rumi's corollaries to the notion of the inseparability of poetry from experience. Universal poetry, for those who can sense it, is an inescapable reality, and the consequences of immersion in it are manifold and at times even conflicting. On the one hand, no lover need go through the labor of putting his sadness into words, for "every particle in the universe is aware of the poetry of his love" (D, 759:12). On the other hand, verbal assertion can be fatal, for it is as "burning as fire" and as "sharp as a sword" (D, 332:18 and 971:18). According to Rumi, this universal poetry permeates everything, including the being of the poet himself (D, 876:10).

This omnipresence endows poetry with a unique property: the ability to bridge the gap between inner and outer experience and to transcend the duality of subjectivity and objectivity. Poetry is a "wave" from the "shoreless sea of love," watering this world and bringing life to earthly bodies (D, 729:18). When the pain of separation from Ṣalāḥ al-Dīn "cuts like a sword," the *ghazals* "bleed"! (D, 588:9); when Shams is present "like a king on the throne," the poems "align in his presence like obedient soldiers" (D, 1077:11). When despair reigns, the words "travel like ants to the palace of Solomon" to summon help (D, 23:4). Short and "without beginning or end," the *ghazals* can carry the reader from the "lowest of the low to the highest of the high" (D, 2025:15).

These examples testify to Rumi's vision of the effectiveness of the poetic force. Furthermore the effectiveness stems from something more enigmatic and more profound than the pervasiveness of poetry. It stems from their ability to blend the Divine with mundane experience. It is not accidental that these poems, which at times are not more than a melody to dance to, at other times become "incantations" that replace the liberating presence of Shams (D, 1854:9). They even form a "plane" whose inhabitants can observe life "freed from time and place" (D, 2009:12). To illustrate this transforming potential, Rumi uses the metaphor of a magician, describing his own poetic utterances as "wondrous birds that grow from the palm of [his] hand" (D, 328:4). Producing the birds symbolizes creation, bringing things into being, an inexplicable intermingling with the Divine to the point that the poetic and the Divine become one and the same. As readers, we never discover (nor are we supposed to) where God's creative process stops and Rumi takes over.[45]

These observations may lead one to expect that the *Dīvān* is an articulation of the power of discourse. It is only natural to expect this poetic confidence to crystallize into a sense of verbal victory. Yet paradoxically this is not the case, because the *Dīvān* is also thematically centered around the inadequacy of verbal expression. Throughout the work we are told that words should be torn apart and speech abandoned, since what is worth expressing is inexpressible. The limitations of a pre-existing linguistic system and the formal constriction of the traditional genre of *ghazal* are emphasized. One can literally feel the inflexibility of the prosodic patterns, the stubborn refusal of words to bend into desired shapes. This is Rumi's testimony to the human paradoxical destiny of being a magician of words and a captive of them at the same time.

It is clear that a criticism pertinent to Rumi's poetry should dispel myths and misconceptions regarding his dislike of the medium. It should focus on the 35,000 verses of mystical lyricism that he left behind, regardless of circumstances that may imply their lack of literary artistry. If the reader treats them as poetry and Rumi as a poet, these verses can reveal much about themselves that extratextual evidence cannot.

CHAPTER 3

The "Footless" Journey in "Nothingness"
The Power of Illogical Tropes

Mystical Poetry as Paradox

In the mysterious and paradoxical universe of poetic discourse "mystical poetry" is by far the most perplexing paradox itself. By its very existence, it promises to express the inexpressible.[1] It employs words to bemoan the inadequacy of words, and in volume after volume it celebrates silence as the true indication of attaining to the mystical goal. This affinity with coexisting opposites in mystical lyricism may well be rooted in, one might even say a textualization of, a larger paradox: the life of the mystic itself. Most mystics live paradoxically in that they attempt to combine complete devotion to God with commitment to mundane daily matters.[2] On an intellectual level, the ability to come to terms with the incongruity of paradox usually results in a more polyvalent vision than one subscribing to the unacceptability of contradiction.[3] While recognition of paradox has produced tangible results in areas such as set theory and mathematics, the poetic impulse it can create deserves special attention. In Rumi's case, standard logical arguments carry little weight where the mystico-poetic experience is concerned. This is not so much because love and rationality are incompatible, as we are often told, as because the "wooden leg" of the "logicians" lacks the agility and the courage to transform the funeral procession of words into the effective whirling of poetry.[4] Here, the productive instability of paradox not only textualizes the instability of mystical experience and expands the poetic horizons, but it disrupts the anticipated flow of the narrative. Through the disruption, paradox creates obstacles that the reader has to acknowledge and negotiate. Thus the reader remains aware of the urge to participate instead of drifting into dreamy inaction at the rhythmic flow of the *ghazals*.

Finally, though rarely mentioned, paradoxes are fun,[5] not so much because they shock and keep the reader awake but because they provoke him to search for a solution. This is a search valued not for the end it achieves but for its own sake, much like the "thirst" Rumi values above the thirst-quenching "water."[6] Good poetry is also fun, among other things, because it motivates the reader to explore, and in exploration there is anticipation. This anticipation, which is at the heart of the poetic impulse in the *Dīvān*, is frequently detectable:

> O singer with a face bright as moonlight!
> tell us what you heard.
> We are all worthy of your trust;
> tell us what you saw.
> O my king! O my garden of joy! tell us what you found in the sanctuary of our souls, tell us.
>
> (D, 2245:1–2)

The intensity of anticipation is often emphasized through repetition in refrain of words denoting expectation, such as *bargū, bargū* (tell, tell) in the following example:

> O the one superior to all! tell, tell;
> O commander at the time of war! tell, tell.
> O the moon everlasting! the royal cupbearer!
> O the speaking soul of all, tell, tell.
> You are the direction to which all pray, the flame of the candle [around which all gather];
> Tell the tale of them all, tell, tell.
> You are full of ruse, O giver of wine to the intoxicated!
> Reveal the secret of the rose garden, tell, tell.
>
> (D, 2246:1–4)

Rumi employs the power of illogical tropes to expand poetic horizons and achieve the above-mentioned effects; or, sometimes he simply employs the device as a "semantic reenactment" of the larger paradox of the human predicament.[7] Let us first look at the use of paradox in the literary tradition in which Rumi's poetry is rooted.

The Use of Paradox in Medieval Persian Literature

Exploring the tradition in which Rumi works reveals that poetic use of paradox is not a prominent feature of medieval Persian *ghazal*.[8] Despite the lack of systematic studies concerning the use of this literary device, a cursory examination reveals its scarcity. It is not surprising that the rhetorician Rashīd al-Dīn Vaṭvāṭ (d. 1182) referred only to *al-mutaḍādd* as the form of paradox used in the literary discourse of his time. In his *Ḥadā'iq al-siḥr fī daqā'iq al-shi'r*, the earliest existing compendium of rhetorical rules in Persian poetry, Rashīd al-Dīn devotes two pages to paradox. Significantly, half of the examples he quotes were not selected from *ghazals*.[9] Shams-i Qays, the author of the next standard manual of rhetoric in the early decades of the thirteenth century has nothing to add to Rashīd al-Dīn's contribution. He calls the device *muṭābaqah*, and the art of juxtaposing contrasting things he calls *ashyā'*.[10] Modern scholarship on classical Persian literature shows no more awareness of paradox as a poetic device. In her latest exploration of Persian poetry, Annemarie Schimmel is even briefer than Rashīd al-Dīn and Shams-i Qays: she devotes one paragraph to "the stylistic form *taḍādd*." The single example she quotes is from Anvarī.[11]

Generally speaking, criticism of Persian lyric poetry has largely been limited to a chronological enumeration of lyricists. The norms and conventions of the *ghazal*, the main vehicle of Persian lyric, except for broad formalistic features such as the number of lines and the rhyme patterns, remain unexplored.[12] In the absence of hard data, a brief detour into the works of some medieval master lyricists to examine their interest in paradox is illuminating. A small random selection of *ghazals* composed by predecessors and contemporaries of Rumi exhibits an almost uniform use of paradox and its variations.

Khāqānī Shīrvānī (b. 1121–2), described as "the master of panegyric *qaṣīdah* and no less of the *ghazal*," is one of the poets whose efforts are supposed to have given the *ghazal* its "final classical form."[13] The first twenty *ghazals* in his *Dīvān* do not show an extensive use of paradox. There are a handful of *mutaḍādds* (contrasts) built on the interplay of opposites, and one instance of a more complex paradox describing the beloved as residing in the *jān* (the vital core of life) and yet being its enemy.[14] Awḥad al-Dīn 'Alī Anvarī (b. 1126), another poet associated with the development and independence of the *ghazal*, was not enthusiastic about the usefulness of paradox, either. Well-versed in all the sciences of his time and praised for the fluency of his panegyric poems, he was best known for the pungent sarcasm that pervaded his work.[15] An examination of the first twenty *ghazals* in his *Dīvān* reveals a moderate usage of *mutaḍādds*, mostly adding a touch of humor to his down-to-earth love complaints. He does not seem to have been aware of or interested in utilizing other possibilities that paradox can bring to literary expression.[16]

Niẓāmī of Ganjah (b. 1141) was acknowledged as the unrivaled master of romance. He left 1,200 fresh and vigorous verses in the form of *ghazals*, though his prominent standing as a storyteller overshadowed his contributions to the genre.[17] He is an interesting example for our purpose because of the unanimous recognition of the quality of his lyricism and because, like Khāqānī, there is an air of intentionality about his craftsmanship in using literary devices. The first twenty *ghazals* in his *Dīvān*, however, exhibit a pattern very similar to those of Khāqānī and Anvarī, with a slightly higher occurrence of *mutaḍādds*.[18]

A near contemporary of Rumi, Saʿdī of Shīrāz (b. 1213–19) is generally recognized as the *ghazal*-writer par excellence.[19] Among other skills, a natural blending of literary ornamentation with simplicity is a prominent feature of his work. The first twenty *ghazals* in the *Dīvān* of Saʿdī show an unprecedented number of *mutaḍādds*, incomparable both in variety and complexity to those used by the other writers mentioned here. In the following typical example, he utilizes contrasts (night/morning, Solomon/Sheba, anger/contentment, peace/enmity, and hope/fear) to accentuate poetic impact:

> O fresh breeze of *ṣabā*! greetings!
> You arrive from the abode of my love.
> O caravan of the night! what did the morning say to you?
> O Solomon's bird! what is the news of Sheba?
> Is my love still angry?
> Or there is hope she may be content [with me]?
> [O breeze of *ṣabā*]! have you come in peace? or in enmity?
> Should I approach her in fear or in hope?[20]

However, apart from the use of contrast and the occasional inversion of commonly used tropes (e.g., the prey seeking the lasso instead of attempting to escape in *ghazal* 10), Saʿdī does not make use of other variations of paradox.[21] Our brief exploration suggests the scarcity of paradox in medieval Persian *ghazal*.

Other Varieties of Literary Paradox

In contrast to the *ghazal*, the genre of *rubāʿī* (quatrain), frequently associated with the poet/mathematician ʿUmar Khayyām (d. 1122), made extensive use of paradox. Khayyām perceived the creation as the paradoxical act of a senseless potter who made the "fine goblet" of the human body only to break it. This sinister outlook alone provided numerous occasions for the literary employment of paradox.[22] Khayyām's *rubāʿīs* are, thus, fraught with paradoxical assertions, such as the warning not to reveal nature's most "guarded secret": withered tulips do not bloom a second time.[23]

Long before Khayyām, however, the genre of *rubāʿī* had found currency among mystic poets. Pūrjavādī traces the circulation of a *rubāʿī* by Abū al-Ḥasan Bustī, the eleventh-century Sufi of Nīshābūr, in later Sufi manuals, demonstrating the popularity of the genre and its smooth intertextual transmission prior to Rumi's time.[24] Abū Saʿīd Abū al-Khayr (d. 1049), the mystic of Khurāsān and a pioneer in Persian verse composition, also made use of paradox in his *rubāʿīs*. Human infidelity and faith, the concurrent attachment and detachment felt toward this world, and the simultaneous absence and presence of the beloved are among the paradoxes he underlined:

> The world is a game in which losing is to win;
> The winning trick is being content with less.
> The world is the dice in the game of backgammon;
> It should be picked only to be thrown.[25]

The poet and mystic Ahmad of Jām (d. 1141), whose *ghazals* show patterns strikingly similar to those of Rumi, used paradox in his *rubāʿīs* to add a touch of sarcasm and achieve a satirical tone:

> Until a hair from your existence remains;
> The religion of self-worship, and the shop [in which to sell yourself], remains.
> You said you destroyed the idol of illusions;
> The illusion that you destroyed the idol remains![26]

The brevity of the genre of *rubāʿī* added to the sharpness of such double-edged messages as the above and provided an excellent vehicle for the ironic impact that paradox creates. Although the *ghazal* possesses different formal features and generic conventions, *rubāʿīs* similar to those quoted above provided Rumi with fine examples for the adoption of paradox for poetic use.[27]

Persian mystical prose written prior to Rumi's time made use of paradox, too. The words uttered by Sufis in moments of rapture known in Arabic and Persian as *shaṭaḥāt* or *shaṭḥīyāt* are a case in point. Some of the best-known Persian *shaṭḥīyāt* were uttered by Abū Yazīd Bistāmī (d. 875) and ʿAyn al-Quḍāt Hamadānī (d. 1131). In these utterances that, according to the Sufis themselves, "overflew from ecstasy and seemed strange in speech," the initiated confronted some of the most paradoxical aspects of their spiritual quest. Carl Ernst's study of the *shaṭḥīyāt* identifies the main topics as the duality of the self and God, transcendence of the created, and the significance of unknowing.[28] It is in this paradoxical vein that ʿAyn al-Quḍāt spoke of the true Muslim as the "infidel Muslim" and attempted to describe certain indescribable aspects of the sacred as the "black light" or "the light of Iblis."[29] In an account of his nocturnal journeys, Abū Yazīd related a mystical experience as follows:

Intoxicated, I threw myself in all lands, melted the body on the fire of the divine jealousy in all crucibles, and galloped the horse of my yearning everywhere. I found no prey better than need and nothing better than despair. I saw no light brighter than dark and no speech more articulate than silence. I resided in the house of silence and wore the robe of forbearance. It reached a point at which He found my inner and outer self cured of the malady of humanity.[30]

Paradox as the Unresolved Duality in Love

The brief examples discussed here underline the affinity between the mystical literature and paradox. The concurrent need for articulation and emphasis on unknowing may be one deciding factor in the employment of this device. The courtly *ghazal*-writer did not require the same expressive tool. He needed to display knowledge, artistry, and above all full control over the artistic medium of *ghazal*. In the example from Saʿdī, as in the works of the majority of the court poets, the superbly polished sonic surface encases carefully regulated poetic impulses communicated in conventionally "appropriate" moments. The result is a smoothness that creates an illusion of ease, as a master acrobat makes ropewalking appear effortless. Disruptive paradoxical expression is not necessarily in demand here.

The mystic, however, sought in paradox a mirror for his own perplexity. Since the perplexity could not be clarified or articulated through rational argumentation, as Michael Sells notes in his study of Ibn ʿArabī (d. 1240), "the language enacted and performed" the paradox semantically in the hope that the "meaning event" would help the experience to be "apprehended." By way of illustrating the point, Sells shows that in the writings of the Andalusian mystic, the semantic enactment of the identity shift from an "ego-self" to a "divine other" reflected in the fusing of pronoun antecedents. In one example, the pronoun "his" refers to God and Adam simultaneously in the way that the mirror of a polished human heart reflects the Divine at the same time. Here the paradoxical God/human duality and oneness are not rationally explained but semantically apprehended.[31]

In Rumi's *ghazals,* we encounter semantic schemes similar to those used by Ibn ʿArabī. To begin with, his *ghazals* are not addressed to courtly audiences and pursue different ambitions. This change of priorities may be deduced in many ways, including the change of the smooth ropewalk into a rough journey on the sea, to use a suitable metaphor. The consciousness of artistry, the pride in manipulation of literary devices, and the orderly march of words, which in Saʿdī's work show everything is safely under control, evaporate. Together with the poet, we are at sea—and a stormy one at that. The reader is presented with more than the finest and most polished accomplishments of a poet who speaks to us from behind a half-closed door. It is more than a plea to admire the artwork, even more than a request to hear, understand, and empathize. It is a bold invitation to everyone to get on the same boat, as it were. This rough sea journey requires no less artistic skill on the part of the poet nor dedication on the part of the reader. However, it is less an exercise in leisure than a struggle not to be engulfed by the wild sea. Why should poetry not be so if its aim is to reflect the stormy journey through the sea of our real lives and the urgency of our struggle with its waves? In Rumi's words:

I said I shall tell the tale of my heart as best as I can;
Caught in the storm of my tears, with a bleeding heart,
  I failed to do that!
I tried to relate the event in broken, muted words;
The cup of my thoughts was so fragile, that I fell into pieces like shattered
  glass.
Many ships were wrecked in this storm;
What is my little helpless boat in comparison?

The waves destroyed my ship, neither good remained nor bad;
Free from myself, I tied my body to a raft.
Now, I am neither up nor down—no this is not a fair description;
I am up on a wave one instant, and down under another the next.
I am not aware of my existence, I know only this:
When I am, I am not, and when I am not, I am!

(D, 1419:1–6)

From this vantage point, with the poet caught in the storm instead of commenting on it with aloofness, the malleable substance of love and the poetry that gives voice to it acquire new and changing roles. This poetry of love is not merely an appeal to the beloved to put an end to separation. It is action in the broadest sense of the term, action that may range from singing and whirling to an outright declaration of war. Love, the unequivocal basis for everything that finds expression in the *Dīvān*, is for Rumi itself a paradox. The contradiction inherent in the oneness of the two, the concurrent separation and unity of the lover and the beloved is a maze with no apparent exit. It is better expressed in the roughness of fighting a storm than in skillful ropewalking. The *Dīvān* echoes the mixture of joy and agony in Rumi's response to this paradoxical experience:

> My life is yours, yours mine;
> Has anyone witnessed one life in two bodies?
> My life is union with you, my death separation from you;
> You have given me unique skills! in two [different] arts.
> (D, 2012:3)

As in any unresolved duality, the question persists: where does the lover stand at any given moment, with the beloved or separated from the beloved? To avoid a sense of hopelessness, fatigue, and resignation, Rumi converts many such bitter complaints into playful anecdotes like the following:

> Last night you poured the wine, then you escaped from me;
> I have caught you one more time, don't do what you did before.
> (D, 1827:4)

Yet in anecdotal language or otherwise, the concurrent unity and duality in love is indescribable. It cannot be paraphrased, in the same way that a paradox cannot be paraphrased. A paraphrased paradox is flat and dull and therefore not a paradox anymore.[32] So is the tale of love told in flat and unparadoxical terms of description and interpretation. Rumi senses this reality; in fact, he refers to it even in the *Maṣnavī*, which, due to its didactic goal, should have closer affinity with description and interpretation:

> Though interpretation of speech makes things clear
> Love free of words is clearer.[33]

Consequently, the *Dīvān*, instead of describing the bewilderment of love, becomes a linguistic manifestation of bewilderment. It does not struggle to paraphrase or unravel the paradox of love, but instead becomes an extended linguistic paradox that operates at the limits of discourse, challenging the absolutes that literary orthodoxy had created and worshipped up until that point. This "playing with human understanding" and "redirecting thoughtful attention to the faulty or limited structures of thought," in fact, constitutes a primary function of paradox.[34] Letting the force of his lyricism demolish terminal and categorical boundaries of existing discourse, Rumi leads us into an enchanting maze that does to our poetic senses what the paradox of love does to our emotions. It prepares us for surprises, keeps us eager to participate in the poetic act, and yet leaves us acutely aware of our limitations. As a result, the *Dīvān* expresses the mystery and the paradox in the experience of love not through description and explication but by letting the reader share that experience in his/her role as the reader of these lyrics.

The Identity Paradox in the *Dīvān*

The perplexity begins with the first encounter with the text. In fact, it begins even before approaching individual *ghazals*. On the cover of the *Dīvān* is usually written *Dīvān-i Shams* or *Kullīyāt-i Shams* (The Complete Collection of Shams's Poems).[35] The standard explanation is that the creative force behind the *Dīvān* was Shams, although the poems were written by Rumi.[36] But if Rumi considered his poetic contribution to be so profoundly dependent on someone else's inspiration that he refrained from claiming authorship, can the poems be considered his, as opposed to Shams's? Indeed, in the closing verses of most of the *ghazals*, the poet gives his nom de plume as "Shams."[37] Perhaps Rumi is suggesting that his identity has fully merged with his master Shams's and that he no longer exists as an independent being? If so, why does he in the same breath protest the pain of separation from Shams? One might even fall into the trap of attempting to uncover what he "really means" by doing this. However, it soon becomes clear that most such questions are irrelevant. Like so many of Rumi's baffling paradoxes, this maze does not have a safe and clearly marked exit. There is no solution but to negotiate the twists and turns, constructing one's own way out with the aid of imagination. But the correctness of the answer, the safety of the path thus forged, are not guaranteed. If one turns to the *Maṣnavī*, another of Rumi's great works, to find verses which may shed some light on the identity of Shams, one is likely to be rewarded with a double puzzle, such as "There is no stranger [*gharīb*, which also means a strange person] in the whole world like Shams."[38] Somewhere during the process of being puzzled, however, it becomes apparent to the reader that it is the process that has mattered all along. Entering through the door Rumi has opened, one has stepped onto an open-ended road that can stretch as far as one's imagination. This is another function that paradoxes are designed to perform, deny limitation and point in the direction of an open-ended road. The process might even be likened to a whirling dance, a turning in circles, in which revolving is all that matters while reaching a destination (in its conventional sense) is irrelevant.

This paradoxical grappling with identity and creativity is only one example of the many such experiences that the *Dīvān* offers the reader. Frenzied, uncontrolled, but articulate, Rumi's Persian lyric expands its generic horizons to become the textualization of the inexplicable. In the process, it accommodates the playfulness, the surprise, the dramatic effect, the dialogical richness, and the unconventional parody that are byproducts of paradoxical games and rarely found in the lyric prior to his time.

> O lovers! O lovers! I have lost my cup!
> I have tasted the wine that does not fit into cups.
> I am drunk with the wine of *min ladunn,* inform the prosecutor[39]
> I have brought him and you some of that wine to taste!
> O king of the truthful! have you ever seen an impostor like me?
> With your lively servants I am alive, with the dead ones I am dead!
> With heart-ravishing beauties, I am in bloom like a flower bush
> With cold-hearted deniers [of you], I am dispassionate like the autumn.
> (D, 1371:1–4)

The *ghazal,* with its potential flexibility to become a vehicle for thematic expression, a string of disjointed or harmonious ideas, or a mere juxtaposition of conflicting imagery, provides Rumi with the suitable playground for playing these lively literary games.[40]

Rumi's paradoxical self-introduction, or his general use of this device, are of course not unique to him. Over the centuries paradox has occupied the minds of many to the point of being called respectfully "the tuning fork of thought."[41] The relevance of paradox to literary expression stems from the existence of basic dualities within human reason itself. As long as our rational system operates in an arbitrary fashion, we have to live with painful inner contradictions. Paradox is the device that can best articulate this intellectual, moral, and psychological confusion. For Rumi, this inner duality, the "identity paradox" that resonates in the title *Dīvān-i Shams,* is the center around which his lyrics gravitate in movements that outline the harshness of the human predicament: confusion.

> This shape that I have, O master, who do I look like?
> One moment I am a fairy, the next an enchanter of one.

Burning with enthusiasms, I am both the candle and the crowd gathered around it;
I am the smoke and the light, together and scattered at once.
(D, 1467:1–2)

Varieties of Paradox in the *Dīvān*

Intelligent Ignorance

The *Dīvān* benefits from a variety of techniques of paradoxical expression. The thematization of intelligent ignorance, for example, usually implies that in the midst of confusion there is a ray of hope. We are not abandoned; rather, we are like pawns in an elaborate game too complex for our understanding. Like a "mirror" we "reflect the image put before us" (D, 1397:5). The game will end at some point and there will be a way out of this maze of existence if we play carefully, sincerely, and by the rules. The most essential rule is to admit that we do not know the rules:

You who have invited me to your house! lead the way!
I am so bewildered, I do not know the way home.
You who have enchanted the city and the village alike!
Where is the house? show it to me! I do not know the way home.
How do you expect knowledge, of the one who is not even alive?
Come forward! do not hurt me anymore! I do not know the way home.
O glorious musician! play your drum with your hands
Play this tune to my heart's content:
I do not know the way home.
(D, 1465:1–3, 6)

Thus, in its playful way, the *Dīvān* performs poetically the concept of intelligent ignorance, the complex notion that "what seems nothing to the intellect is the incomprehensible maximum."[42]

He said: you are not crazy, you don't deserve to live in this house;
I became crazy, I put myself in chains.
He said: you are not drunk enough, give up this pretense, you are not the right type;
I became drunken, I became full of enchantment.
He said: you are a little too intelligent! affected with fancy and disbelief;
I became foolish, I became ignorant, I freed myself of all.
(D, 1393:3, 4, 6)

Sometimes, the point is not presented thematically. Rather, readers are made to see it by participating in a full poem, going through circles within circles to the point of forgetting that any specific destinations await. Yet the closing portions of the *ghazal* demonstrate that an explicit goal has been consistently pursued. In one instance, we participate in a series of invigorating games, including hiding behind trees and mysteriously "turning into their shadows" (D, 1397:6, 7). Then we "soar into the sky," "roll in the direction of the sea like flood," "fall from branches like torn little leaves," "fly like green-winged parrots," and "escape from cracks in the ceiling in the manner of raindrops" (D, 1713:1, 3, 5, 7, 11). Just before our panoramic journey ends, and after we have tested the tricks we know for travelling to distant lands, we "sit still" like a "silent reflective mirror" to receive direction and start the journey (D, 1713:14–15). Travelling or not, fun is an essential part of the affair. No matter how puzzling, the paradox is never joyless or dull. Through the joyous interaction with the poems, we remain hopeful of learning the steps and joining the dance, hard though they may be. The abundance of colorful images softens the ambience and adds to the fun.

Juxtaposition of Contrasting Images

Rumi opens the *ghazal*, known for its traditional restriction on so-called nonpoetic elements, to images as unconventional as a cup of milk, a stove, or a tailor. These images play their part, as the occasion demands, in lively carefree moods or serious philosophical frames of mind. Furthermore, they are often paired with dissimilar images to enhance their poetic effect through radical and paradoxical contrast. In the following example, the image of the tailor provides a useful metaphor for God: the divine dressmaker, fashioning our lives. It also elicits God's transcendent greatness through juxtaposing the tailor's modest existence with His, thereby enhancing His glory:

> I shall go to the store of the tailor of lovers, tomorrow;
> Wearing my long robe made from a thousand meters of melancholy.
> He can cut you off from Yazīd and sew you onto Zayd;
> He can pair you with this one and separate you from the other.
> He can attach you to one to whom you give your heart for life;
> What a fabric, what a stitch, what a miracle-making hand.
>
> (D, 216:1–3)

At times a large number of contrasting images are clustered in uncharacteristically short verses. In the following example, God/wood and stone,

stone/water, mirror/rust, infidelity/faith, peace/war, heart/soul, lion/fox, intellect/love are all paired in short succession:

> The one who has not had a taste of love
> Is but a piece of wood or stone to God.
> Love extracts water from stones;
> Love removes rust from mirrors.
> Infidelity seeks war, faith peace;
> Love sets fire to war and peace alike.
> Love opens its mouth in the sea of the heart;
> It devours the two worlds like a whale.
> Like a lion, love knows no ruse;
> It does not change from a lion to a fox.
>
> (D, 1331:1–5)

The Use of Oxymora

Shrewd and resourceful oxymora are present throughout the *Dīvān*, with their thought-provoking double faces that continuously fight to cancel one another out. Their main function is to disrupt the rhythmic flow of the poems as they appear, like obstacles placed before the reader demanding that their presence be acknowledged:

> I said: "you are that . . . ," he said "silence!
> What I am cannot be expressed through words."
> "Since it cannot be expressed through words" I said
> "I shall be a silent speaker to you.
> I have journeyed in annihilation footless like the moon;
> I shall be a footless runner to you."
> I heard a voice: "what are you running for, look
> at this hidden manifestation that I am!"
>
> (D, 1759:8–11)

In the above example, Rumi not only presents us with a good number of original oxymora such as *gūyā-i bī-zabān* (silent speaker) and *bī- pā-yi pādavān* (footless runner) but constructs extended oxymora in phrases like *mīshudam dar fanā* through deliberate use of the verb *shudan* in the sense of *raftan* (to go). In this manner, he benefits from the contrasting effect of juxtaposing *fanā* (annihilation) and *shudan,* which frequently means "to become" or "to come into existence." The result is that when in the third verse he says, "I was journeying in annihilation," he is at the same time saying, "I was being created in nothingness." In this and similar occasions, Rumi's command of the Persian poetic tradition allows him to combine traditional devices with innovative ways of expression. Thus he uses the diaglossia in terms such as *sharāb* (wine) to cross the boundary between sacred and profane and generate paradoxical shades of meaning. Scenes of dance, similarly, depend for their effectiveness on the interplay between the sacred and the profane.

> Let us hold hands in circle-shaped groups;
> Rush drunken and dancing to the seaside.
> (D, 1719:2)

The above scene evokes playful and profane merrymaking easily accessible to the imagination. It also brings to mind the whirling dance or some form of *samā'*. Caught in the interplay between the two implications and perhaps surprised by their similarity, one is signaled in the following verse to be prepared for the sacred, which in this case receives the main emphasis:

> On the shore of the sea of love, we shall freshly grow;
> Like a garden we shall remain fresh for ever.
> (D, 1719:3)

There is an intentional ease with which in such poems we cross the border between the sacred and the profane. Perhaps it is meant to demonstrate the similarity in these apparently conflicting realities. It is not, however, meant to lead to the illusion of ease and comfort in human expressive efforts. To the contrary, the reader of the *Dīvān* is kept aware of the agonizing struggle that runs like a unifying thread through the entire work. It can be described as a persistent unanswerable question that underlies key poetic moments: how do I dare even attempt to name the unnameable?[43]

Paradoxical *Impossibilia*

It is important to realize that in the *Dīvān*, this declaration of despair in the face of the inadequacy of verbal expression is paradoxical, too. It often transforms into its own opposite, an acknowledgement of the autonomous power that words can carry:[44]

> If you heard the news of the beauty of the beloved;
> My drunken head has been speaking, I know nothing of it!
> The noise of a drum as loud as this cannot be suppressed by a carpet;

> The glory and the light of the moon speaks for itself, declaring "it is me here hidden in the dust!"
>
> (D, 1624:1, 5)

The fear that words will take over, that they will say it all, and more specifically, that they may reveal too much is constant in the *Dīvān*. The depth of this concept, of course, can be adequately investigated only through looking at its full context, including the Muslim belief that God's miracle, the Qur'ān, exists merely in words. What is significant, though, is that Rumi's lyric, by accepting an apparently conflicting reality—the coexistence of the weakness and power of words—creates a paradoxical *impossibilia*. It makes use of the tension contained in the paradoxical combination of poetic power and despair as a propelling force, a fountainhead for its poetic vigor. In fact, the concurrent experiences of triumph and defeat described in the *Dīvān* are not limited to the literary domain. The way the poet relates to himself and to outer reality often fluctates between the two:

> What happened to you again, O my heart?
> What trickery are you engaged in this time?
> Yesterday, you were soaring into the sky like the prayer of the pious;
> Like the light of the stars, you are falling down again.
>
> (D, 2478:1–2)

Where simple affirmative statements fall seriously short, paradoxical *impossibilia*, with their relentless push to bend logical and linguistic bars, can do much to make the "airy prison" of language a more spacious one.[45] Rumi benefits from the power of these illogical tropes, particularly in dealing with matters inaccessible to human speculation, such as the following description of the Divine:

> You are a drop and an ocean, you are kindness and wrath;
> You are sweetness and poison, O do not make me suffer more!
>
> (D, 37:4)

Paradox and the Mode of Contact in the *Dīvān*

The standard critical approach associates lyric with subjectivity, with turning inward and with excluding the audience. In a mysterious and melancholic ambience, the audience is supposed to overhear a poetic utterance not directly addressed to them. In Persian lyric poetry, one typically hears the poet address himself, natural elements, or heavenly forces.

Frye goes so far as to liken this to the poet turning his back to his audience, in contradistinction to the dramatic mode in which the audience is acknowledged and addressed.[46] As we shall frequently observe, Rumi's lyric breaks out of the convention of the poet as recluse and assumes an interactive mode that aims at fully engaging the audience. Much of this dramatic effect, this keeping the reader actively involved, is achieved through successful use of paradox. Paradoxes, as Colie notes, depend for effectiveness on a challenging and surprising quality. In order to challenge and to surprise, there is need for an immediate audience eager to participate in the game.[47] Rumi not only invites his audience to share in the lyrical experience but frequently acknowledges their presence. The result is a close and unusually direct relationship between lyricist and listeners. At the same time, it extends the generic horizons of the *ghazal,* allowing it to say more and to reach a wider readership. To use our metaphor of whirling, this rapprochement with the audience allows the poetry to dance on—even cross—the borders between the lyric and dramatic modes.

The poetic impulse created by mystical love in the *Dīvān* and the direct and paradoxical mode in which it has been expressed is likely to be received with skepticism. This has to do with earlier expressed notions of poetic creativity and its reception in the social and historical context of the Muslim world. There has been a persistent assumption of the Islamic "distrust of the poets." It has been said that Islam, with its "comparative lack of opacity," to use Hamori's terminology, is unable to accommodate the paradox at the heart of the poetic impulse. The literary implication of this, according to Hamori, writing on the generic development of the Arabic *qaṣīdah,* is that for centuries after the advent of Islam, Arabic poetry looked to its pre-Islamic ancestors for a generic model and remained secular. To evaluate Hamori's judgment on the lack of opacity in Islam and the secular nature of early Arabic *qaṣīdah* is beyond the scope of the present chapter. The mystical lyricism of Rumi, however, with its deep religious conviction and its willingness to accommodate paradox as a major poetic propelling force, demonstrates that the two qualities are not mutually exclusive. Furthermore, it highlights the necessity of paying attention to the complexity of diachronic and gradual development of generic paradigms as opposed to settling for easy explanations.[48]

Thus the *Dīvān* brings together a variety of poetic solutions designed to articulate our paradoxical existence. Like fine details of a painted landscape, these images are presented to us in the frame of the larger paradox of adopting Shams's name, thereby pointing to the paradoxical and diffuse nature of poetic creativity itself. I have, in this chapter, made a few major observations concerning Rumi's use of paradox. I have demonstrated that Rumi understood its relevance to mystical lyricism as he appreciated the paradoxical nature of love itself. This appreciation, I have maintained, prevented Rumi from any attempts to describe love by way of elucidation and paraphrasing. He resorted, instead, to paradoxical expression, textually replicating the sensation of confusion in the experience of love. I have shown that in so doing he benefited from promoting the notion of intelligent ignorance, forming complex oxymora and juxtaposition of contrasting images and concepts. I have pointed to the direct and dramatic mode of contact that he adopted to enhance the surprising effect his paradoxes have on the reader. I have suggested that although Rumi's religious conviction was the central core of his poetry, it did not prevent him from accommodating paradox.

The Sense of Play

I would like to conclude by emphasizing that the truly unconventional distinction between Rumi and many of his contemporary fellow poets is less his paradoxical approach to poetry or his skillful use of paradox—many poets have demonstrated innovative use of literary devices. The distinction is in Rumi's ability to make his poetry an embodiment of his life, yet not take it so seriously as to be overwhelmed by its grandeur. The fun and the sense of play persist, even in illustrating matters as grave as the confusion of destiny:

> I am drunk and you are drunk, who is going to take us home?
> I told you a hundred times drink a cup or two less.
>
> (D, 2309:1)

The beloved is not described in somber or oppressive terms, either. In fact, he is often portrayed as the source of all playfulness:

> Who is this? who is this beauty who has arrived sweetly?
> Who has arrived at our house drunken with shoes under arms.
> By way of trickery came that ruby-lipped, asking for fire;
> Who does he intend to burn this time, I wonder. He has come alone.
> O come! you the source of fire, come! how could you ask us for fire?
> By God this is another trick, O you who have arrived so unexpectedly.
>
> (D, 2278:1, 3, 4)

Accordingly, the freedom and open-endedness of paradox is not taken too seriously, either. As a scholastically trained logician, Rumi realized that the noncommitted position of a paradox is only an illusion of freedom, because defying limitation ultimately implies submitting to another kind of limitation. Thus in the midst of Rumi's engagements with paradox, there is the awareness of a more eloquent mode of expression, an ultimate solution to all the unexpressed and unarticulated paradoxes of our existence: silence. Rumi's ultimate tribute to paradox is to devote an unprecedented proportion of his poetry to the theme of silence.

The very mentioning of silence is a paradoxical act, the naming of the presence of an absence, the seductive invitation for interpretation under the cover of emptiness and indifference. Silence claims to have nothing to offer, yet it occupies the space that hides the unspoken. It is a potentially effective literary tool and one that turns the very existence of the *Dīvān* into a major paradox. The chapter that follows will investigate Rumi's recognition of the thematic scope, pivotal role, and the complexity of silence. His intentional adoption of silence as a tool to enhance expression will constitute the core of the argument. Let us, now, observe how the riddle of speaking about not speaking unfolds in Rumi's poetry.

CHAPTER 4

"How Sweetly with a Kiss Is the Speech Interrupted"
Rumi's Poetics of Silence

Rumi's lyric is occupied with the thought of silence. In the *Dīvān,* speech is not worthless, but silence is infinitely more powerful. Words draw strength from the "realm of silence" (D, 124:10); mysteries are transformed because "they are untellable" (D, 183:7); whereas words may be counted silence is "immeasurable" (D, 569:12). One may see the *Dīvān* as an intense expression of the desire to abandon the spoken word and embrace silence.[1]

To produce over 35,000 verses celebrating the absence of speech is not a practice common to medieval Persian poetry. It is, however, a paradoxical scheme typical of Rumi. It is another attempt to demonstrate the fragility of our horizons of expectations by plunging into deliberate self-contradiction. At the same time, Rumi foregrounds silence as the repository for the unsaid. He does not speak of silence because he wishes to remain silent, for he could have done so by not composing poetry at all. He speaks of silence to explore the theme and to emphasize its centrality for the *Dīvān*:

I shall now catch that essence of all images
A good snare I have prepared for that *Kaʿbah* [that beloved] of mine!
The walls may hear, speak in lower voice;
O my intelligence climb up the roof [to guard]! O my heart keep the doors closed!
The enemy, while in ambush, has but one concern;
To hear a thing and to spread it around.
Though invisible, the particles are enemies;
Speak in the bottom of a well [if you must], keep vigil at the time of dawn.

One day the thought of the enemy, not even himself,
Entered in my heart in order to pass through.

He heard just one riddle of my secrets;
Soon he was rushing around, revealing it to one and all.
Since that day, my road companions and I have made the covenant
To hide our secrets, to keep our heads bent down.
We are people, we are not less than stones in a mine;
Quietly enduring agony, it found the gold.

The tightfisted sea! in its willful silence
Says: "I know nothing,
I have not seen any pearls!"

(D, 194:1–9)

In the above poem, silence as an uncharted entity lends itself to imaginative interpretations. It takes many shapes, beginning with a snare in which the essence of all images may be caught. Silence is also an assistant to the intelligence that must stand guard and a necessity for the heart, which has to keep out intruders. This protector of the valuables, then, is transformed into a valuable itself: a mine of gold and the pearl in the sea.

Silence: Independent or Rooted in Language?

Philosophy has long exploited the flexibility of the unchartedness of silence, turning this malleable concept into all manner of shapes.[2] Most relevant to a literary analysis of this concept is Wittgenstein's attempt to withdraw silence completely from the linguistic realm and make it into an island, a unique vantage point. As Bruce Kawin has pointed out in relation to the urge for silence in Beckett's work, silence may be understood not as intermission within language but a category outside it, a different aspect of experience.[3] In this role, silence is not a constituent element of the discourse but an imaginative leap or a ladder to climb up the linguistic system and arrive at somewhere beyond it. Any view expressed in words, Wittgenstein tells us, would be a view of the interior of the world that finds articulation through linguistic expression. Only a flight on the wings of silence can provide access to an external realm in which the means for articulation is different: an absence of articulation. Such philosophical ladders or shortcuts are not alien to Rumi's way of thinking. He utilizes such leaps to achieve what the Viennese philosopher termed "vanishing the problem of life" as a solution to it. In fact, Rumi speaks of a concept similar to the Wittgensteinian notion of "that which cannot be put into words" but which is capable of "making itself manifest" when he refers to Shams as the manifest Sun "under whose rays the snow of words melts away" (D, 132:8).[4]

In its basic form, the view that argues for the independence of silence from the shackles of language has been echoed by many thinkers prior to Wittgenstein. No doubt Rumi's awareness of the fundamental difference in origin and characteristics between the two entities of silence and speech is also rooted in an earlier mystical tradition.[5] He clearly draws on that tradition when he singles out the immeasurability of silence and underscores its independence from the laws of mathematics to which words have to comply. Indeed, it has long been a universal dream of mankind to take refuge in a different universe and gain a new perspective on the world that is given to the illusion of verbal expression. This is reflected in the view found in all major religious traditions that the spoken word is likely to lead to pollution and sin. The monastic rule of silence and similar practices are not idiosyncratic or regional training procedures. They are a manifestation of this universal craving for the special vantage point accessible only to the silent. Such practices were an expression of the need for that uncorrupted opportunity, that pure space, that moment of silence which may provide the room for revelation. Only in uncontaminated silence could the voice of God, that which transcends human speech, be expected to be heard.[6]

Yet, silence as an intermission within language is not any less significant. As moments of absence of discourse punctuating the flow of speech, silence may be turned into a powerful literary tool to turn the funeral of words into the whirling dance of poetry. The following example illustrates such a use through thematization:

> Where is the Musician in my soul? that its singing
> May echo in a thousand heads the enchantments of love.
> I said I will not speak, but I will;
> Fulfilling promises is not a notable
>   virtue of mine.
>
> (D, 223:1–2)

The above *ghazal* begins with singing, yet we realize that the words have emerged from the storehouse of silence as the poet reminds us of his unfulfilled oath not to speak again. Had the poet kept his promise, we would have not had the present poem in hand. These words are, therefore, not ordinary but empowered by the silence from which they have come forth. Having established its special orientation, the poem, then, delivers its main message: the futility of resisting the transformation that love brings about.

If repentance grows on earth, from end to end;
Love shall uproot it, in one instance, like grass.
For repentance is like a shackle
The proud sea waves will not surrender to captivity.
(D, 223:3–4)

The poem continues with praise of love, which is likened to an ailment without a remedy: curing the sufferer of love would be as absurd as attempting to repair the "ceiling of the sky" with "plastered straw" (D, 223:10). The most significant feature of this *ghazal*, and the one relevant to the present discussion, is the fact that these verses remain connected to the silence introduced in the opening lines. The poem ends:

The mouth is full of words, but speaking is not possible;
By the true men's soul, I beseech you to
complete this poem!
(D, 223:13)

And so the words return to the silence from which they evolved following the circular path of emerging, delivering their message, and returning to their fountainhead. One might describe their flow as punctuated by silence (remember that Rumi's last plea is for someone to break the silence again and complete the poem). This punctuation may seem insignificant until we consider more closely what silence does for the whole process of verbalization.

The importance of words in our lives is usually well-understood. However, we hardly realize that without plain silence, how meaningless these words would be. On a literal level, statistics reveal that an average of forty to fifty percent of utterance time is occupied by pauses without which any speech would turn into an unbearably boring and incomprehensible flow of sounds. These pauses are not neutral hollow spaces with identical qualities. They themselves are divided into complex and independent categories of *voiced*, *verbal*, and *silent* fillers with distinct roles.[7] We shall not here investigate the variety and complexity of these pauses. The mere acknowledgement of them, however, reveals the centrality of silence for our verbal game.

Silence in Our Literary Memory

Other factors make silence an equally effective tool in literature. One is the precise way in which we define the concept of silence, or rather the way it resonates in our literary memory. As twentieth-century readers of

Rumi's lyrics, we translate his poetics of silence into our contemporary terms. We are not able to perceive silence unaffected by the central place it has occupied in the modern debate that shapes our concept of poetics. We live in an era that is acutely aware of the dominance of language and its association with the so-called loss of the mythical worldview through which a greater expanse of the imaginary was accessible. Many poets and thinkers in this century have considered language to be at the root of fundamental social problems: political oppression, alienation from the universe, and the narrow vision that results from positing human verbal expression as a unique and universal means of communication.[8] Rumi may not have shared all the above concerns. His poetry does, however, strive to privilege a vision of humans as active participants in a universe populated with a wide range of beings, all of whom possess independent media of communication. For him, love is the universal language, but no one insensitive to the diversity of this universe or blind to the importance of its varied participants will become conversant in that language. Silence as an awareness of the existence of these beings, as an acknowledgement of the vastness of this universe, and as a memory that can contain the unknown is the key to learning love's language. It is the remedy that will resensitize our receptive faculty to the messages these beings send. For Rumi, silence is the moment of realization that the entire universe is within our reach, providing we seek it and learn the language spoken by each of its constituent elements. Love has spread a feast for us, although it is hidden from view by a "curtain." "The intellect" is skeptical, and we are perplexed. "Silence" knows the way, for it can penetrate the "clouds of speech" that cloak the Sun:

> Behind a blood-stained curtain, love has spread its gardens.
> Lovers are busy with the beauty of the love that is beyond explanation.
> Intellect says: "The six directions are the limit, there is
>   nothing beyond them."
> Love says: "There is a road, and I have journeyed on it many times."
> Intellect saw a market and started to conduct business there;
> Love detected markets beyond that market.
> Intellect says: "Do not set foot on the land of annihilation;
>   there is nothing there but thorns."
> Love says: "Those thorns you feel are only inside you!
> Be silent! remove the thorn of existence from the foot of the heart;
> So that you may see the gardens within."
> O Shams of Tabrīz! you are the Sun cloaked by the cloud of speech;
> When your Sun rose, all the words melted!

(D, 132:1–3, 6–8)

This ability of silence to reach behind the curtain when the intellect is mired in confusion is the source of its poetic richness. The fact that it can both conceal and be concealed imbues silence with potential for artistic expression. Like any other artistic tool, it is likely to be viewed with suspicion. It is a double-edged sword, a weapon that can be turned against the holder. Indeed, silence evokes retribution as a moral transgression in which an individual refuses to express himself/herself in terms of universality. As Taylor points out in his analysis of Kierkegaard's *Fear and Trembling,* ethics has often viewed silence as the "snare of the demon," the concealment that fractures the moral structure of the world. From an ethical perspective, to remain silent and to refuse to express oneself is to negate the very possibility of moral relationships.[9]

What is ethically unacceptable may be aesthetically rewarding, however. Silence has much that aesthetically enhances the intricacies of linguistic discourse. Particularly, as the bridge to the inaccessible and the malleable blank that can contain the unknown, it fulfills the paradoxical demand to reveal through concealing, a characteristic feature of poetic utterance.

To begin with, the refusal of silence to comply with the rules of unconcealment in remaining publicly accessible endows each silence with characteristics of its own. Not only are silent moments hidden treasures, invisible tunnels to the Sun through the cloud of speech, they are unpredictable and individualistic. That is, they give individuals the chance to pour the essence of their personal explorations into their molds translating these silences into unique tales. Each of us travels in silence as far as our particular vision allows.

The realm of love and the domain of poetry share one major delight: the unexpected. In both these worlds, there are wonders to be seen, tricks to be exposed, and unknowns to be discovered. Silence is a suitable component to heighten the sense of surprise in this poetic game of make-believe. The contractual relationship that any good poetry imposes on the reader allows a measure of shock but never disbelief. Reversals of norms such as the following are part of a range of surprises used in the *Dīvān.* In this example, thematization of silence becomes a major tool for expression of the shocking event:

> Be silent! be silent! for love behaves
> contrary to normal;
> Here the meaning hides itself if you
> talk too much.
>
> (D, 1138:12)

Thus, silence is the nest of "true" meaning because only under its cover may the hidden be revealed. Yet, silence itself hides more than it ever reveals. In the recesses of its inaccessible inner core, it may contain all that we ever wished for: "words sweet as sugar" (D, 38:7), "innocence" long lost (D, 115:13), the cure for mouths inflicted by the "black demon" of empty words (D, 2631:22). Part of the aesthetic appeal of silence, as we have seen, is its ability to provide the space for revelation of the rare, the pure, and the extraordinary. Another part of its aesthetic appeal, however, stems from precisely the opposite quality. Not only can silence refuse to contain specific meaning, but in fact, it can liberate us from the shackles of the desire for fixed, conventional, exclusively verbal or textual means of expression. This is probably what Rumi has in mind when he pleads:

> Speak without words, so the enemy will not be able to say
> These are other people's sayings, and material from books!
> (D, 2636:12)

In fact, this liberating impact removes more than the apprehension of imitation. It works toward freeing its subject from an idealized concept of language as pure, beautiful, and sacred. It demands that attention be paid to the less attractive aspects of the verbal game such as those voiced by Susan Sontag concerning art's discontent with language. It brings to sharp focus the fact that words are in one sense too few, too many in another. Besides, they are crude and contaminated, and they block our immediate sensual communication with our surroundings.[10] Silence can liberate one from many such inadequacies and imperfections. Obviously, in Rumi's poetry the description of this liberating effect is colored with his specific concerns and fueled with his usual passionate tone:

> Now sleeping, now awake, my heart is in constant fervor.
> It is a covered saucepan, placed on fire.
> O you! who have offered us from a cup a silencing wine[11];
> Each moment a new tale is shouting to be told in silence.
> In his wrath there are a hundred kindnesses, in his meanness a hundred generosities;
> In his ignorance immeasurable gnosis, silently speaking like the mind.
> The words of those whom you have silenced, cannot hear but those whom you have made unconscious;
> I am both silent and fermenting for you like the sea of Aden!
> (D, 1808:6–9)

This is not a silence that is built upon despair or a lack of interest in self-expression, but on fervor, passion, and the desire to make the tale of love infinitely more intriguing by leaving the core of it untold. There is a marked distinction between not speaking and intentionally remaining silent; the former indicates absence of action, the latter qualifies as an intentional act.[12] Much of twentieth-century literature is concerned with silence of the first kind. It tends to underline the absurdity of speech in the face of the void in which the artist feels caught. This silence, though intentional, does not claim to be liberating.

Beckett's writings are a good example of literature preoccupied with this kind of silence. They are also relatively well-explored examples.[13] Because of its impact on our contemporary understanding, the Beckettian demarcation of silence may be the only literary utilization of the concept with which the twentieth-century Western reader is likely to be familiar. To clarify the situation, let us briefly examine the silence that inspired Beckett and contrast it with the silence that poetically motivated Rumi. In *Waiting for Godot* (1952) much of the dialogue only fills the silence without saying anything. Similarly, in *Krapp's Last Tape* (1959), Krapp has no memories. He is "alone with himself, with his nothingness which no other sound can enliven. . . ." As Hubert observes, Krapp's "very act of listening to the voice of his past, as played by the tape, merely becomes a new variety of silence." In a way, in Krapp's case, an inversion has taken place. It is not the silence that is impregnated with hidden speech but speech drained of its ability to express by the ever-present silence of nothingness.

Rumi's tendency to evoke silence does not imply such an emptiness either in the world in which we live or the words we utter. In marked contrast with Beckett, Rumi's silence is a moment of listening to the singing of a lively universe. If Krapp has no memory, every particle in Rumi's universe resonates with a divine memory. Like an intricate and invisible web, this memory connects every created being with the source of everlasting love that permeates the moments of its creation.[14] Human memory may be temporarily obscured by the shades of multiplicity which lead to the illusion of separation from that origin; nevertheless, it is possible to recover that memory. What is more, the literary discourse, far from witnessing the emptiness, has the distinct role of assisting in the recovery of the memory by reviving something of the fragrance of the forgotten past.

Rumi therefore makes a point of emphasizing the intentionality of his silence and the good news masked by its blank surface. He is particularly careful not to create the impression that the silence is a result of emptiness. If anything, it is the fullness and vastness of the experience that hinder expression. The following poem is intended as a testimony to the sky's participation in divine love. The physical characteristics of the sky (i.e., radiance, detachment from the earth, etc.) and its acts of generosity (replenishing the earth with raindrops) are evoked to bear witness to this love. Realizing that the evidence fails to prove the desired sanctified status, Rumi then converts the purity of the sky into a blue *iḥrām* to endow the "actions" of the sky with the sacredness of the Muslim pilgrimage.[15] He relies on the "scientific" theorem that considered the sky to revolve around the sun to attribute to the *iḥram*-wearing sky the act of circumambulation the pilgrims performed around the house of *Kaʿbah*. Having described the sky's endless allegorical pilgrimage, completed with an affirming Qur'ānic citation, Rumi realizes that all he has labored to describe can be reduced to "pretexts" for ulterior motives. The only true "house of God" is the indescribable love itself, and the alternative to the faulty verbal attempts to convey the true magnitudes of this house is silence, a rich intentional silence:

O, the sky who turns above our head!
In love of the sun, you share the same mantle with me.
By God you are in love—and I shall tell what reveals your secret:
Inside and out you are radiant and lush.
You do not get soaked in the sea, you are not bound to the earth;
You do not burn in fire, and are not disturbed by the wind.
O the millstone! which is the water that makes you turn?
Tell me! perhaps you are a wheel made of Iron.
You turn one way and make the earth green [with raindrops] like paradise;
Then you turn the other way and uproot the trees [in a storm].
The sun is a candle and you a moth in action;
  weaving your web around this candle.
You are a pilgrim wearing an *Iḥrām* turquoise in color
Like pilgrims you are in circumambulation of *Kaʿbah*.
God said: "whoever performed *Ḥajj* is safe";
O dutiful wheel [of the sky]! you are safe from harm.[16]

Everything is a pretext, there is love and nothing besides love;
Love is the house of God and you are living in that house.
I will say no more, for it is not possible to say;
God knows how much more is in me crying out to be told.

(D, 2997:1–10)

At times this silence functions like a safety mechanism that prevents the poems from disrupting the order of their composed and controlled surroundings. "Silence!" Rumi warns himself, "for the words are beginning to fly, full as they are, with secrets" (D, 21:18). "Be silent!" he says in another poem, "Do not set fire to the woods" (D, 227:11). In other instances, he is even more specific about the disclosing nature of his poetry and the fact that it may be beyond the capacity of his audience to understand. Once more, silence is not an absence of meaningful expression but a safety device to contain the explosive impact of revealing a secret:

> Be silent! for if it was not for fear of causing a mutiny;
> My speech would tear open a thousand curtains each moment.
> (D, 1722:13)

With such an effective weapon in hand, it is not surprising that in certain moments of intimacy (one might say mischief), Rumi threatens in a half-joking, half-serious tone:

> I shall cry so loud, I shall play such tricks;
> That the rust will be removed from the mirror [of the heart] of every denier.
> (D, 22:1)

After all, as it has been pointed out, silence never ceases to imply its opposite and depends on that presence for its effectiveness.[17]

Some isolated rebellious moments aside, silence in the *Dīvān* reveals itself to us as being instigated by the Divine. This is either expressed directly through the authorial voice or implied in the poem. As human love may have a tendency toward possessiveness, its divine counterpart also involves jealousy (*ghayrah*), which forbids the poetic discourse from publishing the secrets of love. Interestingly, jealousy, which is often personified as a strong figure, is so opposed to verbal disclosure of secrets that he himself appears as a mute character who gestures or acts silently. In one instance Rumi describes the divine jealousy that guards his silence as a bridle that keeps his mouth shut (D, 356:14). In another instance, *ghayrah* gestures by biting its lip, signaling to the poet to stop writing more poems (D, 169:14).[18] Finally, in an even more dramatic confrontation, love physically interferes by putting its hands over the poet's mouth to prevent him from uttering one more word. The threatening move is compensated for by a promise that if the poet remains silent, he will attain to a high status in heaven. In the meantime a playful pun is created with the words *shiʿr*, meaning poetry, and the name of the star *shaʿrā* to diffuse the seriousness of the situation (D, 182:6). Many are the instances in which Rumi explicitly refers to being forbidden to continue speaking (cf. D, 11:11; 1144:17; 1925:16). In these examples, often the metaphor for the effective poetic expression of love is a burning flame. Not only does the image convey the warmth, the ethereal nature, and the glow of love, it facilitates the creation of another useful pun. While the sonic impact of this pun, which involves the words *zabān* (tongue) and *zabānah*(flame), sharpens the semantic impact, its use of the verb *khāmūsh kardan* with the double meaning "to silence" and "to extinguish fire" usually allows the poet to economize in words (D, 332:18).

Side by side with its divine impetus, silence serves a number of specific literary purposes in the *Dīvān*. One of its main purposes is to maintain in the reader an awareness of the open-ended nature of poetry. As we have observed in his adoption of paradoxical modes and in his attention to the experiential nature of poetic creation, one of the ways by which Rumi maintains communication with the reader is to allow them to participate in the act of creation. Throughout his lyrics, he emphasizes the point that poetry is a well-planned game and that readership is an intentional participatory act. The reader can partake of the transforming impact of this heavenly phenomenon only to the degree that he can participate in the performance the words stage in front of him. Ultimately, each reader is a poet who finishes Rumi's poem in his own individual style. Thus Rumi closes a vast majority of his *ghazals* with lines such as " I am silent, my throat is injured. O Sufi singer, you sing the rest" (D, 38:13). In this verse, the voice of the Sufi singer is compared to that of the prophet/musician David, thus allowing the possibility of hearing a miracle in the finishing touch that comes from the reader. Do not shy away, says Rumi to his readers, be your own poet, for what you create may be even better than my own poem. The same richness is implied in the reader's potential contribution in another poem in which Rumi closes by confessing his inability to say more. He then plunges into silence with this final request: "Read this *ghazal* in full from the tablet of my heart" (D, 771:8). The reader feels empowered by the poet's confidence that his incomplete *ghazal* could blossom and attain perfection in the reader's creative mind. Elsewhere, Rumi simply declares that he has arrived at the edge of silence but reminds the reader that far from being an end, this is the spot where the reader's task begins (D, 99:19). It is important to realize that some of these statements are addressed to God. In these examples, it is divine interference that the poet is making a plea for, implying the divine source of all creativity. God alone is able to put the perfecting touch to our imperfect creations. Yet, there is no question that the majority of such closing statements are addressed to ordinary readers, whereas some others are intentionally left vague. The very act of playing on this ambiguity as well as alluding to divine and human creative impulses in parallel situations attests to Rumi's conviction concerning the autonomous role he expects his ordinary human readers to play in shaping and defining the silent spaces he offers them in his *ghazals*.

Notwithstanding the significance of the open-ended atmosphere the silent gaps bring to the closing portions of the *ghazals,* they may be found elsewhere, as well, making a variety of literary points. One of the most prominent themes expressed through such gaps is that of the restrictions imposed by language. Time and again, Rumi points to the obligatory silence caused by the inadequacy of the expressive medium. "I became silent," he says in one instance, "for my feet sank into the mud" (D, 102:15). Elsewhere, he compares the difficulty of verbal expression to that of making the reader see the image of a bird sitting on the branches of a tree itself too distant to be seen with human eyes (D, 154:11). At times, his complaints are even more explicit:

> I am ashamed of describing the beloved's face, by God I shall close my mouth.
> How much water can a water-skin carry from a sea or an ocean?
> (D, 164:11)

The solution is silence, though this time more precisely defined: "Beat the drums and speak no more." The justification is clear, for language cannot find its way when the "heart," the "soul," and the "intellect" have all gone astray (D, 329:6). This example, however, is particularly significant for its detailed reference to the circumstances in which silence is to be observed. The drum may be played, whereas verbal communication is to be withheld. In this way the poem makes clear that the absence is that of speech and not of sound. This is a point worth further exploration.

Using the term silence may imply an absence of any sound, a kind of auditory void. This kind of complete stillness has its own literary overtones. The desire for and the fascination with the phenomenon of death, reflected in much prose and poetry of this century, is an artistic expression of the desire for such silence. This kind of silence is utterly alien to the *Dīvān,* where the *ghazals,* which make us aware of the need for silence, themselves vibrate with a wide range of lively sounds. Like the murmuring of a nearby city, the sound they produce contains both harsh noises and soft melodies. In fact, the range of sounds heard in these lyrics is considerably wider than those common to the genre of *ghazal* in general. As we shall see in the section on imagery in the *Dīvān,* not only do nightingales sing and flutes play sweet melodies, but thunder roars, mountains echo, the earth shakes violently, and floodwaters flow noisily. This is not to mention the "green-robed preachers of Spring" with their eloquently "silent" speech (D, 1134:27) and other apparently mute inhabitants of the universe who become articulate in these poems. The "lamp of the day and that of the night," for instance, give voice to their respective solar and lunar messages with their radiant glow (D, 45:18). As for flowers, each of their petals is a tongue, if only we could achieve the kind of silence that enables us to hear their words (D, 1624:14).[19] In the poetic universe that Rumi builds, there is neither absence of sound nor the desire for it. Instead, there is a desire for that absence of speech which allows entrance into a higher state of consciousness. This is the state in which human beings realize and acknowledge the imperfection of their verbal medium of expression. Abstinence from self-expression through language will, it is hoped, cure us of the illusion that we possess a powerful, autonomous, and exclusively human expressive tool. We will come to realize that our sense of freedom and independence is a self-delusion, for we are completely dependent for our inner experiences on the universe and the divine force that created it. To put it in the language of metaphor, we are like a "flute, a piece of wood imprisoned in its muteness," which can sing its inner music only through the divine lips that blow in it (D, 1641:3). That we are all, seemingly, one instrument does not deny us our individuality, for no two flutes will sound exactly the same. Nor does this silence diminish our roles as participants in the cosmic dance. If anything, we have joined the company of those who speak through even more powerful media like the "green-robed preacher of Spring" and the "many-tongued lily." We have done more than simply add to the range of our communication skills. We have transformed and reached the highest level of intelligent articulation. There is no limit to what we can now express; it is possible for us to stop "reciting the *Qur'ān*" and "be the words of God himself" (D, 1665:16).

The Varieties of Silence in the *Dīvān*: A Thematic Exploration

To describe silence in the *Dīvān* as a divinely inspired phenomenon says something about how Rumi's lyrics consciously explain their origin. It does not, however, shed any light on the diversity and poetic signficance of this silence. In his "Sounds of Silence," Mark Taylor provides an illuminating discussion on Kierkegaard's consideration of reflective silence in problem III of *Fear and Trembling*. "Aesthetic silence," Taylor observes on the basis of Kierkegaard's analysis, "assumes many forms, ranging from the seemingly necessary silence of the sensuous-erotic genius to reflective silence willingly kept for *playful, deceitful, demonic* and *heroic* purposes."[20] Few works of literary art effectively utilize all of these forms of silence as tools for expression. Furthermore, other varieties of silence, stemming from the above main categories or independent from them, may be detected in literary settings. In what follows, we shall proceed to examine the varieties of silence detectable in the *Dīvān*, as well as their overall literary implications for this corpus of poetry.

Kierkegaard's playful silence refers to a kind of intentional secrecy that is at the heart of comedy. As Taylor points out, it finds a variety of manifestations, ranging from mistaken identity, careful disguise, and white lies to puns and irony. To search for comic intentions in the *Dīvān* may initially sound like a farfetched idea. Hardly any other body of Persian poetry treats the plight of humankind and the tragedy of the separation from its origin with as much seriousness. Yet the work shares many features with comedy. It has a lighthearted, fast, and rhythmic tempo. Topics of deep and profound significance are often treated with uncharacteristic brightness and humor. For instance, the comic element is at work when Rumi describes his plea for divine intercession as a visit by a melancholic "long-robed" customer to the workshop of the "tailor of the lovers" (D, 216:1–2). Elsewhere, just as the poet is being driven to madness with perplexity and fear, love appears disguised as a sage and suggests a solution. The solution, which is also meant to serve as a model for our relationship with Rumi, is to observe silence. This otherwise noncomical episode is given a humorous aura through simplicity and overdramatization. The comical ambience is enhanced by exaggerating its seriousness. The tearing of the clothes, the whispering of hidden words, and the silent nodding all point to entertaining nuance in the episode. The silence here does not conceal much. Indeed, it is there to reveal the intimacy of the relationship:

> I went crazy last night, love ran into me and said:
> "I am coming, do not shout, do not tear your clothes, speak no more."
> "O love!" I said: "I am afraid of other things."
> "There is nothing else" it said: "speak no more.
> I shall whisper hidden words into your ear;
> You just nod in approval! except in secret speak no more!"
>
> (D, 2219:3–5)

This kind of happy ending, where love uses its charm to solve major problems, is something else that the *Dīvān*, despite its seriousness, shares with lighthearted comedies. Many of Rumi's *ghazals* demonstrate a clear and detectable pattern: despite the difficulties on the path, if we sincerely wish it, in the end love will "pull us by the ear" to a "corner" and recite to us an "incantation" (*fusūn*) whereby our lives will be transformed (D, 1829:15–16). Though this is not a situation which would lend itself to description in a *ghazal* easily, the reader feels convinced of the happy ending. Such poems use light metrical patterns and images that radiate a sense of hope, warmth, and safety. Thus playfulness is a familiar dimension of silence that the *Dīvān* adopts to brighten its vision of love and of the poetry which is an expression of that love. The following is an example of mistaken identity in which love is taken to be a thief, intentionally wearing a thin disguise:

> I have seen thieves who steal money and possessions from people;
> This thief steals the thieves themselves!
> One pleads to the king for justice, when the thieves become too many;
> Where should one look for justice, when the thief is the king himself?
> Love is that king with whom even thieves fall in love!
> To that overseer God takes the arrogant—dragging them by the hair.
> Love is that thief stealing the heart of all guards;
> In the service of that thief there are countless guards.
> I shouted last night, "O sleepers! there is a thief in the house!"
> In the midst of that, he stole the tongue from my mouth!
> I said I would tie his hands, in fact he tied mine;
> I said I would put him in a prison, but he would not be contained in the world.
> From the pleasure of his theft, every night a new guard turns into a thief;
> Intelligent ones are hiding for fear of his tricks.
> In the middle of the night, you see a crowd gathered asking where is that thief?
> He is in the midst of the crowd asking the same question "where is that thief?"
>
> (D, 1810:1–8)

Of the other forms of silence mentioned by Kierkegaard, heroic silence is probably the only one that is clearly detectable in the *Dīvān*. Heroic silence is painful, willingly chosen to protect others. Abraham's silence before the planned sacrifice of his son falls into this category. We have seen many examples in the above paragraphs in which Rumi alludes to the necessity of silence to protect his audience. Sometimes, this is more than an allusion, as in the following verse:

> I obey the order, when he says "silence!" I remain silent;
> For one day that king will explain this in person.
>
> (D, 1122:15)

Rumi's silence may be compared to that of Abraham in another respect: the way it is erected like a wall to conceal and protect the extraordinarily personal nature of his relationship with God. This form of reluctance to speak, what Kierkegaard calls the silence of faith, has to do with the inexpressibility of "the direct, unmediated and radically privatized relation of the believer to God." A relation of this nature "cannot be conveyed in the universal categories of thought and language," and any attempt to capture the unique experience of faith would only result in a misrepresentation of it.[21] Furthermore, as David Wren has observed, Abraham's lack of interest in speaking about his planned sacrifice of his son stems from the fact that any explanation would turn this "peculiarly personal" relationship with the divine into a public affair, a much less valued circumstance.[22] This variety of silence may also be compared to what we singled out in Rumi's lyrics as the urge to refrain from speech imposed by the divine jealousy or *ghayrah*. The pattern recognizible in both cases is the urge to preserve a "peculiarly personal" relationship by protecting it from the public.

However, in Rumi's lyrics there is an additional factor at work. Whereas in Kierkegaard's silence of faith, the faithful is struck dumb by the inexpressibility of the individualistic nature of the experience and the fear of its trivialization through publicity, in our examples from the *Dīvān* the divine *ghayrah* actively imposes the silence. Another notable point here concerns the question of the inexpressibility of the experience. Interestingly, Rumi, despite all his complaints concerning the inadequacy of language, is more optimistic than Kierkegaard's faithful in that he does have faith in some form of verbal expression. This may stem from the conviction that while ordinary speech may be ineffective, poetry with its divine source of inspiration offers a solution to the problem. The solution, at least in Rumi's case, frequently involves overlooking canonic conventions and adopting unorthodox schemes that radically depart from tradition. Nevertheless, he demonstrates a confidence in the possibility of achieving this end. Here, silence figures highly among the effective tools of expression. In one instance, he likens ordinary speech to "screaming" while one is drowning in the sea. A "skilled diver" keeps his mouth shut so as "to preserve enough air" in the lungs to survive (D, 565:14). Elsewhere Rumi is explicit about the fun, magic, and tricks of poetry that can help stretch the expressive ability of language. This stretch of the imagination, made possible in a poetic ambience, renders the unseen visible through the process of make-believe:

> Speaking has become so fine, so precise, there is not even room
> for the breath in the mouth [for the fear of distorting the speech];
> I shall resort to sophistry, since here tricks are justified!
>
> (D, 27:30)

Silence can refer to the "perpetually unstated meaning, the unformulated conception," observes Hubert in relation to Beckett's play *Waiting for Godot*. He further describes this kind of hollow silence as "the mute perplexity of man in a given situation or the lack of response on the part of the creator or creation."[23] We have established that Rumi's silence, in marked contrast with that of the twentieth-century writer, is a pregnant silence that points to fullness and abundance. It is a cloud ready to rain, with promises of freshness and growth to follow. The heart is a "fermenting sea" (D, 2170:17). If the "mouth is silent," it is in the hope that the "divine storyteller" may take over the responsibility of telling the tale (D, 1086:8). In this sense Rumi's poetry is more concerned with the future than with the past:

> The heart is full of words, Alas! with no ability to speak;
> O the beloved of the Sufis! you open your mouth and tell the story.
> Tell us of those states which we have not yet gone through;
> It is not a habit of the Sufis to speak of the past.
>
> (D, 198:5–6)

Obviously the other characteristic of Beckett's silence, namely its sense of ineffectiveness and failure, is not present here either. Hubert reminds us of the overpowering, one might say defeating, nature of the silence in *Krapp's Last Tape*, which is empty speech played back on a tape recorder to replace the missing "inner voice of the past and fill the void of the present." Here, a mechanical device is used to populate a realm of "maddening silence" with words. Hubert rightly contrasts this with the "lyrical outbursts" of the so-called "hero" prevalent during the Romantic period which usually contributes to a sense of triumph over silence.[24] It is clear from the above examples that Rumi's silence does not point to stagnation or defeat. Not only is this silence more dynamic than its counterpart in words, but the absence of speech opens the way for the unlimited dynamism of the potential discourse that may fill this blank space. Silence has thus furnished the discourse with an opportunity constantly to renew itself and remain relatively immune to the ravages of time.

Nevertheless, we are twentieth-century readers. At a time when Beckett's silence speaks for our bewilderment and life's absurdity, the dynamism and playfulness in Rumi's silence may come as a surprise. We may find it shallow in the face of our suffering and naive in offering such simple-sounding solutions. In the age of solitary discontent we are only too familiar with a world rapidly losing the awareness of the Divine. This is the civilization that, in the words of Wallace Stevens, "consists only of man himself."[25] To reduce the pain of this extreme loneliness, the arts have been promoted to fill the void. With the crown of divinity on the head and the agonizing burden of human consciousness on the shoulders and destined to become the modern era's "project of spirituality," contemporary art has predictably found little time to play.[26] It should not come as a surprise that this state of affairs has affected our critical understanding of playfulness as an effective literary device. We have approached poetry much too seriously. Of course the profoundly moral and spiritual purposes that infuse all of Rumi's poetry, including the *Dīvān*, are serious in that they are central to his poetic creation. Yet the universe, as he sees it, is imaginatively designed and prudently run by God. In it, there is room for everything. Silence is sweeter than honey (D, 75:8), but words too are divine magnets which attract one to God (D, 1710:14). In this setting poetry occasionally has the childlike opportunity to find a chance to play. This playfulness is by no means incompatible with seriousness. Indeed, as we shall see, it becomes a key device that enhances the poetic impact of the discourse in which the "spiritual" has a prominent part. Differently put, in Rumi's "project of spirituality" there is ample room for purposeful play. This applies to his manipulation of the poetics of silence, too. In the following poem, the reader is transformed into a young boy whom the poet addresses with utmost informality. To this young companion, whose existence Rumi describes as mingled with his own, he offers himself to be read like a book. The special gift which the fatherly poet gives to the boy, however, is the mirror of silence, a seemingly simple present to a young child who has not had much chance to explore the wonders of his own face. Yet there seems to be no limit to what may be heard in the heart of that silence or seen in that silent mirror:

> I have come without a heart, without a soul;
> Look at my color, read the lines on my face, O my boy!
> No, I am wrong, I have not come at all, you came to me;
> You came with me, hidden in my existence, O my boy!
> Smile in the face of fire like a piece of gold;
> And good fortune will smile at you, O my boy!
>
> In the tavern of my heart there are thoughts
> Fighting each other like drunks, O my boy!
> Bear [with me] and listen to the clamor of the intoxicated;
> Ah, the door broke! the doorman run away! O my boy!
> I have come, and I have brought you a mirror;
> Look at yourself, do not turn your face, O my boy!
> My blasphemy is a mirror for your faith;
> Behold the blasphemy that is faith! O my boy!
> I cry out in silence;
> I have come to be a silent speaker, O my boy!"
>
> (D, 1098:1–8)

As readers of twentieth-century literature, we are familiar with another variety of silence, known as stunned silence. Stunned silence is usually caused by extreme fear and mistrust. The most obvious example in this century is the silence of the Holocaust survivors in the face of unspeakable horrors they witnessed, a silence reflected in much post-Holocaust literature.[27] It is important to bear in mind that Rumi's moments of silence in the *Dīvān* do not reflect a sense of being stunned. His are confident and controlled silences, even when they illustrate an inadequacy or a dilemma. They are often conscious and purposeful rather than unexpected and bewildering. To us, the readers, he offers the experience of that silence like a carefully wrapped gift, not an unintentional fruit of a moment of surprise or confusion. It is something we are expected to appreciate and exploit to the fullest. This silence is a tool, both literary and spiritual, to be put to careful use. Rumi's display of poetic authority and composure has profound implications for his lyrics. First, it maintains a sense of order in the midst of the most baffling moments of intoxication. Furthermore, it reassures us of the authority of the text and the trust we may put in it. The *ghazals* become more than an invitation to join the whirling dance of love. They become a source of wisdom, a wise counselor, a guide who can be trusted. Indeed, one might say the lyrics use these moments of silence as islands in a stormy sea to counterbalance their dynamically changing nature. We, the readers, rest on these islands and let the poet within use these quiet moments to take his/her own imaginative leap, confident that the destiny of our experience is in safe hands.

The above poetic use of silence also promotes Rumi's experiential perception of poetry. Through an evocation of intentional and controlled silence, the poetic voice is constantly invigorated and empowered. For his/her part the reader has to fill these gaps of intentional silence during the process of reception. He/she is, therefore, kept permanently engaged in reconstructing the poems in his/her mind. The reader soon learns that full benefit from Rumi's poems requires active participation in the poetic game, i.e., a continuous and dynamic re-creation of what is buried beneath the silent surface. The interaction has no end, the poems are read on a regular basis, even those that the reader knows by heart, and the process of reconstruction is different each time. It is a coming full circle to the starting point, not unlike whirling, in which, just as in poetry, the destination is secondary to what the participants explore during the experience. Taking the analogy a step further, just as the silent whirling figures do not appear to be doing very much, whereas the experience is otherwise for those engaged in the action, the dynamism of this text/reader interaction is felt by its active participants. Active participation, however, should not be difficult, for, as Janice Sanders Moreno has pointed out, "silence infects its subjects with its atmosphere and the products of this atmosphere are made eternal."[28]

Silence as Beginning and End

No poet can ignore the significance of silence in its purely textual sense. Poems begin in silence and end in silence. Their brief existence is caught between two unlimited stretches of silence. As metaphors, these blank spaces speak for our limited opportunity to live and to voice the plight of our captivity between our births and our deaths. Poems make use of these metaphors, but at the same time, they have to cope with the anxiety of their own textual finiteness. In a discussion of silence as the demarcation of limits of narration in the poetry of the French middle ages, McCracken refers to these beginnings and endings as spots filled with poetic anxiety.[29] Different poets deal with this anxiety in different ways. A common strategy is to make use of what McCracken terms "narrative silence." Narrative silence refers to direct intervention by the poet to disrupt the normal flow of the poem by introducing silence as a theme. These instances are, obviously, important not only because we witness the poetic action in diffusing tension but because we hear the poet reflect on the relation of silence and poetry.[30] In them we have concrete examples of silence as a space impregnated with meaning rather than being deprived of it.

In Rumi's poetry, beginnings do not seem to be overly anxious moments. He does, however, benefit from thematization of silence to overcome the anxiety of ending the text. "I stop here," he says in one instance and justifies the suspension by reminding "short speech is more pleasant" (D, 103:11). In another instance, "be quiet [O Rumi!]," he warns himself: "for you said much and no one listened" (D, 215:14). However, these are his less frequent, as well as less complex, ways of declaring that no poem may go on forever and that texts will have to come to an end just as everything else does. More often he uses a dynamic way to deal with the anxiety of ending a *ghazal,* which is rather unusual: he ends the poems by introducing a completely new theme which the reader will have to follow in his own imagination and which transforms the *ending* of a poem into a *beginning*. In other words, although the text physically ends on the page it continues to resonate in the mind of the reader, who is stimulated to follow the newly introduced theme:

> I stop here, now rise everyone!
> The cypress figure beloved is calling unto us.

O the king of Tabrīz, O my king Shams-i Dīn!
I have closed my mouth, you come and open yours [to speak].
(D, 60:15–16)

Elsewhere, this is achieved differently. In a *ghazal* devoted entirely to a description of the poet's relationship with the Divine, self-praise is used as the central theme. In the second to the last verse the poet likens himself to a Sun that, in the shadow of the beloved, has conquered the world. Then, in what seems to be a standard closing statement, Rumi addresses himself: "Enough of boasting, abandon this, say your prayers instead." The last hemistitch, however, instead of ending, begins a new motif: the elevating theme of ascension. "Jesus," the verse continues, "ascended to the fourth heaven." Then, by way of furnishing details, we are informed that "the wings of prayer" were the means of transportation for this heavenly expedition (D, 226:11). Thus the poem ends when we begin our visualization of the prophet's journey on the wings of prayer. In another fascinating example of such endings, Rumi pleads with us not to ask for the ending of the story. He suggests that we go, instead, to his disciple Ṣalāḥ al-Dīn for a full description of the "beauty of the king." While these lines indicate that Ṣalāḥ al-Dīn has provided the inspiration for their creation, their main role is to inspire a new beginning by inviting us to speculate on what Ṣalāḥ al-Dīn's version might entail (D, 239:11–12).

Rumi uses the above scheme not only to deal with the anxiety of closing the poem but to benefit from the "interpretive opening" that silence inserts into the text. He helps us explore such "openings" and experience their expressive effect.[31] Hence, we may remember once more, it is not his distaste for poetry but his faith in the poetic potential of such "interpretive openings" that inspires him to say that a silent love is clearer than one which is aided by commentary.[32] Ultimately, it is not the linguistic skills but the transformational magic of love that with the aid of divine grace enables us to penetrate the deep silence of incomprehension. The less we depend on the verbal medium, therefore, the more receptive we shall be to this empowering force, this silent love. We shall thus be more likely to overcome the silence of incomprehension when we learn to read the silent, the unwritten.

One does not have to deal in mystical poetry to appreciate that the most significant part of any poem is the unwritten. What is on paper is of importance only insofar as it is a preface to this unwritten poem. The written portion will remain extremely limited if it fails to guide to the portion that resonates beyond the page. Rumi echoes his frustration with this dependency on the written. But just as the recognition of the silent layers of a poem does not diminish the significance of the words, frustration with this limitation is not a statement of disrespect concerning poetry. It is an acknowledgment of the complexity of poetry and the limits of its boundaries that are as real as the boundlessness of its impact.

The fascination with silence, for Rumi, is at the same time a declaration of freedom. In this way he reminds us that although words as his artistic medium of communication are important, even alluring, his real loyalty is to that portion of the poem to which words are only a preface: the silent part. Rumi, familiar as he was with the Persian literary tradition, knew well that poets often become captives of the intricacy of the medium with which they work. The words become idols whose attraction enslave their own creator:

> Before, I wished customers for my poems;
> Now, I wish you would buy me back from those words.
> I carved many an idol to attract everyone's attention;
> Now, I am intoxicated with Ibrāhīm, I am tired of being [an idol maker]
> like Ādhar.
> There! a colorless idol has arrived, my hands are busy with that one;
> Find another master for your idol carving store!
> I cleaned the store of myself, I threw away all figures;
> I came to appreciate the value of madness, I abandoned all thought.
> If an image comes to mind, I say "get out O deluding one!"
> I destroy it if it challenged my authority.
>
> (D, 2449:1–5)

Since the medium of expression may itself become a hindrance—even a prison—for Rumi it is important to make clear his refusal to become a captive of his own words. If need be, he will abandon words and opt for the poetics rooted in silence; verbalization is a medium, and it will remain so. At times, however, Rumi's fascination for silence is meant to be more than a declaration of personal freedom from the spell of words. As has been the case in the work of some twentieth-century poets, the centrality of silence for Rumi is, in part, a "testimony to his belief that human language ought not posit itself as the optimal avenue by which meaning might find expression."[33] When not praising silence, Rumi demonstrates his loyalty to this ideal through engaging in what Sontag has termed "participating in the ideal of silence." That is, he displeases, provokes, shocks, and frustrates the audience through violation of canonical literary conventions.[34]

The present chapter testifies to the depth and the variety of ways in which Rumi celebrates silence. It makes clear that Rumi's fascination for silence does not stem from a wish not to speak but rather a desire to foreground the significance of the phenomenon of silence in spiritual growth and literary expression. The chapter continues with an exploration of the unchartedness of silence from two different philosophical vantage points: as independent from language and as rooted in the verbal system. Since as twentieth-century readers we have a definite and rather gloomy understanding of silence, the discussion focuses on contrasting Rumi's brand of silence with the one generally understood as built upon despair and emptiness, best demonstrated in the works of Samuel Beckett. The specific literary values of silence, such as preserving the open-endedness of poetry, are discussed next and followed by a review of the ways in which the *Dīvān* benefits from thematization of silence (i.e., as playful, as heroic, etc.). Silence in a purely textual context as the blank that frames the beginning and ending of each poem and the anxiety of dealing with this textual finiteness in Rumi's lyric is dealt with next. The chapter closes with a discussion of the freedom that silence can bestow on a poet such as Rumi; a freedom not only from idealizing one's own poems but of positing human language as the optimal avenue for expression.

The fact remains that sound and silence need each other for a meaningful existence. In the actualization of the poetic event, they are convertible polarities that are engaged in a constant interplay. The tension that exists between the two provides the propelling force behind poetic creation. The poet is not just a manipulator of words but also a master of silence. By reaching out and capturing the moments in which silence speaks more eloquently than words and by contrasting them with instances of lyrical outburst crystallized in verbal discourse, the poet weaves the fine tapestry of poetry. In the finished product, the transformation is so complete that the work may not be meaningfully studied through an analysis of its constituent parts. Only the tapestry, and not the threads with which it is woven, can relate the artistic tale it has been created to tell.[35]

Knowing that silence does something more than blend with words to weave the tapestry of poetry, Rumi utilizes it to achieve a goal beyond words: an undefined and unlimited poem. He makes his poems a preface to the "immeasurable" silent poetry, unaffected by time and capable of exploring new horizons. In the chapter that follows, we shall observe the ways in which Rumi builds colorful and dynamic images to give a visual dimension to this "silent" poetry, an act he describes as "growing wondrous birds" from the palm of his hand.[36]

CHAPTER 5

"Wondrous Birds Grow from the Palm of My Hand"
The Dynamism of Imagery in the Dīvān

The wondrous birds of images that grew in astonishing numbers from the palm of Rumi's hand never failed to sing a new tune.[1] That is to say, the one unchanging feature of the images in the *Dīvān-i Shams* is that the poetic message they send changes from poem to poem. For example, the moon that we have encountered in the section on paradox, journeying "footless" and brave in "nothingness" (D, 1759:10), is a powerless, isolated lover in another poem (D, 2326:6). In the second poem (which, in contrast to the first, does not evoke lunar movement), the stationary moon melts away in the dark night of love. In another instance, not the last of the guises in which the moon appears in the *Dīvān,* it represents the radiant face of the beloved, a metaphor with which readers of Persian lyrics are familiar:

> The heaven and earth are but mirrors;
> The moon of your face reflected in them.
> The mirror has come to life with the reflection;
> To catch a glimpse of the beauty.
>
> (D, 2278:10)

It is significant that critical works on the *Dīvān,* instead of reflecting this diversity and its monumental poetic implications, attempt to reach a single fixed interpretation for each image (for example, all the moons in the entire corpus of Rumi's lyrics). This approach limits the generic horizons of the *ghazals,* overlooks their richness and variety, and reduces them to a conventional hard core.[2] The present chapter will demonstrate that Rumi's lyrics do not warrant this critical method. On the contrary, their freshness, their appreciation of change, their dynamic nature, and the playful ambience they attempt to create are all indications of a need for a more resilient and creative criticism. The pages that follow will strive to present an example of such criticism, with special emphasis on the function of the imagery.

There is, of course, no question that the verbal surface of any literary creation is pregnant with latent concepts which might be made more accessible through critical analysis. The attempt to reach beyond the verbal surface and search for latent concepts is not in itself misplaced. The problem here lies in understanding the critical process as assigning the image a permanent meaning that deprives it of its diverse and dynamic function. The false assumption that an image, regardless of its varying postures in different poems, can be interpreted in terms of a single unchangeable concept (or, in some cases, concepts) is the chief error in this approach.

There are other major flaws in the existing critical literature on the imagery in Rumi's lyric works. The first and foremost is a lack of generic appreciation. The vast corpus of Rumi's works is often dealt with as if all of it was written in the same genre.[3] The result is that the imagery employed in the *Maṣnavī*, despite its different generic purposes, conventions, and audience, is lumped together with that in the *Dīvān*. When convenient to the critic, examples from the *Fīhi mā fīh*, Rumi's discourses in prose, are also included. Each of these works, however, must be analyzed separately in the light of its unique generic characteristics.

Secondly, the search for symbolic meaning is usually carried out by sifting through standard manuals of speculative mysticism in pursuit of parallel imagery. The gaps are then filled with extratextual evidence extracted from biographical and other sources. In the meantime, poems that themselves offer major clues to our understanding of their poetic function are relegated to the margin. The incorporation of extratextual material, of course, does not pose a problem if it contributes to the reader's grasp of the context yet remains in the background. In the criticism in question, however, it becomes the major instrument for extrapolation of authorial intention and is therefore fatal to a poetic reading of the *Dīvān*.[4] Furthermore, conventional adoption of the Sufi idiom, which itself is supposed to have rigidified over time, dictates specific readings as the only possible ones.[5] In this hermeneutic reading, every heart is a mirror for the reflection of the beauty of the beloved, and wine always points to the intoxicating effect of divine love.[6] The playfulness and the vitality of such images are lost when they are assigned these permanent readings. At the same time, the criticism which has treated them as fixed entities evinces a lack of interest in the different roles they play in each new poem: their uniqueness in their new poetic surroundings. Once this criticism settles for a "correct" and "final" interpretation of the images common to all of Rumi's lyrics, it considers the process completed.

The reductionist attitude discussed above explains why the critical investigations of some of the liveliest and most playful examples of Persian lyric poetry are themselves devoid of playfulness. It also explains the absence of fresh readings of these lyrics, despite the large number of books published on the subject. The hermeneutic process has lost its critical edge, and much of secondary literature on Rumi's poetry has turned into the mechanical process of deriving timeworn "meaning" from the standard reservoir of predictable Sufi imagery.

The basic function of an image is to bring us an "immediate sense experience."[7] Poetic imagery, however, with its potential complexity and the force it can draw from its unique relationship with various elements in the poem, may achieve more than that. A symbolic image serves as a way to contact a world with codes and meanings of its own. An exuberant image, to use an old-fashioned term, can through the force of its energetic presence set an otherwise quiet poem into motion.[8] Allegorical imagery carries in itself mysterious qualities of allegory, not the least of which is ironic subversiveness. As Fletcher points out, when speaking in an allegorical mode we "say one thing and mean another," thereby destroying the expectation that words mean what they say.[9] This subverts the most fundamental conventions of linguistic expression. It is not surprising that, as we shall see, Rumi, with his constant urge to explore the limits of linguistic discourse, makes ample use of this device. Yet allegory is not merely subversive. It is also a powerful literary device which can make us aware of the latent ability of language to say more than it appears to be saying. This is empowering, not only because it demonstrates that language can do more than what we realize at the outset, but because to say one thing and mean another is enigmatic. This enigma at the heart of allegory is not always decipherable. A good allegory, much like a good poem, may be infinitely explored.[10] Enigmatic allegorical imagery may be employed to enrich the ambiguity of the poetic message and lend it an indecipherable quality that inspires perpetual inquiry as opposed to settling for a finalized interpretation. This enigmatic allegorical quality, deserving of endless exploration, is at the core of the poetic message in the *Dīvān*.

Love Defies Interpretation

Love, as enigmatic and indecipherable as allegory, also defies description and clarification. Instead, it seeks a mode of articulating itself without destroying the enigma, of "saying" without giving all the mystery away. Hence the *Dīvān,* despite its disjointed narrative flow, becomes an enigmatic allegorical tale that gives expression to the various manifestations of love. However, it would be a grave mistake to assume that a catalog of the work's most common love imagery, such as that of wine, would adequately explore this colorful tale of love. To start with, these poems often articulate the experience of love best when they appear not to be directly engaged in doing so. Furthermore, they progress beyond the utilization of layers of symbolic meaning in individual terms to exploit the visual and dynamic effect of the interaction of the images in crowded and lively collectives. At times, they march in dozens in the space of a few verses, creating a vivid sense of motion. At other times, they participate in repetitive phrases or appear in unexpected spots and bring about an experience of novelty and change. They may also appear as disorderly piles of images, causing critics to accuse Rumi of being unable to produce polished, diamondlike verses. In such instances, they successfully textualize the perplexity and disorderliness of love. Through these and similar features, the poet becomes the choreographer of what might be described as a linguistic dance in which words whirl to dizziness and break rules of syntax. In return, however, they gain unprecedented effectiveness and resonance.

The sense that Rumi's lyrics have a specifically allegorical nature, that they say things other than what they appear to be saying, is frequently present in the *Dīvān*:

> Should I tell you of sugar candy?
> Or do you want the story of the fountain of life?
> But if you sit face to face with me, I shall tell you
> Why the King got you in a checkmate position.[11]
> (D, 368:1–2)

At times, there is a clear sense of commitment, an awareness on Rumi's part that his poetry has been chosen to deliver an important message. Still, the poetic element is not to be sacrificed in the seriousness of a messianic ambiance. References to the matter find expression in little playful anecdotes with false confessional tones:

> The sweet beloved fooled me on the way here;
> He said "write fresh verse and take old wine instead."
> What to do? Whatever he says I have to obey;
> How can I say no to life, and to a ruby mine?
> (D, 1312:1–2)

Besides reminding us of their allegorical role and poetic mission, these playful recollections or anecdotes also serve to keep us aware that the tale of love shall never be fully told. Time and again, the poems take us on a journey, and just as we think we are going to reach a much-awaited destination, they leave us stranded. The closing verses of such *ghazals* do not create a sense of finality. They urge us to take over from that point and explore the last step ourselves. No matter how detailed the description of the various stages of the journey is in these poems, the nature of the destination remains unarticulated. It may be argued that this reticence has to do with the inexpressibility of the ultimate experience. I maintain that it also serves to urge the individual reader/listener to be the architect of the final "truth" he/she is going to discover. This is part of the same expectation Rumi often has of the reader: to be the poet who completes the poem in his or her own way.[12] The following is a typical example:

Get up! do not sleep! we have come close.
We have already heard the dog and the rooster of that neighborhood.
By God they were signs from the village of the beloved;
All the flowers that we grazed on.
Get up! do not sleep! it is daytime.
The morning star has risen and we see the footprints.
It was night and the whole caravan was locked up in a caravanserai;
Get up! for we have rid ourselves of the dark and of the prison.

As we hold our breath to see what is waiting for us beyond the walls of the prison in bright daylight, we are told:

But be quiet! so that the sun the Preacher may speak;
For he is in the pulpit now and we are all his disciples.
(D, 1480:1–2, 8–9, 16)

Hence love may be many things, the barking of the village dog that tells you the village is within reach, the footprint that leads to the village of the beloved, or the preacher sun, who has a pulpit so high he can preach to us all at once. What love may not be is a fixed, describable entity, for if it were, it would be defined, thus deprived of its enigma:

I swear by love that love is finer than the essence of life itself;
That for lovers love is the food and the drink.
My soul and love have exchanged a thousand secrets;
In them there has been no room for the coherence of speech.
(D, 1733:3, 8)

The same is true of the *Dīvān*, the body of lyrics that strive to be a poetic representation of love. To interpret them and to understand them in the context of standard entrenched ideas is to overlook the heteroglossia (to adopt a Bakhtinian term) which is by definition unresolvable.[13]

Observing the Poems in Action

The key to a critical understanding of these poems is to observe them "in action." To represent the changing state of love, Rumi endows the *ghazals* with changing messages. Images and ideas must be treated as meaningful in relation to the poem in which they "act." By following the shifting context through a number of poems, the reader would discern recognizable patterns that, in turn, enhance the overall understanding of the work. The element of reception is crucial, too. The *Dīvān*'s predominantly allegorical nature demands that the individual reader ultimately decodes and "completes" each poem. The orientation of the reader, a unique individual, will therefore influence the details of the patterns as they emerge in different readings. Despite their differences, however, these readings share a general strategy of observing the way the lyrics as a whole "act," as opposed to what their various elements "mean." The goal of such readings would be to understand how the *Dīvān* gives expression to the force of love that sets its universe in motion. The present work, for instance, suggests that the *Dīvān* mirrors that force. In this mimetic reading the lyrics are seen as staging before us a "whirling dance of words" which can be appreciated only in motion. This approach confirms Collins's suggestion that reaching a "poetic interpretation" of the *ghazals* requires understanding them as a "performed realization."[14] One further point needs clarification. The whirling dance of words, a metaphor for the force of love, is meant to do more than evoke the basic mimetic function of poetry, mere "representative versification" and its iconic quality of imitating objects and events.[15] Not only is the mimetic process in the *Dīvān* more complex than plain imitation, it participates in the formation and development of love as much as it helps articulate that experience. That is why Collins's concept of "performed realization," with its connotation of interactive relationships not only of various elements in one poem but of entire poems with one another and with the reader, is applicable. Let us now turn to the images in *Dīvān* to observe them in action and to highlight recognizable patterns in their poetic roles.

Creating a Sense of Motion

In the *Dīvān*, Rumi utilizes poetic imagery in a number of ways, making the poems into a panoramic screen that reflects thousands of minute, colorful images and upon which performers are engaged in constant movement. Nothing stands still: natural elements, creatures, and objects jump, roll, fly, and run.

> Get up! O lovers, let us soar into the sky;
> We have seen this world, let us pay a visit to the next.
> Let us rush to the sea prostrated like the flood;
> Then clapping hands let us journey on the waves.
> We are like raindrops on a ceiling full of cracks;
> We shall escape from the cracks and find the drain pipe.
> (D, 1713:1, 3, 11)

Just as the universe is crazed with the frenetic "dance of the sea, the flood and the raindrops" (D, 1713:3, 11), so we, readers of the *Dīvān,* begin a dance of our own. With each *ghazal* we enter a new whirling scene crowded with large, small, quick, and clumsy images that enter and exit the dance as they continue to whirl. To reflect faithfully the experience of change that characterizes the nature of our interaction with love, it is important that the influx of the new imagery be maintained. We sense the motion, even have to hurry to catch a glimpse of the imagery that rushes out as hurriedly as it is summoned in. If any image were to linger, it would slow the pace or dispel the illusion of motion:

> You roam around in my heart keeping the light of the soul and the body burning:
> Well done, O eye and lamp of the heart, O light of vision in my eyes,
> Well done, O sea full of pearls, skies full of stars,
> The plain full of jasmine, the garden full of lily.
> The heavenly bodies take their swiftness and the souls their intoxication from you.
> O you who have filled the lap of the earth with jewels!
> I am burning with love like firewood in fire;
> Except for love, I am alien to all like water to oil.
> (D, 1847:1–3, 10, 11)

Not only do the variety and the quick march of the imagery underscore dynamism and change and thereby present a lively picture of love, but the parallel drawn between the swiftness of the heavenly bodies and the intoxication of the soul further emphasizes love's dynamic nature. That the proliferating imagery in the *Dīvān* is never described in detail has been commented upon in passing by a number of scholars. In her study of allegorical gardens in the Persian poetic tradition, Meisami refers to this as a "lack of concrete description" without further comment.[16] This lack of focus on individual images is, I believe, part of Rumi's effort to sustain the sense of motion and exploration I have just described. Its primary function is to keep the reader involved in dynamic interaction with the poems, mirroring the dynamic nature of love that keeps us engaged with the universe. Furthermore, the imagery of the *ghazals* is frequently more detailed than it appears on initial consideration. This is the result of their complexity, indirectness, and interplay with one another. The following is a good example:

> I have come back, like the new moon;
> To break the lock on the door of the prison.
> And [I have come back] to break
> The teeth and the claws of this man-eater firmament.
> (D, 1375:1)

The above verse does not create anticipation of description. Action takes center stage with a sense of urgent mission. The scene is crowded with the new moon, the lock, the door, teeth and claws. One might add the interrelationship between some words and concepts (for example, the parallelism between the brokenness of the new moon and the breaking of the lock). As this complex web of images and ideas is packed in one verse, the reader may not at first notice the "monster firmament" with a maneater's teeth and claws in a dark corner of the poem. Upon further reflection, however, the details of this description prove to be crucial for the rest of the *ghazal*. Not only does the maneating firmament create the tension which necessitates the poet's fight against evil in the next sixteen lines of the poem, but it provides a parallel for the image of death as a parrot-eating owl, part of a cluster of bird images that highlight the vitality of the poet's efforts:

> From the arm of the king everlasting, I flew like a hawk;
> To break the parrot-eater owl [of death] living in the ruins.
> From the beginning I had promised to give my life for the king;
> May the back of my soul break, if I break that promise now.
> (D, 1375:3–4)

In this regard, another essay, this one by Rehder, requires comment. The study, which is concerned with Rumi's style, is based on a close reading of one *ghazal*. The reading leads Rehder to the general conclusion that Rumi is not a "painter of pictures."[17] The most immediate problem with Rehder's analysis is that his judgment of Rumi's entire poetic corpus is based on one short poem. Furthermore, Rehder speculates that Rumi's lack of interest in describing details was due to his conviction that "the world being in a state of flux makes it both impossible to observe and not worth apprehending."[18] While this assessment is in line with the standard analysis of the Sufi desire to remain detached from this world, Rumi's lyric poetry tells us otherwise. In the *Dīvān* alone Rumi eagerly introduces more objects, plants, animals, and people than probably any other lyricist in the medieval Persian tradition.[19] In his *ghazals,* for the first time tailors, cooks, and shoemakers with their feet firmly on the ground appear as frequently as do poets, theologians, and mystics dealing in higher levels of existence. One may hold the standard notion that these ordinary participants were used as allegorical tools to direct us to loftier concepts, worthy of attention only insofar as they were manifestations of the Divine. Manifestations of the Divine or otherwise, it is clear that Rumi did not ignore the world that surrounded him. Similarly, answering the question of whether Rumi was a painter of pictures calls for a more rigorous approach. While his lack of interest in detailed description disqualifies Rumi as a painter of portraits, the panoramic landscapes he paints through the juxtaposition of colorful, minute images must not be ignored. By overlooking these busy landscapes, critics neglect a key source of insight into Rumi's poetics.[20]

Images with Built-in Dynamism

To replicate the vitality of love, the *Dīvān* makes use of another poetic strategy that captures a vivid sense of motion. This is to utilize actions that have built-in propelling forces. The secret is not to employ randomly verbs that denote motion, such as flying, running, and the like.[21] It is, rather, the sensitivity to the inherent dynamic power of images and the ability to give leading roles to those which have their own "engines." Once launched, they can sustain the momentum, breathe life into the poem, and create a sense of moving beyond the individual *ghazal.* One example of an action with such an inherent propelling force is laughter. Once it is induced, laughter may not be stopped until it has run its natural course. The forcefulness of this exclusively human habit may not come readily to mind because the sensations mostly associated with it are gentle and peaceful. If used properly, however, the image of bursting into laughter can give visual representation to the release of a vibrant force with a momentum of its own. One may state with certainty that few Persian lyricists prior to Rumi allowed the sound of laughter to echo so frequently in their poetry. The traditional Persian lyric concentrated on the laments of a suffering lover and rarely made full use of the imagery of laughter. If anyone laughed, it would be the carefree beloved, whose laughter mocked and obscured the sad melody of the lover's endless cry.[22] In the frenzied universe of Rumi's lyric, however, laughter is a way to participate in the joyous movements of the world. It is a lifeforce that animates people and objects alike. In the following *ghazal*, laughter assumes an allegorical role, drawing attention to less audible laughters such as blooming, growing, speaking, artistic creativity, and tearing apart:

> If the flowers of His face, from the garden they are in, burst into laughter;
> The spring of life would be renewed, the tree of body would burst into laughter.
> If that essence of the essence of life appeared all by Himself;
> My body would come to life with the grace, my soul would burst into laughter.
> If that speaker par excellence opened His mouth to speak;
> The dead body would gain the power of speech, the stuttering heart would burst into laughter.
> If that beloved of the beloveds looked [at us] with uncanniness and skill;
> The souls would all become masters of skills, and each skill would burst into laughter.
> If that master of all beauty revealed the beauty of His face;
> All the robes of beauty would [be torn apart] burst into laughter.
>
> (D, 2525:1–2, 4–5, 7)

Here, laughter is a metaphor for a myriad of activities and accomplishes a number of goals. It articulates those actions while emphasizing their lively nature. As a result, it turns a seemingly passive and silent universe into an animated one. At the same time, it trains us as readers to look for movement beneath stillness and listen for sounds beyond silence. Finally, it urges us as occupants of the same noisy universe to break out of our shell of passivity.

Rumi uses imagery of light in a parallel fashion to that of laughter. Light "spreads" with a dynamic quality similar to that of laughter. When released, light moves forward. It ends the silence of the night and celebrates the beginning of action in the morning. It has a bright transforming quality with which restless "dust particles are in love" (D, 1195:3), but most of all it is a pervading force that tears apart the veil of darkness:

> The night wove a veil in front of your moonlike face;
> I tore apart the veil of the night, every night, like the moon.
>
> (D, 300:3)

The spreading light recognizes no earthly boundaries.

> Behold the full moon which broke into our sleep;
> From the seventh sphere it shone on our ruined land.
> (D, 48:1)

The same penetrating quality is elsewhere found, through association with the moon, emanating from the human soul:

> Your body is the Night of Qadr through which fortunes can be found;
> Your soul is the full moon which penetrated darknesses of all kinds.
> (D, 55:1)

While the light imagery maintains its basic vibrant quality throughout the *Dīvān*, it shows versatility in origin and personality. One moment its source is the "conquering" sun, determined to eradicate all darkness (D, 340:4); the next it emanates from a moon shockingly close and intimate.

> When that moon circles in my breast, I say:
> O the orbiting moon behold my moon!
> (D, 76:2)[23]

In this last example, in addition to the pervasiveness of the light and the mobility of the moon, other factors are at work to contribute to the liveliness and fun of the image. One such element is that of surprise. Fletcher has noted that metaphors in general depend for effectiveness on the surprise they generate through unexpected associations.[24] The fact that the moon may draw near in the guise of a companion is surprising enough, but to have it circling where the hands can reach is to make full use of the fictive nature of poetry.

Sound waves are as agile and pervasive as rays of light (at least to us, who are not at this instant concerned with tedious scientific details, and to Rumi, who measured velocity with a poetic yardstick). Sounds break the silence and discourage stillness. They excite and create an impulse for action. They can form sophisticated combinations and turn into charming melodies. But most of all, they have a built-in desire to spread and to travel. Once released, they are unstoppable. Invisible to the eye, they can penetrate, move, destroy, or bring to life. The *Dīvān* is animated with sounds that transform the poems into scenes of action. In a way, in Rumi's lyric sound and movement are the basic modes of expression and can be translated into one another. If only we could "see" and "hear" properly we would notice that

Your kindness [O Lord!], like a musician, with the slightest of his songs,
Animates the Sufis of the skies into their whirling dance.
The spring breeze comes running, singing;
It makes the world laugh and the autumn leave.

(D, 196:3–4)

Again, participation is essential to a full appreciation of this noisy universe. One is best advised to choose an instrument to play, the drum, perhaps, to pursue one of Rumi's recommendations. Part of the fun in playing the drum for him is that it "cannot be played in secret," just as love refuses to be contained (D, 213:13). So "play the drum of your love in the open," Rumi tells us, and the "ear of your heart" will hear the "cries of love" that have filled the "blue dome of the sky" (D, 213:14). Love as the urge to defy control is often represented in the *Dīvān* by the image of a "roaring sea" rather than the lamenting nightingale, the conventional metaphor for the crying lover (D, 224:11). Vibrant sounds closely articulate the dynamics of love; thus Rumi confesses: *a hundred drums are being played in my heart* (D, 246:1). Additionally, in the *Dīvān* there is an awareness that Rumi's verbal articulation of love is itself another variation of the musician-like kindness of the beloved that finds expression in the roaring sea, the drum, the bagpipe, and thousands of other sounds that shake the blue dome. To produce poetry is to be drawn to this frenzied universe to echo its songs rather than perform a willful act. This lack of choice is articulated in another one of Rumi's personal confessions: *this bagpipe has no control over its singing*. In this particular example, the central theme of the *ghazal* is the uncontrollable urge to join the noisy ensemble:

There is a fire that keeps my saucepan boiling,
That will crack open the ceiling of the sky, if it reaches there.
A river of blood is running from my being;
I know not where are its beginning and its end.
What should I say to this river? "do not flow?" how can I fight it?
You go and tell the sea: "do not be agitated O sea!"
By those sweet lips with which you blow in me;
This bagpipe has no control over its singing.

(D, 227:6, 8–10)

A significant point is that the tune of love that animates the universe, as represented by Rumi, is far from delicate. If anything, it is jittery and confused, just as our reactions to it are. Everything in the *Dīvān* works in the direction of defying a smooth, polished, idealized image of love. Love is dynamic and playful, but it is also chaotic and paradoxical. It makes the lover run around in circles until confused enough to see the clarity beyond the confusion. The *Dīvān* attempts to textualize the constructive destruction of love by mimicking the instances of excitement, haste, conflict, and confusion. It successfully demonstrates that these instances are imbued with creativity and may lead to clarity of effective expression. The sound imagery, at times acquiring a sharp edge, plays a sensitive role in this process. In such instances, instead of the roaring seas and bagpipes that declare their love, we listen to the piercing cries of souls from *sū-yi bī sū'ī* (the direction of indirection) that "penetrate our sleeps" in the darkness of the night (D, 224:6). Elsewhere, the mystery of the dark and the familiarity of music are combined in the image of a gigantic harp that fills the midnight skies with its music (D, 255:4). The reader is left free to appropriate the majestic mystery of such a harp through the discovery that he may be "transformed into a harp," if the "musician of love" deems him worthy of becoming an instrument (D, 302:5–6).

The quick march of the images that bring us a sensation of movement, the dynamism of laughter, the rays of light piercing darkness, the sound waves agitating silence, and other attempts to articulate movement in the *Dīvān* find culmination in the complex imagery of dancing. Nothing describes better than dancing the chaos that is simultaneously harmony. Again, we can fully sense this harmony only if we join the dance like the dust particles we can observe in a ray of the sun. Rumi's use of such imagery can be partially explored in those poems in which he speaks of *samā*ʿ, the Sufi ritual of dancing.[25] Much of the dancing in the *Dīvān*, however, occurs elsewhere. Not only do the more expected candidates such as the "tree branches" and the "raindrops" dance in the breeze and "whirl" in the sky (D, 189:1, 5), but when Jesus performs his miracles on "the deaf and the blind," he in fact restores to them the ability "to dance" (D, 189:12). Surprised at first, we are persuaded by the lighthearted atmosphere of the *ghazal* to visualize as a joyous dancing the release of a blind person from darkness. Later we realize that the participants in the whirling scene that constitutes the *Dīvān* are many:

> No one shall dance, unless he sees your grace;
> For in the womb the fetus is by your grace dancing.
> When the soul can dance in the confines of the body,
> How well shall it dance when free from the heavy shackles?
> (D, 186:3, 6)

In general, the dancing imagery with its soothing quality compensates for the harshness of quake, storm, and flood sounds that are often evoked in the *Dīvān*. In Rumi's words, dancing is the "shaking of the cradle of the body" that calms down the "baby of the heart" (D, 143:5). The effectiveness of the imagery of dancing is in part due to its complexity. It can in a single verse give visual representation to a large dance floor with numerous participants. Furthermore, the interaction of the participants with the music, which provides the propelling force for the dance and extends the action beyond the willful motions of individual dancers, provides the image with additional dynamism. This quality makes the image suitable for a portrayal of the paradoxical experience of love. The lover pursues the beloved willingly. Yet, is it not the invisible string of love that pulls the lover, as the invisible stream of music directs the flow of the dance? Should the dancer stop and question every move? After all, the advantage of "love" over "thoughtful planning" is that it takes the traveler home faster (D, 146:3). When dancing to the tune of love, "thoughts" are but "huge boulders in the way of happiness" (D, 146:6). So "let go of your personal wisdom" is the poem's message: be pulled by the invisible string of love, let the stream of music guide your steps, and you will arrive at the colorful destinations that await you.

> He plays a beautiful tune, I dance to it;
> Love plays a new game on me every instant.
> He teases me sometimes: "go sit in a corner!"
> Just as I sit in the corner, he calls me back.
> Today, he is going to fly me like a hawk again;
> What does he want to capture by me?
>   who does he want me to go after?
> I am as generous as thunder, as talkative as the cloud;
> Raindrops fall when he embraces me.
> My cloud is generous because it partakes of his sea;
> I know not on whom he shall make me rain.
> When he makes me rain, it is never in vain;
> For he lets me, then, live in a hundred plants.
>
> (D, 208:4–9)

Dust particles are among the more conventional dancing figures in classical Persian literature. We encounter them in the *Dīvān,* too, in love with the sun which "rises neither from the East nor the West."

> A sun neither from the East nor of the West rose from the soul;
> Our world begun to dance like dust particles [in the array of that Sun].
>
> (D, 136:6)[26]

Many dancing figures featured in the *Dīvān* are not as familiar to the genre of *ghazal*. The planets whirl in the sky above, the winds blow from page to page, the rivers flow noisily between the lines, and earthquakes shake entire *ghazals*. Everything works to maintain visual contact with a universe in motion and a sense of active participation on the part of the reader. That aim explains why dancing is a central image in Rumi's lyrics: it is the one activity that allows human beings to mimic and experience the constant whirling of the universe (and its poetic parallel performed in the *Dīvān*):

> I am a mirror, I am a mirror, I am not a man of writing;
> You shall see my state, if your ears turn into eyes.
> (D, 38:8)

The readers are aware that if their ears turned into eyes, there would be much to see. Similarly, as the reader is taken on an experiential journey from *ghazal* to *ghazal*, there is a sense that the journey is toward a specific destination, even though it is frequently said that indirection is the journey's true direction. As the beloved in the *Dīvān* may take the shape of almost anything in the surrounding world (D, 37), descriptions of his beauty give no clue to what might await at the destination. Nevertheless, the reader remains confident that the ambiguity of this indirection is not empty and meaningless. This confidence is mainly the result of a powerful sense of personification of the cosmos in the *Dīvān*. While we do not meet any specific persons in this universe, we sense that it is animated with a wisdom and an inner drive.[27] In other words, as readers we can completely let go, following the cosmic drive regardless of the fact that we are not sure where the move will take us. We are certain that the rivers, the winds, the planets, and other constituents of the cosmos know well where they are going. In simple language, being a part of this universe means we are in safe hands. There is hardship and smallness in the presence of the beloved, but as the trees, the birds, and the skies know, there is a magnet to which all particles will ultimately be drawn:

> All the images in the world are running after His image;
> Like pieces of iron pulled toward a magnet.
> Rubies turn into stone, lions into wild asses;
> Swords turn into shields, and suns into dust particles in His presence.
> (D, 33:14–15)

This cosmic awareness and sharing in the wisdom of love may adopt specific warning goals, as with the sky that sends "hourly messages" of awareness to those in the "right state of mind" (D, 2442:1). It also may remain a strong but vague presence that despite its visual absence exerts wisdom and control. Through this awareness we understand that sitting still is a waste of time, and we maintain our sensitivity to cosmic motions and our search from *ghazal* to *ghazal*:

> There is someone here, invisible to the eye, holding onto me.
> Someone who does not show himself, has seized the front of my robe.
> There is someone here, invisible to the eye, like life and sweeter than life.
> He has shown me a garden and taken away my house.
> There is someone here, invisible to the eye, like an image in the heart;
> But the radiance of his face has taken over my existence.
> There is someone here, invisible to the eye, like sugar in sugar cane;
> A sweet sweet-seller who has taken over my store.
> Like sugar and rosewater drink, we are mixed.
> I have acquired his spirit, he has obtained mine.
>
> (D, 2388:1–5)

The Motion of Change in the *Dīvān*

The greatest of all motions, yet the hardest one to detect, is change. Change is the constant movement we go through irrespective of personal choice. Everything that surrounds us changes, too. Laughter turns into crying, night into day, youth into old age, winter into spring. No other constant so accurately reflects the nature of our existence and the dynamics of our interaction with love. Indeed, one way to understand the ongoing movement of the universe is in terms of change. Love itself, Rumi's lyric would have us understand, can be appreciated only if its kinetic and changing nature is acknowledged. This will in turn lead to the understanding that we act differently at different stages of our lives because we are a different being in each stage:

> I was dead, I came to life. I was a cry, I turned into laughter.
> The fortune of love fell upon me and I turned into everlasting fortune myself.
> He said: you are not crazy, you do not deserve to live in this house.
> I became crazy, I put myself in chains.
> He said: you are not drunk enough, give up this pretense, you are not the right type!
> I became drunken, I became full of enchantment.
> He said: you are not dead, you are not smeared with joy!

Before his life-giving face, I died and fell.
He said: you are a little too intelligent, affected with fancy and disbelief!
I became foolish, I became ignorant, I freed myself of all.
He said: you have become a light-giving candle, you have become a kaʿbah to these people.
Not a candle, not even together, I became dispersed like smoke.
(D, 1393: 1, 3–7)

A central message of the *Dīvān* is that it is not an arbitrary exertion of power that leads the beloved to expose the lover to hardship. It is, rather, an attempt to force the lover out of his safe hiding place to experience and understand change. The beloved himself changes and becomes different things to different lovers in order to maintain his dynamic relationship with them in different stages of their growth. Thus Rumi speaks on behalf of the beloved:

If you build two hundred houses like bees;
I shall make you as homeless as a fly.
If you are [as stable as] the mount Qāf;
I shall make you whirl like a windmill.
If you are [like] Plato and Luqmān in knowledge;
I shall reveal my face and make you ignorant.
(D, 1665:2, 4–5)

Physical stillness is alien to this changing state of affairs, while whirling mirrors it. Referential language, flowing without disruption in a quiet descriptive mode, would similarly fail to capture the dynamics, the constant change, of this relationship. Poetic discourse, however, is able to give expression to it by becoming an embodiment of change itself or, one might say, a textualization of it. The *Dīvān* becomes a linguistic manifestation of this change by substituting a change-oriented aptitude for obedient loyalty to generic and other conventions. To achieve this, it breaks when necessary every conceivable rule that governs the universe of poetic discourse.[28]

The march of a wide range of images and the utilization of exuberant imagery, which we have mentioned as techniques to create a sense of motion, also serve to evoke change. The *Dīvān*, however, adopts more specific techniques to highlight the effectiveness and continuity of change. For example, the verb *shudan*, which denotes a change of state, is frequently used. This includes *shudan* as a simple verb meaning "to come into existence" and as a constituent of a compound verb, usually in conjunction with adjectives, nouns, and prepositions, meaning "to become."

Pīr shudan (to grow old) is an example. In the *Dīvān,* out of 404 *ghazals* with rhymes or *radīfs* ending with the letter *dāl,* 50 end with the words *shud* (past tense) or *mīshavad* (present and future tense). If the instances in which the term occurs elsewhere, and not only in rhyme, are taken into consideration, the number of examples would be significantly higher. In addition, there are many cases in which a change of state is expressed by verbs other than *shudan.* In the following *ghazal,* in which the poetic self once more personifies love, change is evoked vividly:

O lovers! O lovers! I turn dust into jewel.
O musicians! I fill your instruments with gold.
O thirsty ones, I shall be the water-bearer today;
And I turn this dry dusty land into paradise, into the river Kawsar.
O lonely ones, relief has come!
I turn everyone afflicted with sadness into a king.
O the elixir, look at me! for I
Turn a hundred convents into mosques, a hundred gallows into pulpits.
O unbelievers, I shall release you all;
For I am in full command, I give faith and I take it away.

(D, 1374:1–5)

Not all descriptions of love as celebration of change are as comprehensive and as direct as the above, but in general the idea of change pervades the *Dīvān.* We constantly witness things changing into one another or something other than themselves. Not only do "grapes" change into "sugar" and "stones" into "rubies" (D, 644:6), as we might more conventionally expect, but the "earth" becomes the "sky" and "left" turns into "right" when least expected (D, 644:7). While this keeps the element of surprise alive, another of its functions is to emphasize that the poetic boundaries are changeable. As readers, therefore, we should prepare ourselves for a changing message, just as the lover should be prepared for the unexpected in the discourse of love. The following verses are a more explicit expression of the same idea:

The four elements are in fervor like a saucepan [on fire];
Neither is the fire still nor the earth nor the air.
Sometimes the earth slips into the garb of a plant;
Sometimes water turns into air because of love.
The water in oil turns into fire, then fire turns into air similarly because of love.

(D, 202:15–17)

More often, however, to observe the articulation of the centrality of change in these lyrics, one must go beyond descriptive examples and notice how the poems become enactments of change themselves. In these instances, the *Dīvān* itself becomes the arena in which the implications of change are demonstrated. The poetic message conveys the positive implications of change by demonstrating that itself can undergo fundamental changes and maintain, even enhance, its poetic effect. The *Dīvān* offers us a range of such examples including the frequent skillful inversions of the trope. In one instance, the moon, that journeyer in darkness, that witness of long nights of separation, changes role to pay a visit to us:

> At the twilight, a moon appeared in the sky;
> Then it landed on earth to look at me.
> Like a hawk stealing a bird at the time of prey;
> That moon stole me and rushed back into the sky.
> I looked at myself, I did not see me anymore;
> For in that moon, my body turned as fine as soul.
> The nine spheres disappeared in that moon;
> The ship of my existence drowned in that sea.
> (D, 649:1–3, 5)

In this freshly constructed lyrical universe, a new set of images, many of which would be considered profoundly unpoetic in the traditional Persian lyric, give visual representation to people and concepts. Lovers, no longer dressed as sickly beggars, run like "streams of fresh water" to reach union (D, 314:3). Insignificant objects such as the "dust settling on the furniture" are allowed to play a poetic part (D, 315:5) in a frequently surreal world in which "thoughts fall like leaves from trees" (D, 315:5) and "wondrous birds grow from the palm of [the poet's] hands" (D, 328:4). Sharing these features keeps the *ghazals* connected, despite their thematic independence from one another. Each *ghazal,* in its own way, opens like a window on to the corpus of the *Dīvān,* which embodies thousands of explorable moments. At the same time, the *ghazals,* like numerous pictures each containing visual novelties of their own, are contained within the great frame of the *Dīvān.*

There is yet another way in which the *Dīvān* brings us into contact with change and with our shifting role in the world. This is achieved through the versatility of the poetic persona and the variety of the sources from which the poetic voice arises to address us. For over a thousand years, the traditional Persian lyric has prepared us as readers to overhear the poetic voice. As the poet/lover, spiritual or otherwise, talks to himself or complains to the beloved, the door is left half-open for us, sitting outside, to overhear parts of the verbal exchange.[29] In the classical Persian *ghazal*, even when brief anecdotes of a seemingly personal nature are told and scenes of action are discussed, the presence of the audience is not directly acknowledged by the poet. A typical example is the *ghazal* of Ḥāfiẓ in which the singing, happy, and drunken beloved makes a nocturnal visit to the poet.[30] Not only are the words of the beloved, in the third line, whispered in the poet's ear to underscore their private nature, but the entire visit is described in such conventionally familiar terms that it hardly reveals any personal detail.[31] In the *Dīvān*, on the other hand, the poetic message is made personal not only through revealing personal details but by including the reader in events that unfold in the poem:

> Come! join us! we are lovers.
> [Come] so that we may let you into the garden of love.
> Come! live in our house, like a shadow;
> For we are neighbors with the sun.
> You are water, but you are a whirlpool, [you are] imprisoned.
> Come! join us for we are the flowing flood.
>
> (D, 1536:1–2, 6)

This direct and fairly informal relationship with the reader, which is maintained throughout the *Dīvān*, encourages the reader to seek the personal presence of the poet. It is then that the versatility of the poetic persona and the shifting roles it assumes makes its impact. This is yet another textualization of change, through an alteration of the dynamics of the poet/reader relationship.[32] We no longer anticipate our poet to appear always in the guise of a suffering lover, though he does wear that familiar garb from time to time (D, 2077:1). We do not even expect him to always speak to us in human form. Instead, we find Rumi once again departing from convention to explore new territory. Such poems may open in conventional fashion with no signs of unexpected events until thoroughly unexpected imagery begins to change the familiar patterns. An example of this is the *ghazal* which begins with "I became a confidante to the Sufis on the path." We expect this poem to maintain a simple narrative tone, informing us of the poet's personal experience in establishing relationships with other Sufis. Instead, we find ourselves following his footprints to unlikely places:

> I became blood gushing forth in the vein of love.
> I became tears in the eyes of his lovers.
> Sometimes, like Jesus, I became all tongue.

Sometimes, like Mary, I remained a silent heart.
Hear the voice of the eternal flute from me,
though I am bent like the back of a harp.
(D, 1661:3–4, 10)

As a lover Rumi's poetic voice demonstrates the same diversity. In one instance, he is the lover whose "saffron-colored cheeks" are a map to direct the seekers to the Divine (D, 2077:1). In this role, his art as a poet is foregrounded, since his finite words lead others to *baqā'* (subsistence) (D, 2077:6). In another instance, he is the fortunate lover whose parents are "good luck" and "generosity" (D, 1638:1). In this office, "dust" turns into "gold" in his hand and ugly "wolves" transform into "Joseph" in his presence (D, 1638:3, 5). As a lover of a different kind, he becomes the "dark night" that is "angry at the moon" and the "naked beggar" who is "at odds with the king" (D, 1703:1). Rumi's message is simple, clear, and contrary to what standard criticism of his work suggests: there are no stereotypical lovers (mystical or otherwise). Lovers are as varied as love itself, and love is a constantly changing situation. In order to indicate the true magnitude of this change, the poetic voice that issues from the mouth of the beloved at times evokes images of harshness and destruction:

You are in love with me, I shall make you perplexed.
Do not build much, for I intend to have you in ruins.
If you build two hundred houses in the manner that the bees do;
I shall make you as homeless as a fly.
(D, 1665:1–2)

This in itself is not unprecedented. Speculative mysticism has grappled time and again with the concept of lovers losing their identity and acquiring that of the beloved. Rumi's poetic instinct, however, tells him that speculative mysticism may not articulate the point as well as the "saffron-cheeked" lover who appears in the next poem as the mouthpiece of love itself: *my light has taken over the world, look into my eyes!* (D, 1700:1). Elsewhere, he declares:

If there was not light, how could the dust particles be seen?
O dust particle! how would you escape my manifest charm?
The world is a moth flying around my candle;
Now I give it splendor, now I take away its wings.
(D, 1699:4–5)

In still another instance, the poetic voice goes beyond the lover, the beloved, and even love itself to speak for pure joy:

I am joy, joy is me. Venus plays my tune.
Love plays its tricks on the lovers for my sake.
When love is drunk and happy, ecstatic and free;
Like lovers it reveals to all its desire for me.
(D, 1825:1–2)

The process of change is endless. We hear the poet speak as the moon above (D, 1518:1), the birds flying in the sky, and the earth underneath our feet (D, 1400:1). The magnitude of change is no longer surprising. As readers of the *Dīvān,* not only do we come to terms with the many faces of the poetic persona, but in fact we draw pleasure from the freshness and unpredictability of the poet's many roles in his poetic games.

Uncovering the Symbolic Meaning of the Images

The monumental implications of the versatility of the imagery in the *Dīvān* will be appreciated only if we understand that the process of uncovering symbolic meaning and purpose of these images is equally unlimited. The critical exploration of this rich mine of symbolic and allegorical expression (to rename it in contemporary terms) must also be open to constant change. These poems cannot be separated from their historical and cultural context, but what *we* find in them is what they convey to *us.* The generations to come will explore and redefine Rumi's versatile persona in their own terms.[33] Perhaps what endows these lyrics with such endurance in the face of time and changing approaches is their own appreciation of change and of the inexpressibility of what is essential to poetry. In relation to the manifold identities of our poet, for instance, we soon notice that even though he assumes all of the above roles and many more, in the end he confronts us with more questions than answers. Although in some *ghazals* he is a "pigeon that flies higher than hawks" (D, 1428:1), the topic is renewed frequently to remind us that his real identity will remain disguised, to be uncovered by different explorers in different ways:

What do you know of the kind of bird that I am?
And of what I am whispering under my lips in each breath?
How can anyone come to own me?
I am at times a treasure and at times a ruin.
The firmament is whirling for my sake.
For this reason, I keep turning like the firmament.
(D, 1767:1–3)

Thus, the topic of illusiveness of identity becomes one of the most significant subjects in the *Dīvān*. Numerous *ghazals* begin with exclamations such as: *O Lord! tell me! who do I look like, who do I look like?* (D, 1488:1) or *Out of these two thousand of "me's" and "I's," I wonder which me is me?* (D, 1397:1)

Change requires many conditions. One essential catalyst for it is freedom, the necessary space in which the process of becoming something else takes place. Closed and controlled environments discourage activity, while freedom encourages movement and change. The medieval Persian lyric, despite its overall outstanding quality, exhibits signs of strong conventionalism. Not only is the dominant poetic persona that of a suffering lover resigned to the cruelty of fate, but the weight of generic conventions and stylistic considerations often curb freedom and playful activity. Works of the great masters, such as Ḥāfiẓ and Saʿdī, of course, demonstrate an impressive ability to respond to the challenges posed by these conventional limitations. More often than not, though, even these masters remain within the boundaries of convention and preserve the tame and smooth appearance expected of the *ghazal* in this period.[34] It is this quality that Schimmel describes as "refined" and "diamond-like" in the poems of Ḥāfiẓ and Jāmī.[35]

In Rumi's lyric, however, the idea of freedom is central. "Refined" and "diamond-like" words do little in the way of textualizing the shaking and transforming experience of love. If wrapped in the smooth silk of stylistic splendor, the harshness and the intensity of the experience would lose its sharp edge and fail to touch us in the way that Rumi wishes it to. It is not surprising, then, that Rumi's lyric poetry contains few examples of such "refined" *ghazals*. Signs of Rumi's acute awareness of the overwhelming nature of his message and the necessity for conveying the roughness of our predicament are apparent in the imagery he selects. In the following example, the image of fermenting wine rather than that of a singing nightingale evokes the poet in action:

> I am the wine that cannot be contained in the cask of this world;
> The barrel of the Nine Firmaments cannot endure my effervescence and fervor.
>
> (D, 263:9)

Breaking out of captivity and reaching for freedom remain major ambitions of Rumi's lyrics. There are many explicit references to this urge to search for an open space in which one may experience continuous change. "Be crazy" is the *Dīvān*'s message for lovers (D, 1848:1; D, 1194:1), and images such as that of a "drunken lion" are frequently presented as a true model of the aggressive behavior required of them (D, 1848:3).[36] Rumi's own role as a poet is at times described in almost violent tones. In such cases, the imagery suggests stronger tendencies to break out of captivity than that of fermenting wine contained in a barrel. An example is the previously quoted:

> I have come back, like the new moon
> To break the lock on the door of the prison.
> And [I have come back] to break
> The teeth and the claws of this man-eater firmament.
>
> (D, 1375:1)

The Enactment of Freedom in the *Dīvān*

The complexity and illusiveness of freedom do not, however, lend themselves to description. Good poetry is not naive enough to attempt such a feat. At any rate, a description of freedom would mean little to captive readers who wish to be liberated from the narrowness of their world through the medium of poetry. Here, too, Rumi's lyric gives expression to the complex notion of freedom through textual enactment or performance. By struggling with the limitations of linguistic discourse, and attempting to bend the bars of convention in the prison of language, these lyrics offer an example of how the urge and the struggle for freedom may lead to triumph.

Much of the imagery that elicits the sensation of freedom in the *Dīvān* is drawn from nature. Nature with its might and liveliness, with its tendency to defy control, and with its awareness of cosmic love provides Rumi with a useful reservoir of imagery. Particularly notable is the fact that the nature imagery in his work preserves its versatility. That is to say, natural phenomena are not assigned fixed roles. They represent varying and at times conflicting ideas in different poems. This may happen even in the space of one verse, as in the following example. In the first hemistich of this verse, a stone serves as a surface for a carved image, the epitome of stillness. In the second hemistich, a stone becomes the fountainhead for a spring that gushes forth to freedom:

> Like an image carved in stone
> you are captivated in your physical needs.
> You may leap forward like the spring water gushing
> forth from the heart of stones.
>
> (D, 165:4)[37]

Flood, earthquake, and storm-related imagery are forceful images in the *Dīvān* that evoke freedom and change bordering on destruction, while the breeze and streams of water frequently represent freedom of an effortless and smooth kind. Listing the images, however, is only a first step in understanding their complex poetic performance. Let us observe some of them in action in one specific *ghazal*. In the following example, the images are given additional force through the establishment of a unique *personal* relationship between the poet and nature. The transforming quality of this relationship endows the might and mystery of nature with a sense of accessibility, safety, and love. Against this background, such ordinary images as that of a fish or a parrot acquire renewed poetic force:

> I arrived, once again, like the spring breeze;
> I rose like the sun visible to all.
> I am the Sun in mid-summer, contrary to the old season;
> I have brought liveliness and joy to gardens.
> A thousand ring doves are searching for me in their songs;[38]
> A thousand nightingales and parrots are flying in my direction.
> The news of my arrival reached the fish in the sea;
> The ferment of the sea created a thousand waves.
>
> (1140:1–4)

Allegorically speaking, the poet is standing between us and nature with open extended arms to bridge the gap that separates us from the freshness of the breeze, the innocence of the birds, and the vastness of the sea. It feels almost possible for the arm extended toward nature to sprout leaves and bear fruit, while the other arm extended in our direction remains a familiar human hand inviting us to join the dance. Thus we discover that the sun has something in common with the warmth of Rumi's poetic presence. Similarly, in our enthusiasm for his presence, we have something in common with the fish in the sea. By establishing a personal relationship with the constituents of the universe, the poems succeed in creating a warm and familiar ambience in which we feel connected to our surroundings. The planets whirl just as we do, the rivers rush to merge with the sea just as we yearn to unite with the beloved, and the spring breeze shares our urge to sing in moments of happiness. The only danger is that we may neglect this lively universe and miss not only its beauty but also the message it sends us. Paradoxically, the central message it sends urges us not to get too attached to this abode, for there are better ones along the path of love. But it also says that love may be found in this familiar universe, every particle of which is as worthy of love as it is worthy of poetry. One way in which Rumi gives expression to his urge for freedom is to disregard the poetic decorum that recognizes only a part of the universe in which we live as worthy of mention. In his freely reconstructed universe, almost everything has a license to play a poetic part.

Rumi's all-encompassing view of poetry is evident in his treatment of animals. Persian poetry in general has not been too kind to animals. Birds, as Schimmel's study of "fantastic beasts and other creatures" in Persian poetry demonstrates, receive a better and more comprehensive treatment.[39] Beasts and insects, however, are for the most part presented as lowly ignorant creatures devoid of refined qualities. Often they are but slaves to their instincts and to their material needs. When it comes to lyric poetry the treatment of animals becomes even less sympathetic and more selective. While nightingales, ring doves, gazelles, lions, and a handful of other animals are frequently and positively featured in the poems, others such as donkeys, cows, or insects are rarely mentioned. Ḥāfiẓ's contemptuous admonition to a fly that tries to roam the skies in the fashion of the legendary bird Sīmurgh is typical of the lyric poetry of the time.[40]

Rumi's treatment of animals is notably different. Not only is the frequency of the use of animal imagery in his poetry much higher, but the kinds of animals that are allowed to participate fully in his poetic world are also entirely different. A study of one hundred randomly chosen *ghazals* from the *Dīvān* reveals sixty-three mention of animals, of which only half are birds.[41] The rest are animals which would rarely, if at all, appear in traditional Persian lyric poetry, including whales, donkeys, cows, snakes, mice, and even lice. It is interesting that a similar study of the first one hundred *ghazals* in the *Dīvān* of Ḥāfiẓ reveals only two references to animals. The first is a gazelle which symbolizes the beloved and the second, a horse which is a metaphor for the wind.[42] The rest of the animal imagery adopted in the *ghazals* of Ḥāfiẓ are those of birds such as nightingales and parrots, regular features of conventional lyric poetry of the time.[43] Even more significant than the preponderance of unusual animal imagery in Rumi's lyrics is his tendency to assign them unconventional roles. In the above *ghazals*, for instance, the whale becomes a metaphor for a strong and persistent lover who has no need of "ordinary nourishment" and can "swallow the sea" if need be (D, 1631:9). The mosquito does not represent a small and insignificant creature with a tendency to bite, but rather the "restless lover" (D, 1650:7). In the same *ghazal*, a grasshopper becomes a metaphor for the beloved's constructive destruction of the "plantation of the lover's existence" (D, 1650:5). Similarly, a fly stands not for insignificance or impudence but for "homelessness" (D, 1665:2) and a fish not as one of a vast swarm but as an individual recipient of love.

Despite overlooking many principles of literary decorum (for example, letting outsiders such as grasshoppers into the poetic arena dressed in respectable garb), Rumi's lyric still strives for further freedom. His grievance over the inability to express himself in the face of limitations imposed by linguistic and poetic discourse, which is often taken as a sign of his lack of interest in poetry, is another form of the struggle to highlight the significance of freedom in poesy and in love. So while Rumi expands the generic horizons of the *ghazal* to make room for ideas unprecedented in the genre, we still hear his cry of frustration at how much more could be expressed if the limitations of convention were removed. This linguistic rebellion borders on chaos at times. In these instances, verses resemble a pile of isolated images, to use Fletcher's terminology.[44] These chaotic-looking piles are not less polished poems but celebrations of disorderliness. They are textualizations of the chaotic world of multiplicity in which we live. More than that, they reflect our need to be freed from the superficial order imposed by human rationality. If we will surrender ourselves to the perplexity of love, we will in turn understand the order at the heart of this chaos. Likewise, we shall appreciate the interrelationship of these images, governed by the overall logic of the allegorical world they bring to us, if we see them in relation to the whole *Dīvān* as we may see isolated movements as parts of a stage performance.

Finally, it would be wrong to create the impression that Rumi's repertoire of imagery does not include conventional examples. In fact, in his lyrics there is an abundance of familiar images such as *nargis-i mast* (the drunken narcissus), *lālah-'i dāgh'dār* (the bereaved tulip), and *sūsan-i hizar-'zabān* (the many-tongued [but silent] lily). His use of such images is so extensive that Meisami observes a lack of originality in his garden imagery.[45] While a separate discussion of originality, in light of what the present chapter has demonstrated, seems unnecessary, a major point deserves mention. The originality of an image in a poem cannot be assessed solely on the basis of its novelty. The quality of the imagery must be studied in relation to other constituent parts of the poem. In other words, we can say little about the originality of an image, whether conventional or unprecedented, without considering its performance within the complex web of images and ideas that constitute the poem. Rumi's conventional imagery, for instance, may be seen as a familiar and reassuring element that lends stability to his revolutionary poetic vision. To use a metaphor, these familiar images are the abode in which the reader of the traditional Persian lyric feels at home. At the same time, they serve as a solid but largely unnoticeable background that throws his innovative imagery into sharp relief. It is against the predictable and familiar background of the "drunken narcissus" and "bereaved tulips" that the "wondrous birds growing from the palm of [the poet's] hands" acquire a striking quality (D, 328:4).

A General Rubric for All Images in the *Dīvān*

By way of a final note, I would like to suggest a general rubric that best characterizes the effectiveness of Rumi's imagery, as brought to a focus in the present discussion. Such a rubric would risk a serious reductionist effect if it concentrated on poetic orthodoxy or innovation. It would have to highlight a broader quality than the conventionality of the images or the lack thereof. Admittedly, any rubric would have a labeling and thus restricting effect on our understanding of his poetry. In return, it would emphasize a specific point of view, privileging a particular reading of this poetry over others. Out of a range of possibilities, the present study has brought out one general characteristic as the dominant feature of the *Dīvān*. In the light of what we have so far observed, this feature is clearly "playfulness." Creating a playful poetic ambience is one of Rumi's major achievements in his lyrics. It is within the boundaries of this playful world that the reader enters a gamelike relationship with the poet. As the walls between fact and fiction or wakefulness and dreaming crumble, we the readers grow more eager to accept the rules of the game in order to penetrate more deeply into this world. Needless to say, fresh and dynamic use of imagery is the main instrument in creating this playful ambience.

One may add that Rumi's view of our childlike position in the game of love is not a poetic accident. It fits well with his vision of our constant perplexity in the face of the paradoxes we do not understand. After all, what does a creature separated from his origin resemble more than a child in search of a mother? But there is more than a superficial likeness contained within this analogy through which we are restored to our lost innocence, endowed with a powerful childlike drive to pursue the object of our desire. In other words, Rumi's answer to our harsh fate and perplexed mind is to resurrect in us the child so immersed in the fun of play as to stubbornly pursue the goal heedless of perplexity or pain.

Yet the success of the present chapter will depend on making one point clear: Rumi's lyrics are capable of lending themselves to varying interpretations. Such readings may infinitely enrich our appreciation of his poetry so long as they do not claim "correctness" or "finality." Like all good poetry, Rumi's lyrics will be deciphered in numerous readings by generations to come and yet will remain cryptic. His readers will continue to hear his voice echoing from century to century—*Out of these two thousand "we"s and "I"s, I wonder which me is me?* (D, 1397:1)—with the ring of an almost childlike laughter: catch me if you can!

CHAPTER 6

"A Hundred Drums Are Being Played in My Heart"
The Intricacies of the Sonic Game

Those who find a music chamber filled with the noise of a hundred drums an unlikely metaphor for a poet's heart may feel differently if they listen closely to Rumi's lyrics. In the *Dīvān,* there is a constant and deliberate foregrounding of the rhythm that works either through manipulation of the sonic surface or thematization:

> Every morning, play your organon, like this!
> Yes, my beauty! like this, like this!
> Leave your harp next to Venus, O my moon!
> Enter, stamping your feet joyfully, like this!
> When the crowd asks for fragrant musk;
> Untie your hair [in a dance], like this.
> If the firmament turns against your will, for one instance;
> Set fire to the turning wheel, like this.
> It is the day of assembly, O love hold my hand!
> And guide me to the royal celebration, like this.
>
> (D, 1953:1, 3–6)

While Rumi's general attention to rhythm is known to critics, many questions have remained unattended.[1] What are some characteristic features of rhythm in his poetry? Does it echo the rhythm of the poet's inner feelings, or does it mimic some external music? The present chapter, the first of a two-part study of rhythm in the *Dīvān,* will focus on questions of this nature. In it I shall attempt to unravel some of the sonic intricacies of Rumi's lyrics. My objective is to demonstrate that the metaphor of the heart and the drum is not accidental. The choice of the heart (rather than the ear or some other organ) as the source of music is a reflection of a general tendency in these lyrics to evoke the biological rhythm of human life to rival the movement of the stars and the ebb and flow of seas in reverberation of the universal rhythm of love.[2] It is not accidental, either, that in the thematization of music in the *Dīvān*, the human figure of the musician is always the focus of attention:

> O God! give musicians sweet honey!
> To play the drum, give them tireless hands!
> They give their physical strength [to play] for love;
> Give them true strength in return.
> They fill my ear with your message;
> Give their fortune a hundred eyes to see the king!
> Like pigeons they coo in love;
> Give them the safe sanctuary of your kindness.
> They sharpen the intellect with your praise;
> You, too, praise them in return.
>
> (D, 2342:1–5)

I maintain that the *Dīvān*'s emphasis on the human interaction with music is a reflection of a more significant feature of this work: its general underlying rhythm, the painful and playful rhythm of human struggle. The second part of the present study aims at establishing that this rhythm is intertwined with moments of exploration and quest in childhood. But let us cut and fashion our concept of poetic rhythm first.

That Which Is Heard Must Be Interrupted

The more immediate and tangible definitions of rhythm involve sound. Interestingly, a significant detail concerning our relationship with sound waves is not how well our ears receive them, but rather the fact that we cannot conceive of them except in terms of their division into parts. In other words, that which is heard must be interrupted by periods of silence.[3] Discussions of rhythm concern themselves with all aspects of sounds, from duration, force, sharpness, etc., to formation of complex patterns (even to underlying sounds that are not readily heard). The fundamental preoccupation of such discussions, however, remains the interplay of sound and silence. This preoccupation has acquired such technical dimensions that in certain studies of poetic rhythm it is impossible to recover the poetry from the pile of phonemes and morphemes whose intonation, duration, accent, and pitch are measured and analyzed to the finest detail. On the other side of the spectrum is the view that the study of meter and rhythm in poetry is a futile pastime because of the lack of adequate technical terminology to deal exhaustively with concurrent intricacy and simplicity. The shortness and length of syllables, it is said, are not easy to categorize. Furthermore, meter is not a mere geometric scheme but a progression of sound. The momentum measures and echoes itself.[4]

A way to see the limitations of either extreme is to look at the diversity of poetic rhythm. Dealing with the sound of words or the so-called acoustical formation of the vowels and consonants that shape the sonic surface of poems speaks to a small fraction of what constitutes poetic rhythm. Whatever an analysis of the interplay between plosives, fricatives, and liquids might achieve, it will fall short of explaining the "melodious guile" that poetry can display.[5] In fact, in certain poems sound as aural perception is barely foregrounded.

Sound, however, may be considered in a wider sense, as the structural rhythm of the lines or the bigger portions of a poem.[6] Nevertheless, this would still not include the more entrenched rhythm, what has been called the "fundamental organizing impulse deep within the poetry."[7] This deeply ingrained poetic rhythm presupposes a direct relationship between meaning and the way we hear a poem. The recognition of this relationship may be seen as one of the crucial achievements of literary criticism in this century, with respect to the dynamics of rhythm in language.[8]

Indeed, insofar as it does not preclude the sonic surface or the structural harmony in a poem, the concept of a fundamental organizing impulse deep within a poem can function as a definition for poetic rhythm in general. One advantage of such a broad definition is that it includes the wide range of rhythmic techniques that various languages adopt. The stress in iambic pentameters is not a universal method to generate rhythm; it is the way metrical rhythm is formulated in the English language. In Chinese, pitch is the main factor, and in Greek, the quantity of syllables. Czech poets utilize word limit and obligatory stress, leaving quantity at an optional level. In Persian poetry the number and length of syllables are equally significant; and recent studies indicate that stress in Persian prosodic meter may be more important than usually acknowledged.[9] This scanty list should serve to suggest the complexity of the concept of melopoeia or poetic creativity through rhythm.

Modern criticism has placed sonics, or the study of systems and structures of complex sounds that contribute to a work's aesthetic effect, at the heart of its concerns. The primary orality of poetry is usually given as justification. It is argued that aural iconicity is historically and generically prior to visual iconicity in literature.[10] At the turn of this century, certain proponents of this view went so far as to define poetry as merely "elements of sound appealing to the ear in order of time."[11]

The breakthrough, however, came with the recognition of the interrelationship of prosodic structure and semantic meaning. The primary implication of this for criticism was to acknowledge that linguistic methods can give explicit formulation to subjective impression. At the same time, the Russian formalist view that poetic rhythm and the significance of sound patterns may not be studied in isolation played a prominent role in drawing attention to the sonic effects in poetry as a whole.[12] Around the same time, the Italian Luigi Ronga compared this transformation of verbal symbols within a poem to the magical power of words in an incantation. As a result of transposition of visual reality into sound, he maintained, verbal symbols lose their precise meaning and convey a vaster mystical message.[13] A decade later, Hollander underscored the same alchemical transformation with his notion of poetry as a kind of crucible in which the trope is cooked.

In all this, despite the differences in approach, a general change of course is notable. The change tends to elevate the notion of poetry from a pile of crude phonemes and morphemes to a crucible with a considerable transformational ability.[14] Even more significant than this change is the increasing emphasis during the past decades on the centrality of rhythm as an instrument in poetic creativity. Rhythm is now seen as creating its own opportunity and raising its own kind of expectations in the reader. Even the subject matter of poetry, if such a thing can be defined, is according to some determined by a successful dialectic of raising and fulfilling expectations mainly achieved through poetic rhythm.[15] In the meantime, the formalist notion of versification as "organized violence committed on everyday language" has gently crystallized into the more complex perception that "the correlation between verse *rhythm* and *grammar* are reciprocal." In simple terms, while rhythm is acquitted of one-sided organized violence, it maintains its centrality for a discussion of syntax and morphology as much as it does for poetry.[16]

All this is extremely relevant to the rhythmical features of Rumi's lyric. As the present chapter unfolds, we shall observe how Rumi manipulates the sonic surface of his poetry, utilizing rhythm as a major instrument of mimesis. We shall then proceed through examination of his sound symbolism to explore how subjective impressions are given verbal representation to supply the music for the performing imagery. The pragmatic aspect of his work (to use Abrams's terminology), that is, his use of rhythm as an instrument for the transformation of the self, will also be briefly examined.[17] After an analysis of the sound system we will then pursue the rest of our exploration of rhythm beneath the sonic surface. Let us now narrow our attention momentarily in scope and focus on the specialized subject of Persian prosody.

Persian Metrical System and the "Musicality" of Rumi's Lyrics

Most of the approaches to poetic rhythm mentioned above were formulated on the basis of English poetry. To successfully adapt them to Persian, we are best advised to look first at some characteristic features of the metrical system in this language. Over two hundred prosodic patterns may be used in Persian metrical verse.[18] The basis of prosodic rhythm is the number and length of syllables as well as the order in which they appear. The syllables include short, long, and overlong.[19] These metrical patterns are themselves made up of smaller units that are similar but not identical to the English foot. The Persian foot is usually represented as a derivative of the Arabic verbal root *faʿl*. Thus, a foot consisting of four syllables of which the second is short would be represented as *fā/ʿi/lā/tun*. *Fāʿilātun* is the term conventionally used to refer to this basic metrical pattern. One unique feature of the system, in which the difference between the Persian and English foot is most apparent, is the correspondence between the spelling of the metrical pattern words and the spelling of the word for which they stand.[20] For this reason, in Persian poetry any change in spelling or choice of words results in a modification of the basic foot, which in turn leads to a change in meter.

Like all his classical counterparts, Rumi knew this complex prosodic system well.[21] It is not just an excellent pun when Shafīʿī Kadkanī, the latest native critic of Rumi's work, in his brief but well-written treatise compares the role of rhythm in the *Dīvān* to the force of gravity that holds the solar system together. It is an accurate, if poetic, reflection on a body of tangible facts.[22] These facts include the unusual variety of meters used by Rumi and the affinity between them and a lively musical beat, as well as the frequent references in the poems to music and to whirling.

While the critic's awareness of the prominence of rhythm in the *Dīvān* is remarkable, its immediate impact on the study of this rhythm has not been beneficial. The above-mentioned peculiarities of rhythm in these lyrics have given rise to persistent speculation that Rumi was an accomplished musician.[23] The existing biographical anecdotes concerning his love for music have further perpetuated the idea.[24] More important than the anecdotes, however, is the textual evidence found in the *Dīvān* which may be somewhat parallel to what in Western criticism is termed "verbal music." The concept, which pertains to an interrelationship of music and literature, usually refers to a literary presentation of an existing musical composition. A contemporary example of this is the novel *The Time of the Angels* by Iris Murdoch, which is permeated with allusions to Tchaikovsky's music. Mettler's study of this novel shows how parallels may be established between themes in the novel and major motifs in some of Tchaikovsky's well-known ballets such as *Swan Lake* and *The Nutcracker*.[25] Admittedly, the structure of a nineteenth-century Russian ballet is very different from the fluid improvisational nature of Sufi music as performed in Rumi's time. So are the tangible narrative patterns in a contemporary Western novel from the elusive interplay of concepts in a traditional Persian *ghazal*. However, the idea of music and its performed manifestations as a theme for poetry is exceedingly familiar to Rumi's lyric. In this sense, "verbal music" resonates throughout the *Dīvān*. *Changs*, flutes, and *rababs* personify happiness and lamentation while episodes from everyday life are superimposed on whirling scenes. In addition to these allusions, which usually require no more than a general knowledge of music, Shafīʿī Kadkanī traces in the *Dīvān* over twenty technical musical terms which demonstrate Rumi's expertise in the field of music.[26]

For all the above reasons, whenever the question of rhythm in Rumi's work arises, his fascination with music and love for whirling occupy center stage while attention to the verses themselves fades away. No matter how interesting it may be to examine Rumi's career as a musician, for the purpose of the present chapter our concern with his musical expertise is secondary and need not be too technical. Indeed, the exploration of the rhythmical peculiarities of the *Dīvān* may be carried out completely independently of this extratextual knowledge. Whether Rumi played the lute or not, his poems can tell us about their own rhythms. Through them we can find out how much of a musician he really was and to what extent he was able to sense and echo poetically the music that surrounded him.

To examine the musicality of Rumi's poetry, we must look beyond the verses that describe the Sufi ritual of *samāʿ* or other musical events. We shall, then, observe a general awareness of rhythm in reference to apparently nonmusical activities. We are drawn into a complex web of intertwined rhythms where silence and stillness lose their conventional meaning, and we become aware of the presence of music in everything. It is not playing the lute but the ability to hear and to echo this music in objects and events, sacred or mundane, that makes Rumi a musician poet. In the following example, he thematizes Nature's contribution to the cosmic music. Hundreds of similar poems in the *Dīvān* point to our immersion, and the immersion of the world in which we live, in rhythm:

The sun, the moon, and the stars are dancing in the sky;
We are all in the midst of a dance, let your body sway to the music.
Your kindness [O Lord!], like a musician, with the slightest of its songs,
Animates the Sufis of the skies into their whirling dance.
The spring breeze comes running, singing;
It makes the world laugh and the autumn leave.

(D, 196:2–4)

Simultaneously, Rumi encourages us to appreciate the pervasive music that every one of us participates daily in creating. This is the verbal rhythm of our inner feelings, the language we speak. Rumi shows his sensitivity to natural speech by rejecting complex metrical patterns and opting instead for simpler patterns that allow a preservation of the natural syntactic rhythm of speech. In this area, which will be further explored in pages to come, we shall see examples in which he breaches conventions of prosodic meter to preserve the aesthetic flow of easy ordinary speech.

Still in relation to the musicality of Rumi's poetry, mention should be made of his characteristic ability to make use of the so-called physicality of words. His sensitivity to their concreteness, shape, shade, and size as well as the noise they make may be a result of the closeness of his poems to experience. There is no question that part of this experience consisted in listening to music and whirling to it; many poems speak to us about their inseparability from the musical experiences during which they were composed:

Playing the drum has injured my hand;
You are sitting there guarding your wallet! move an arm!
Come, move your body, you are not a piece of stone;
Even from a stone springs of water gush forth.
Has generosity been washed away with floods;
Is there no sign of it to be found?
If your hands are tied, but your beard is free,
Move your beard instead, move your beard!
Ah, my voice is gone, so loud I have been singing;
Are the ears of my brethren all sealed?
Is any water still flowing into this mill?
Why are, then, the millstones not turning?
If the stones are turning, where is the flour they should produce?
What a feast! with no bread and no water!

I am teasing you, do not be offended;
Do not take too seriously my humorous words.

Sing gently if you wish, do not hurt your throat;
The song would still fill your mouth with pearls and rubies.
God is the ultimate provider,
Keep silent for his generosity is boundless.

(D, 1–3, 5–11)

Even in examples such as the one above, whether the poetry and the musical experience were temporally concurrent or slightly apart is not the crucial issue. In fact, it is time to transcend such preconceptions and focus on the poems, something we are about to do for a close examination of their so-called sonic surfaces. Our first example is a *ghazal* in which the smoothness of the rhythm foretells a good ending even as the poem metaphorizes the harshness of the human predicament as running bare feet in a desert covered with thorns. There is not exuberance but serenity. The confidence that hardship is about to come to an end is conveyed by the slow and smooth interplay of the polysyllabics and the succession of long vowels:

Ey bande bāzgard be-dargāh-i mā biyā
Beshnaw ze āsemān'hā: ḥayye ʿal-al-ṣalā
Dar'hā-ye gulsetān ze pey-e tu gushāde-īm
Dar khārzār chand davī ey birahne-pā!

(D, 197:1–2)

(O our slave! return to our threshold!
Hear the cry: "Rush to prayer" ringing in the sky!
For you we have opened the gates to the garden;
How long are you going to run in the desert covered
with thorn? O barefoot one!)

At other times, one may hear in the interplay of the voiceless and the plosive consonants shaped into monosyllabics, the short staccato beats on the drum (or the sound of the coppersmith's hammer, which according to Aflākī first inspired the poet to whirl).[27] In the following verses it is significant to note that where monosyllabic terms are not used, the choice of words is such that the same desired rhythmic beat is achieved within each word. The slashes mark brief pauses which cross morphological boundaries to contribute to the staccato effect:

Del az tu shar/he shar/he, ben/shīn ka/bāb mī/khur
Khūn chūn mey ast jū/shān, ben/shīn sha/rāb mī/chesh
Gū/shī keshad ma/rā mey, gū/shī de/gar ke/shad vey
Ey del dar īn ke/shā/kesh, ben/shīn u bā/deh mī/kesh.

(D, 1267:2–3)

(O my heart torn apart by you, sit and eat your kebab!
Like wine, my blood is fermenting; sit and taste your wine!
The wine is dragging me by one ear; He by the other!
O my heart! in the midst of this struggle, sit and drink wine.)

With these examples we open our discussion of the intricacies of form at the sonic level exhibited in the *Dīvān*. We shall of course reach beyond these complexities of bond density and sound symbolism to examine the creative use of rhythm at the nonaudible surface. Although the more deeply entrenched, less audible rhythm is important, hearing the sonic intricacies of these poems is equally significant in appreciating their melodious guile. These intricacies are particularly important in the case of Rumi, whose refusal to subordinate creativity to convention has been frequently confused with a lack of formal sophistication and artistry.

Sound Patterns and Semantic Effects in the *Dīvān*

The emotional and psychological effect of sound on living things has long been known. Poets have learned that selective arrangement of types and patterns of sounds will create or enhance certain semantic effects. However, the sonic surface of the poems are not always deliberately fashioned by the poets. Indeed, the more complex and varied the surface, the less intentional it is likely to be. The question of intention aside, these sound patterns and textures often serve as a mark of individuality or a personal signature for the poet. In Rumi's case the repertoire of melodic surfaces that encase the inner intricacies of his poems is vast. The sonic texture of some of the *ghazals* can be described as thick, complex, heavy, and clashing. The following verses are from a long *ghazal* which opens with a declaration of the poet's desire to make the beloved his through verbal description of his manifest glory:

Ey sanjuq-i naṣr Allāh, vey [va ey] mashʿaleh-ye Yāsīn
Yā Rab cheh sabuk'rūḥī, bar cheshm u saram binshīn
Ey tāj-e hunarmandī, meʿrāj-i kheradmandī
Taʿrīf che mī-bāyad? chūn jumle tu'ī ta'īn.

(D, 1863:2)

(O flag of "Naṣr Allāh," O the torch of "Yāsīn,"[28]
Light as you are, your abode is my eye and my head.

O the crown of artistry! O the heavenly journey of wisdom!
There is no need for description, you are so manifest.)

The excitement of this seemingly achievable task gradually fades as the poem's ambition to provide a description of the beloved proves unattainable. How can the sea be contained in a barrel?

Guftam ke: chenān daryā dar khumreh kujā gunjad
Guftā ke: che dānī tu īn shīve u īn āyīn!
Yūsuf be bun-i chāhī bar haft falak nāẓir
Vandar shekam-e māhī Yūnus zebar-e Parvīn
Gar fawqī u gar pastī, hastī ṭalab u mastī
Ney bar zibarīn vaqfast īn bakht na bar zīrīn
Khāmush ke nemī-gunjad īn ḥiṣṣe dar īn qeṣṣe
Raw cheshm be-bālā kun, rūy-e chu mahash mī-bīn.

(D, 1863:12, 14–16)

(I said: how can such a sea be contained in a barrel?
He said: what do you know of this manner and custom [of doing things]?
Joseph observes the seven spheres from the bottom of a well;
And Jonah is above the Pleiades while in the belly of a fish.
Whether you are in a high or low position, seek life and intoxication;
For these good fortunes are not to be taken for granted
by the occupants of either place.
And be silent! for this share [of what we are discussing] cannot be contained
in a story;
Lift your eyes! and behold his moonlike face!)

The central theme of the poem is the paradoxically concurrent ease and impossibility of spiritual pursuit. The overall message, which further complicates the paradox, is that despite the ineffability of the matter we must attempt verbal expression, for in the final analysis it is not how adequately we express the spiritual quest, but our desire for expression that matters. Furthermore, in the fictive atmosphere created by the poem, an assessment of the human position is even more perplexing. Whereas Joseph can observe the seven spheres from inside a well, most poeple can see nothing at all. The solution offered in the closing stanza is in line with Rumi's general tendency to actively explore love instead of philosophizing about it. Here, his recommendation is to gaze at the moon instead of trying to capture it in the net of verbal description.

Rumi's wrestling with these clashing concepts at the semantic level is reflected at the sonic surface, where a smooth flow of liquids and long vowels regularly clashes with dense clusters of fricatives and plosives. In the same way that the poet's expressive attempts run into the barrier of inexpressibility, the reader's path gets blocked by tongue-twisting clusters of sounds just as the verbal journey appeared to be progressing smoothly:

gar fawqī u gar pastī, hastī ṭalab u mastī
Nay bar zibarīn vaqfast īn bakht na bar zīrīn.
(D, 1863:15)

This kind of clashing and impacted surface, however, is by no means typical of Rumi's sound symbolism. In fact, Rumi proves to be as interested in juggling sounds as we know him to be keen on exploring the broadest possible choice of prosodic meters. The result is that the *Dīvān* is filled with a vast array of contrasting sound patterns and textures. When the whirling dance of love is progressing smoothly, happiness abounds and serenity reigns. On these occasions, long gliding vowels and polysyllabics build a light, smooth, and harmonious surface which calls for recitation and causes a sensation of comfort and ease:

khushī khushī tu, valī man hezār chandānam
Be khāb dūsh ke-rā dīde-am nemīdānam
Ze khush'delī u ṭarab dar jahān nemīgunjam
Valī ze cheshm-e jahān hamchu rūḥ penhānam
Derakht agar nabudī pā-be-gel, marā justī
kazīn shekūfe u gul ḥasrat-e gulestānam.
(D, 1740:1–3)

(You are happy, happy, but I am a thousand times happier!
Whom have I encountered in my dream last night? I know not.
I am so happy, I cannot be contained in the world;
But like a spirit, I am hidden from the eyes of the world.
If the foot of the trees were not tied to earth, they would be pursuing me;
For I have blossomed so much, I am the envy of the gardens.)

To prevent the flow of long vowels and polysyllabics from becoming tedious or monotonous, occasional consonantal alliteration is used. The consonant *shīn*, for example, is repeated seven times in the single verse given below. This verse is the fourth stanza in the *ghazal* and follows the last stanza quoted above without interruption. The consonant *shīn* appears in the initial, middle, and final positions to preserve variety while bringing freshness and change to the relatively slow pace of the poem:

Hamīshe dāman-i shādī keshīdamī sū-ye khīsh
Keshad kunūn kaf-e shādī be-khīsh dāmānam.

(D, 1740:4)

I have always pulled the skirt of happiness to attract it towards me;
Now, the hand of happiness is pulling my skirt to allure me towards itself.

Comparison and contrast have long been ways of creating music in language. Comparison brings short, long, accented, or unaccented syllables together to create harmonic effects. In contrast, the opposite is achieved through juxtaposition of unlikes such as short syllables with longs and the accented with the unaccented. Needless to say, more complex patterns may be fashioned through different combinations. We shall here examine an example of lively rhythm achieved through the contrasting juxtaposition of accented and unaccented syllables in one of the best-known *ghazals* in the *Dīvān*. The present example highlights two significant points. First, it demonstrates that, contrary to what is usually said of Persian prosody, stress can play a remarkable role in Persian prosodic rhythm.[29] In this example, the contrast between the accented and the unaccented creates an effect of fast movement in a meter which could otherwise have a fairly slow pace. Second, by falling on the interior rhymes, the accents further enhance the repetitive effect of these rhymes, contributing to a sensation of harmony as well as speed. In the following lines, the accented syllables are in italic:

Yār marā, *ghār* marā, *eshq-e jegar'khār* marā[30]
Yār tuʾī, *ghār* tuʾī, *khāje* negah*dār marā*
Qaṭre tuʾī, *baḥr* tuʾī, *luṭf* tuʾī, *qaḥr* tuʾī
Qand tuʾī, *zahr* tuʾī, *bīsh* mayā*zār marā*
Ḥujre-ye khurshīd tuʾī, *khāneh-ye nāhīd* tuʾī
Rawẓe-ye ummīd tuʾī, rāh *deh ey yār marā.*

(D, 37:1, 4, 5)

(The beloved is mine, the cave is mine, the heartrending love is mine;
The beloved is you, the cave is you, O my Lord! keep me with you!
The drop is you, the sea is you, the kindness is you, the wrath is you;
The sugar is you, the poison is you, do not make me suffer more!
The chamber of the Sun is you, the house of Venus is you,
The garden of hope is you, let me inside O beloved!)

In this chantlike *ghazal*, the location of stressed syllables demonstrates a clear relationship between the occurrence, the morphological boundaries, the syntactical pattern, as well as the pattern of the interior rhymes. In other words, through accompanying the rhythm of repetition and the rhythm of syntax, which are intertwined with the metrical one, the accented syllables highlight the metrical music while performing their semantic roles.[31]

Lexical Symmetry in the *Dīvān*

In the *Dīvān* Rumi demonstrates an awareness of symmetry as a stabilizing factor in the frenzied moments of love. When things seem to be getting out of control because simple linguistic conventions and elaborate rules of prosody have been overlooked, a sense of symmetry defies chaos and replaces the lost order. In its basic form this symmetry is achieved through repetition of lexical elements, as in pairs of nouns and verbs where the prosodic decorum does not require such a repetition:[32]

Berānid, berānīd ke tā bāz-namānīd
Bedānīd, bedānīd ke dar ʿeyn-e ʿayānīd
Betāzīd, betāzīd ke chālāk savārīd
Benāzīd, benāzīd ke khubān-e jahānīd
Che dārīd? che dārīd? ke ān yār nadārad
Beyārīd, beyārīd dar īn gūsh bekhānīd
Parandūsh parandūsh kharābāt che-sān būd?
Begū'īd, begū'īd agar mast-e shabānīd
Sharābīst, sharābīst khudā-rā be-nehānī
Ke dunyā u shumā nīz ze-yek jurʿe-ye ānīd.
(D, 637:1–5)

The following is a literal translation, loyal to the word order in the original where possible:

Ride on! ride on! do not remain behind,
Know this! know this! your situation is most clear.
Gallop! gallop! you are fast riders;
Be proud! be proud! you are among the beauties in the world.
What do you have? what do you have? that the beloved does not have?
Bring that! bring that! whisper it in my ears.
The night before last, the night before last, what was the tavern like?
Tell me that! tell me that, if you are drunken wanderers of the night.
God has a wine, God has a wine hidden from all;
You and the world were created from a sip of that wine.

Further in this *ghazal* there are verses that consist almost entirely of repetitive patterns:

> *Khamūshīd, khamūshīd, khamūshāneh benūshīd!*
> *Bepūshīd! bepūshīd! shumā ganj-e nehānīd.*
>
> (D, 637:15)
>
> (You are silent, you are silent, drink silently!
> Remain concealed! remain concealed! you are a hidden treasure.)

In a similar example, each hemistich begins with a pair of imperatives that mock, in a friendly manner, the beloved's careless shrugging of the shoulders at the pain suffered by the lover:

> *Biyā, biyā u bāz ā, be-ṣulḥ sū-ye khāneh*
> *Maraw, maraw ze pīsham, ketef chenīn majunbān.*
>
> (D, 1889:2)
>
> (Come, Come! come back to the house peacefully!
> Do not go! Do not leave me! Do not shrug your shoulders so!)

Elsewhere in the same *ghazal*, symmetry acquires a more complex manifestation when three consecutive lines attempt to illustrate the human potential to perform wonders if subjected to divine alchemy. Each line consists of four distinct parts. The first alludes to a prophet and the second to the object with which the prophet in question performed a miracle. The third part of the symmetry refers to the exact nature of the miracle, and the fourth part, to its outcome for human beings. Only the last verse disturbs the symmetry by using the negative mode. The resulting contrast, however, further emphasizes the content. These three verses are fascinating examples of reinforcement of an argument through symmetrical arrangements of parallel concepts. The following is a literal translation of these lines that preserves the symmetry of the parts:

> You are a substitute for Moses, we your rod;
> Except when in the hands of Moses, no rod made such a demonstration.
> You are the sweet-breathed Jesus, we a bird made of clay;
> Breathe in us for a moment! and watch us negotiate the heights.
> You are the Noah of all times, we the inhabitants of the ship;
> If Noah leaves, how can the ship survive the Flood?
>
> (D, 1889:12–14)

Obviously, verses with such symmetrical patterns will be more appreciated in the context of the complete *ghazal* which brings all instances together and makes the patterns visible. The idea of a *ghazal* operating like a frame to bring the symmetrical details of the verses together (which incidentally is a major challenge to the conventional notion of *ghazal* as a series of unrelated verses strung together with rhymes) is illustrated elsewhere in the *Dīvān*.[33] In these elaborate examples of playing with patterns, not only do the commensurate parts match in terms of the parallel ideas they express, but they mirror each other lexically and syntactically:

> O Lord, I wish to know what is my beloved's desire;
> He who has blocked my way to escape, has stolen my heart and my composure.
> O Lord, I wish to know why my beloved is stone-hearted;
> That kind king of mine, that forbearing beloved of mine.
> O Lord, I wish to know whether ever hears my beloved;
> My sigh, my moan, my saying "O Lord!" and "Beware!"

Here, an examination of the translation will not do justice to the poem. In the Persian original, it is clear that the semantic effect is enhanced through sonic harmony and symmetry in lexical elements. Once the repetitive music of the rhyme and the refrain are added to this interwoven and orderly collection, hardly anything disturbs the complete symmetry:

> *Yā Rab, man be-dānamī: chīst murād-e yār-e man?*
> *Baste rah-e gurīz-e man, burde dil u qarār-e man*
> *Yā Rab, man be-dānamī: sang'delī cherā kunad?*
> *Ān shah-e mehrbān-e man, delbar-e burdbār-e man*
> *Yā Rab, man be-dānamī: hīch be-yār mī-resad?*
> *Dūd-e man u nafīr-e man, yārab u zīnhār-e man!*
>
> (D, 1837:1, 3–4)

In each verse, there is an echo of the earlier verses in the repeating phrase: *Yā Rab, man be-dānamī*. This is followed by a complete sentence which appears in the interrogative mode in all three lines in which it occurs, reinforcing the sense of symmetry. Similarly, the first half of the second hemistich, which consists of an incomplete sentence, contains possessives with the unconnected first-person pronoun *man*.

The Reverberation Effect in the *Dīvān*

One important corollary of the lexical symmetry in the *Dīvān* is the effect of reverberation. In reading the collection, one regularly comes across poems which contain portions of other poems much like visiting places that revive memories of the past. In this way, recurring patterns and sounds resonate in what one might call the memory of each poem. As one progresses in the *Dīvān*, the number of familiar voices, and with it the reader's sense of anticipation, grows. There are of course new ideas and unfamiliar lines, too, but that does not create disturbance. The new blends in with the familiar and revitalizes the poems to some extent, but the patterns are well-established and recognizable to the attentive reader.

The reverberation effect is at times more deliberate, closer to the surface, and therefore easier to detect. In these instances, whole verses or even larger portions of a poem are followed by a repetition of their own final parts. The repetitive pattern does more than provide the structure: it is foregrounded as a literary strategy, reminding us of the role that repetition plays in raising and fulfilling poetic expectations. These poems do more than deliver their semantically encoded message. They demonstrate a poem expand and relive in its own echo. Many themes resonate in such poems, doubled and tripled through playful repetition:

Come, come, O my beloved, O my beloved. Enter, enter busy yourself with
  me, with me.
You are, you are, my rose garden, my rose garden
  Reveal, reveal my secrets, my secrets.
Wherever I go, you go with me, you go with me,
  in every stage you are the confidant, you are the confidant.
Day and night you are my companion, you are my companion.
For my trap you are a befitting gazelle, a befitting gazelle.
O my candle! you are so bright, so bright. In my house,
  you are like a window, like a window.
When the arrow of disaster targets me, targets me,
  you are both armor and a shield, and a shield.

(D, 1785:1, 3–4)

The rhyme and the metrical rhythm make the reverberation of the sound patterns even more musical in the original:

Biyā, biyā, deldār-e man, deldār-e man. Darā, darā, dar kār-e man, dar kār-e man
Tu'ī, tu'ī, gulzār-e man, gulzār-e man. Begū, begū, asrār-e man, asrār-e man
Har jā ravam, bā-man ravī, bā-man ravī.
Har manzelī maḥram shavī, maḥram shavī
Rūz u shabam, mūnes tu'ī, mūnes tu'ī.
Dām-e marā khush ahū'ī, khush ahū'ī
Ey sham'-e man bas rawshanī, bas rawshanī.

Dar khāne-am chūn rawzanī, chūn rawzanī
Tīr-e balā chūn dar-rasad, ham esparī, ham jawshanī, ham jawshanī.

Rumi's use of repetition reaches its pinnacle in entire *ghazals* that echo one another, sharing complete verses. In this way the *Dīvān* forms an overall memory, a vast repository of familiar poems and clusters of thematic associations that resonate beyond the page in the reader's memory. There are numerous examples of *ghazals* that look familiar even at first encounter because very similar versions of them exist in the collection. There are enough differences between the versions to make them independent poems, and yet they are clearly echos of one another. In a fascinating intratextual transmission, portions of earlier poems resurface in new and varying contexts. Such *ghazals* are, in a way, statements affirming continuity and change. While they create a sense of familiarity and intimacy, what they really underscore is variety and change. They are important enough to be repeated, but not too important to surrender to change. Two enchanting examples of this are *ghazals* 1681 and 1684. The first two identical lines tell us:

I shall not leave this house,
I shall not journey from this town.
All that is left for me is my beloved and the rest of my life!
From here, I shall not go anyplace else.

In one version the third line offers the philosophical and seemingly profound explanation:

Earthly creatures seek [God's] impressions [in their journeys];
I am ethereal, I am not concerned with [material] impressions.
(D, 1684:3)

Not only does the poem make an allusion to the Quranic verse "We will show them our signs in all the regions of the earth and in their own souls" (Q, 41:53), but, in the process, the words *athīr* (ether) and *athar* (impression) are punned, thereby making an allusion to the esoteric interconnectedness of words. For the other version, Rumi chooses an entirely different solution. The explanation for the reluctance to move expressed in the third line of this version is as follows:

By God, I am a parrot and a baby one at that!
I shall not seek anything but a bowl of sugar.
(D, 1681:3)

This leaves us with the intriguing thought that maybe the first version is not the more profound one, after all.

The instances discussed in this chapter testify to the intricacies of the so-called sonic surface of poetry in the *Dīvān*. They point to the fact that Rumi was less concerned with prosodic regulations than with his own creative stylistic preferences. The findings of this chapter suffice to note that attention to the role of sound patterns in lyric poetry would enrich a study of Rumi or the Persian lyric in general. They also reinforce the previously stated fact that the intricacies of these sound patterns and their function at the surface are closely related to what the whole poem has to offer. The interplay of the syllables, the harmony or the clash of vowels and consonants, as well as the more structural rhythm of poems may be meaningfully observed only in relation to what the entire poem sets out to achieve. A similar interconnectedness between the rhythmical performance of single poems and the general rhythm of the larger corpus is also detectable. In turn, further insight into individual *ghazals* will be acquired through examining the general functions of rhythm in the *Dīvān* as a whole. The following chapter, which continues the study of the rhythm in these lyrics, will attempt to capture the broader perspective.

CHAPTER 7

"The Rhyme and the Sophistry, Let the Flood Take Them All"
The Rhythm of Childhood in the Quest for Love

We have seen the colorful "sophistry" of poetry at work in the *Dīvān*. It is time to examine the "flood," the undercurrent which we shall identify as the main rhythmic impulse behind Rumi's entire lyrical corpus. This undercurrent, closely intertwined with the rhythm of childhood, has a sweeping quality. The aim of the present chapter is to conceptualize the way in which this flood of energy runs through the *Dīvān* and breathes a spirit of playfulness into things. Indeed, it will become exceedingly clear that "the flood" does "take them all," the "rhyme," "the sophistry," and everything else that stands in its way.[1]

The investigation of the vowels and consonants will now be directed toward a search for significant patterns in the rhythm beneath the sonic surface. We shall, by the end of this chapter, be able to reach an explicit formulation that best characterizes the "fundamental organizing impulse" deep within Rumi's lyric. First, let us place our search in a wider and more general context, the context evoked in the closing lines of the previous section: the general functions of poetic rhythm.

Mimesis in the *Dīvān*

Good poetry fulfills multiple and complex purposes. That certain poetic functions are highlighted as the key functions at certain times reflects more the particular preoccupations of the critics than it does the poems themselves. This is true for our understanding of poetic rhythm, too. In the Aristotelian, Pythagorean, Platonic, and Boethian poetic traditions, all of which emphasize the moral purpose of poetry, harmony and rhythm were considered major instruments of poetic mimesis. In these traditions, poetic rhythm was nothing but an allegory for the divine music, the harmony of the spheres. In the universe, there existed a "true harmony" for which the poetic rhythm functioned as a mirror.[2] This view of poetic rhythm, however, declined during the Baroque era and was gradually replaced by the less heavenly and more human notion that the main function of poetic rhythm is to sensually please.[3]

In a sense, and for a variety of reasons, we may still meaningfully apply the mimetic theory to Rumi's lyrics. First and foremost, although the *Dīvān* is not overtly didactic, it is filled with a sense of moral purpose: to convey to us the concurrent harmony and discord of love and to prepare us for the experience. Second, we must not understand mimesis as the only purpose served by the rhythm of these lyrics. Finally, the notion of a mirroring quality in poetic rhythm need not be avoided due to a fear of oversimplification. This age-old notion can be renewed, just as our understanding of poetry is constantly revised. If by the mimetic function of poetic rhythm we mean its simplest manifestation, "onomatopoeia" or mimicry as an approximation of sensual experience, the notion is insufficiently comprehensive and complex. But if the mirror, in the poetic action of mirroring, is understood as "rather like a part-transparent, part-clouded, part-reflecting glass, variously stained and colored," as suggested by Hollander, for instance, then there is nothing archaic or simple about the notion.[4]

Rumi shows a clear awareness of the mimetic function of his poetry and its moral purpose. Interestingly, his notion of this function comes closer to our later and more complex understanding of it:

> My essence is an image of your attributes;
> It is as if I am a description of your essence.
> If your kindness bestows miracles,
> I am every part your kindness and your miracles.
> My images and thoughts are breathed in me by you;
> It is as if I am words and phrases that you have uttered.
> (D, 1683:3–5)

The wide range of mimetic instances in the *Dīvān*, and the awareness in the poems of their specific function, makes this topic worthy of further exploration. Some poems are mimetic in the simple onomatopoeic sense. In this category are those poems that bring unpleasant combinations of discordant sounds together to mirror the harshness of the cacophony of life. In the following example, our blind ignorance is the fetter that keeps us tied to our destiny, just as a shackle ties a mule to a millstone. In the repetitive guttural *kh,* and the interplay of the dental consonants *s, sh,* and *ch,* we can hear the creaking noise of the mill and the hardship of the endless circling that the blindfolded animal has to endure:

Bar "dānam" u "na-dānam" gardān shude-ast khalqī
Gardān u cheshm'baste, chūn astar-i kharāsī
Mī-gard! chūn kharāsī, khāhī va-gar nakhāhī
Gardan mapīch!, zīrā dar band-e eḥtebāsī.

(D, 2938:3–4)

(A large crowd moves about on the basis of [a simple] "I know" or "I do not know";
Blindfolded, moving in circles like the mule tied to the millstone.
Turn in circles! whether you wish it or not;
Do not twist your neck [do not disobey] for you are a captive in chains.)

There are less obvious mimetic patterns in the *Dīvān* which frequently pertain to structural characteristics. One example of this is the haphazard lengths of the *ghazals,* disproportionately short or extended to mimic our perplexity, unevenness of feeling, and sense of uncertainty. For example, one *ghazal* opens with the lines:

Captivate in the bottle those wise Jinnis,
Shed the blood of the red-handed caught in the cup!
They have stolen the crown of a thousand kings,
They have adorned my face with a ruby color.
Displaying beauty like a peacock, they have perplexed intellects;
Spreading their glamorous tails like the heart of the lovers.

(D, 212:1–3)

The poem grapples with the metaphorical idea of divine wine and its trasformational quality for twenty-three lines, only to conclude:

A half a *ghazal* is left unuttered in my mouth;
Alas! I am in a state of complete chaos.

(D, 212:22)

The poem ends with a plea for help to Shams. On the opposite page to this poem, however, there is a contrasting *ghazal.* It is a cheerful short invitation to the beloved which has a humorous and confident tone and consists of only three verses:

You who have knocked on my door! you are the light of the house, enter!
My heart is yours, you are the owner, enter!
The house is melted, it has become luminous,
O, my heart and life your abode, where are you? enter!
O, the idol in my house, the cause of my madness!
All fine things belong to you, who do you belong to? enter!

(D, 209:1–3)

In relation to the universe at large, the rhythm of numerous *ghazals* mirrors the outer reality of cosmic fervor and ecstasy. To mimic the ecstatic dance of the universe, various elements in the poetic machinery must work together. For instance, the inrush of colorful images that quickly disappear from the view contributes to a sense of movement. On a sonic level, the vigor of the rhythm is heightened through a use of monosyllabics and short vowels carefully strung together and interspersed with interior rhymes. The process is complex but the interior rhymes are quite central in mimicking the pulse of a cosmos in love. The following description of the universe, alive with ecstasy, is an example. In the two hemistiches of the last verse the interior rhyme *be-dīdam* is further reinforced as it echoes in *davīdam, ṭalabīdam,* and *nashenīdam.* The extra repetition is neither customary nor required by the rules of prosody.

Hame dharrāt parīshān, hame kālīve u shādān
Hame dastak zan u gūyān, ke tu khurshīd leqā'ī
Hame dar bakht shekufte, hame bā luṭf-e tu khufte
Hame dar vaṣl be-gufte, ke: "khudāyā tu kujā'ī?"
Chu man īn vaṣl be-dīdam, hame āfāq davīdam
Ṭalabīdam, nashenīdam, ke che bud nām-e judā'ī.

(D, 2826:2–3, 5)

(All particles perplexed, all baffled and overjoyed,
All clapping and singing: "You the one with a face like the Sun!"
All blooming with good fortune, all reposing in your kindness;
All chanting in union: "where are you, O the Lord?"
When I saw this union, I ran to all corners;
I sought but I did not [even] hear the word "separation."

Mimesis of Inner Realities: Remaking of the Self

The complexity of poetic mimesis will be further appreciated if we note that this "variously stained and colored" mirror may also reflect internal cosmic realities. Our anger, passion, enthusiasm, and fear have rhythms of their own which turn our feelings into a complex web of tunes hard to disentangle or reproduce. In the *Dīvān* our cosmic role and our nature, specially insofar as they reflect human nature in general, constitutes the primary focus of attention. For this reason, Rumi examines personal emotions only to the extent that they shape the patterns significant for the development of the cosmic self. However, there are moments in his poetry in which purely personal feelings are foregrounded and magnified. In these moments Rumi slips out of his garb of the mace-bearer, the one who knows the way that lies ahead. These are moments of perplexity, perhaps not in the Sufi sense of a stage on the spiritual path, but rather a kind of deep personal perplexity, even amazement at the poet's relationship with himself and with his growing inner voice. In these uncharacteristic moments, he addresses others less and whispers instead to himself:

Īnjā kasīst penhān, dāmān-e man gerefte
Khud rā sepas keshīde, pīshān-e man gerefte
Īnjā kasīst penhān, chūn jān u khushtar az jān
Bāghī be man nemūde, eyvān-e man gerefte
Īnjā kasīst penhān, hamchūn khiyāl dar del
Ammā furūgh-e rūyash arkān-e man gerefte
Īnjā kasīst penhān, mānand-e qand dar ney
Shīrīn shekar'furūshī dukkān-e man gerefte
Jadū u cheshmbandī, cheshm-e kasash nabīnad
Sawdā'garīst mawzūn, mīzān-e man gerefte
Chūn gulshekar man u ū dar hamdegar sereshte
Man khūy-e ū gerefte, ū ān-e man gerefte
Dar cheshm-e man nayāyad khūbān-e jumle 'ālam
Bengar khiyāl-e khūbash mudhgān-e man gerefte
Man khaste gerd-e 'ālam darmān ze kas nadīdam
Tā dard-e 'ishq dīdam darmān-e man gerefte
Tu nīz del'kabābī darmān ze dard yābī
Gar gerd-e dard gardī, farmān-e man gerefte
Dar baḥr-e nā-umīdī, az khud ṭama' burīdī
Zīn baḥr sar bar-ārī marjān-e man gerefte
Bishkan ṭelesm-e ṣūrat, bugshāy cheshm-e sīrat
Tā sharq u gharb bīnī sulṭān-e man gerefte
Sāqī-e ghayb bīnī peydā salām karde
Peymāne jām karde, peymān-e man gerefte
Man dāmanash keshīdeh, key Nūḥ-i rūḥ'dīde
Az gerye 'ālamī bīn ṭūfān-e man gerefte
Tu tāj-e mā u āngāh sar'hā-ye mā shekaste
Tu yār-e ghār u āngāh yārān-e mā gerefte

Gūyad: "zi gerye bugzar! zān sū-ye gerye bengar!
ʿUshshāq rūḥ gashte, reyḥān-e man gerefte
Yārān-e del'shekaste bar ṣadr-e del neshaste
Mastān u mey'parastān meydān-e man gerefte"
Hamchūn sagān-e tāzī mīkun shekār khāmush
Ney chūn shagān-e ʿaw ʿaw kahdān-e man gerefte
Tabrīz Shams-e dīn rā bar charkh-e jān bebīnī
Ishraq-e nūr-e rūyash keyhān-e man gerefte.
(D, 2388)

In this *ghazal,* the fast and staccato sentence structure gives way to an interplay of long vowels with a meditative slow pace that lends it a melancholic emotional texture. There is a sense of knowing and yet not knowing, something that cannot be easily shared with a general audience. The poet has sensed a presence, vivid and invisible at the same time. He whispers to himself:

There is someone here, invisible to the eye, holding unto me;
Someone who does not show himself has seized the front of my robe.
There is someone here, invisible to the eye, like life and sweeter than life;
He has shown me a garden and taken away my house.
There is someone here, invisible to the eye, like an image in the heart;
But the radiance of his face has taken over my existence.
There is someone here, invisible to the eye, like sugar in sugar cane;
A sweet sweet-seller who has taken over my store.
A magician, a master of tricks whom no eye can see;
A skillful merchant who has taken away my scale.
Like the sugar and rosewater drink, we are mixed.
I have acquired his spirit, he has obtained mine.
The beauties of this world can no longer attract me;
Look at his fair image holding my eyelashes together.
Ill though I was, I found no remedy anywhere in the world,
Till I encountered the ailment of love possessing my cure.
You are broken-hearted too, you shall find cure in love;
If you listen to me and pursue that ailment.
In the sea of despair, ready to be drowned
You shall emerge alive, jewels in your hands.
Break the spell of form, open the eye within;
So that you see the East and the West taken over by my king.
You shall see the hidden cup-bearer openly greeting you;
With a filled cup and the covenant of my friendship.
I pull Him by the skirt: "O Noah! intimate with my soul!

See the flood of my tears that has taken the world.
You are the crown on my head! do not let my head be broken;
You are my companion in the cave, do not let my friends be taken from me."[5]
He says: "cease crying! look beyond tears,
See lovers turned into souls, enjoying my gardens
Broken-hearted friends taking pride of place in my heart
The drunken and the wine-lover taking over my domain."
Like a hunting dog, go after the prey silently,
Not like noisy ones barking in the barn.
O Tabrīz, you see the sun of religion in the sky of the soul;
The illumination of his face has brightened my universe.

Let us focus on smaller portions of the poem to see how rhythm works to enhance the expression of feelings:

Īnjā kasīst penhān, dāmān-e man gerefte
Khud rā sepas keshīde, pīshān-e man gerefte.

(D, 2388:1)

(There is someone here, invisible to the eye, holding onto me;
Someone who does not show himself, has seized the front of my robe.)

The long vowels *ī* and *ā* contribute to the slowness of the pace and mark the absence of the fast, rhythmic beat generally characteristic of Rumi's lyric. Although he is not addressing us, we sense that something important, something that requires our sincere interest and undivided attention, is about to be revealed. The nasal in *penhān, dāmān,* and *pīshān* creates a low, whispering effect. We feel special, one of a select few who are going to share this experience: the presence of an invisible being. We anticipate learning more about the nature of this mysterious being. The next verse fulfills our expectation:

Īnjā kasīst penhān, chūn jān u khushtar az jān
Bāghī be man nemūde, eyvān-e man gerefte.

(D, 2388:2)

(There is someone here, invisible to the eye, like life and sweeter than life;
He has shown me a garden and taken away my house.)

The occurrence of sibilants *sīn* and *shīn* in *kasīst* and *khushtar* contributes to the sense of mystery and works like an invitation to silence. Yet we overcome our apprehension concerning this unknown presence not only because he is "like life" and even "sweeter than life," but also because in the verses that follow the combination of the long vowels that flow smoothly to form polysyllables creates a sense of ease and serenity. The emotional texture of the sounds is that of joy and trust, not anguish or discomfort. This is in accord with what the lines tell us, namely, that the radiance of this presence engulfs the poet's entire being:

Īnjā kasīst penhān, hamchūn khīyāl dar del
Ammā furūgh-e rū-yash arkān-e man gerefte.

(D, 2388:3)

(There is someone here, invisible to the eye, like an image in the heart;
But the radiance of his face has taken over my existence.)

The poem includes many other fine examples of utilizing sound to express feelings. In the fourth line:

Īnjā kasīst penhān, mānand-e qand dar ney
Shīrīn shekar'furūshī dukkān-e man gerefte.

(There is someone here, invisible to the eye, like sugar in sugar cane;
A sweet sweet-seller who has take over my store.)

The repetition of the consonants *shīn* and *re,* which are associated with the words *shikar* (sugar), *shīrīn* (sweet), and their derivatives, in the expression *shīrīn shekar'furūsh* (the sweet sweet-seller), emphasizes the irresistible sweetness of what the sweet-seller has to offer. In the sixth verse:

Chūn gulshekar man u ū dar hamdegar sereshte
Man khūy-e ū gerefte, ū ān-e man gerefte

(Like the sugar and rosewater drink, we are mixed.
I have acquired his spirit, he has obtained mine.)

Where the lover and the beloved unite to the point of acquiring one another's character, the second half of the line is divided into two short sentences that mirror each other: *man khūy-e ū gerefteh, ū ān-e man gerefte.* With the exception of the word *Khū* (character, conduct), which is replaced in the matching sentence by the pronoun *ān,* every word that is in the first sentence appears in the second, too. *Man* (I) and *ū* (he) change position or become one another, a sonic illustration of the inner transformation the poem describes. Likewise, in the ninth verse:

Tu nīz del'kabābī darmān ze dard yābī
Gar gerd-e dard gardī, farmān-e man gerefte.

(You are broken-hearted too, you shall find cure in love;
If you listen to me and pursue that ailment.)

The confusion involved in the "pursuit of the ailment of love" is reflected in the four consecutive words *gar gerd-e dard gardī* (literally, if you pursue the ailment). The words contain no letters other than *gāf, re,* and *dāl* and form a mazelike combination, a tongue twister.

Generally speaking, the slow and melancholic tone of this poem may be less typical of Rumi's lyric than his regular short, fast rhythm. Its sense of transformation and the awareness of a kind of underlying magical current, however, are typical of the *Dīvān*. In verse 11 in the above *ghazal,* the secret of meeting the invisible presence is given as breaking the "spell of form." Although no solutions are offered for the breaking of this spell, except for the simultaneous ailment and cure of love (D, 2388:8), the poem fulfills its rhythmic anticipation and ends on a positive note. If the "eye within" is opened, the "hidden cup-bearer" will appear to "greet" and "to offer" us the wine (D, 2388:12)

The function of rhythm, and the rhythmical impact of the poems themselves, is a recurring motif in the *Dīvān*. Not only does the poet, in moments of lethargy, urge the musician to play so that "life may return to the lifeless body" (D, 1981:1), but throughout the *Dīvān* there is an understanding that the poems themselves possess a life-giving quality. As the "wondrous birds of images" grow magically from the "palm of [the poet's] hand," the words "pour out of his lips" with the intoxicating power of "wine" (D, 328:4). For the poet himself, these are moments of ecstasy in which the "height of his flight" is the "envy of birds" (D, 324:5). Their impact on others is no less. They can set the universe on fire (D, 89:2). With rhythmic magic as its inner life, poetry not only mirrors a universe in love, it becomes an instrument for looking within and for remaking the self.[6] This rhythmical magic is frequently inseparable from the meanings of words. Chanting Shams al-Dīn's name to music, for instance, can breathe life into the dead and cause them to dance in their coffins (D, 1981:5).

The Source of Poetic Rhythm

The rhythm of remaking the self in the *Dīvān* is not always that of joy and triumph. Often a sense of captivity and helplessness is interwoven into it. Instead of causing stagnation, however, the pain of captivity becomes the necessary opposite pole. In the tension between triumphant and desperate moments, there is a propelling force, a source of creative energy. The choice is between becoming a speck of dust drifting aimlessly between the two poles or taking action to control one's destiny. Through generating the rhythm for this action, the lyrics in the *Dīvān* provide the "soul for the lifeless body." Theirs is the rhythm of search, of endless struggle, and of change. Most of all, it is the rhythm of freeing oneself from the illusion of lifelessness in order to submit to love.

What is the source of this tireless struggle? Where does the dynamic and playful mimicry of the universe draw its energy from? What is the fountainhead for the sense of make-believe that pervades these lyrics? These are compelling, if diverse questions. Yet they fit together, as if they all belonged to a larger all-encompassing pattern.

It is not unusual for poetic rhythm in the works of one poet, or a group who represent a certain epoch, to exhibit certain recognizable patterns. The phenomenon may be described as rhythm being influenced by an external reality. It is as if the poetry borrowed, the rhythm of a certain event, activity, or mode of experience that happened to have normative qualities for the era or for the poet in question. In his study of English religious literature of the seventeenth century, Louis L. Martz demonstrates that in the mystical compositions of Southwell, Herbert, and Donne the structure of the poems is heavily affected by the tripartite structure of the meditative practice of the time. He identifies these parts as *composition, analysis,* and *colloquy*. Martz shows the existence of formal units in the works of the above writers that correspond to the sections in the meditative structure. That the structural rhythm of poetry should correspond to the patterns of a well-ingrained spiritual practice comes as no surprise. Yet the greatest significance of Martz's study, I believe, rests in his attempt to penetrate more deeply than the structural rhythm and explore the role of meditation as a fundamental organizing impulse deep within the poetry.[7]

Martz is attentive to details. He accounts for the religious significance of the act of meditation and the paradigmatic nature of its object, Jesus Christ. Yet he does not overlook the artful and imaginative dimensions of the practice. He is aware of the advantage of meditation in offering poetry a firm and well-tested structure to adopt. And yet he does not deny the dynamic quest for self-knowledge in either meditation or poetry. All in all, Martz's observations are insightful. One is even tempted to adopt them, with some modification, to Rumi's lyrics. After all, the latter was deeply attached to similar ritual practices such as the *dhikr* (meditative remembrance of God) and the *samāʿ* (mystical dance of ecstasy) in Sufism. Indeed, we have demonstrated in the course of the previous chapters that the practice of whirling to music forms one of the central images that successfully embody many key poetic concepts visually articulated in the *Dīvān*. Whirling expresses the dynamism, the playfulness, and the harmony that characterize this large corpus of poetry. In addition, there is the persistent question: what other activity but whirling is suitable to serve as the model for inner rhythm particularly in the poetry of the one who invented the practice? (Not to mention that he made it a central theme in his poetry, too.) I would maintain that while whirling constitutes an appropriate visual articulation for many things in the *Dīvān* and has been evoked as such in the present work frequently, it is inadequate as a model for the inner rhythm of the work. The following are a few of the problems in giving whirling such a fundamental role. For one thing, it presents itself too readily due to its visual accessibility. The same quality, however, leaves no hidden or remote corners in it to be explored. Mathematical problems may demand full explanation, but good poetry never lends itself to a full unraveling. In addition to this, there are prominent characteristics in these lyrics that cannot be accounted for if we consider their inner organizing impulse to be best characterized by the practice of whirling.[8]

The Rhythm of Childhood in the *Dīvān*

Let us now begin an examination of some such trends and look for recognizable patterns in them.

Patterns of Repetition

Exaggerated patterns of repetition, which at times border on nonsensical utterance, are characteristic of Rumi's lyrics. Repetition has long been known as a rhythm-creating literary device. Technically speaking, it produces sets of likeness/difference discriminations that utilize binary contrast.[9] In poetic terms, repetition is the "rhythm of recurrence" which operates in a fairly complex and paradoxical manner.[10] It moves between the two extremes of becoming redundant as a result of predictability or increasingly meaningful due to emphasis. We have seen in chapter 5 that Rumi was well aware of this dialectic of memory and anticipation and utilized repetition through widening the selection of refrains or other repeated patterns, creating a resonant effect.[11] However, in the *Dīvān* there are examples of repetition which go beyond the boundaries of the functions described here. In their extreme form, these are merely sound patterns, resembling nothing more than a child's babbling. Instead of generating meaning, as verbal symbols usually do, they seem to serve a purely musical purpose:

Guft: man nīz tu rā bar daf u barbaṭ bezanam
Tananan tan, tananan tan, tananan tan, tananan.
(D, 1991:14)

(He said: then I shall play you! on the *daf* and *barbaṭ*
Tananan tan, tananan tan, tananan tan, tananan.)

In other examples, the patterns are not themselves devoid of meaning but lose much of it through exaggerated repetition:

Ey ziyān u ey ziyān u ey ziyān u ey ziyān
Hūshyārī dar miyān-e bī-khudān u bī-hushān.
(D, 1955:1)

(What a loss, loss, loss, loss it is
to remain sober among the intoxicated and the unconscious.)

In the following example, the repetitive pattern appears in the second hemistich:

Qaṣd-e jafā'hā nakunī! var be-kunī bā del-e man
Vā del-e man! vā del-e man! vā del-e man! vā del-e man!
(D, 1817:1)

([I hope] you do not intend to be unkind to my heart, for if you do
Woe unto my heart! woe unto my heart! woe unto my heart! woe unto my heart!)

In the above examples, the medium of sound, while staying within the modality of words, intentionally breaks through the symbolic function of language. It is as if the poet were attempting to express himself even as he simultaneously mocks the expressive inability of language. One might see it as an alternative to silence, a way to defy ineffability without completely surrendering to the illusion that linguistic discourse can fully represent inner feelings.

What is certain is that these words do not represent mindless babbling or carelessness with language. They are intentional, as is the babbling of the young child who uses mimicked sound patterns to repeat an experience and to reach out for things beyond his grasp. Such an analogy should not lead to an underestimation of the complexity of Rumi's poetry. Indeed, "access to childhood" is often seen as a necessary component of creativity. Many poets have benefited from this line of access. The use of such rhythmic-intonational patterns in the works of Gerard Manley Hopkins, for instance, has been the subject of a study by Emilie Sobel.[12] Concerning the poetic function of these sounds, Sobel observes that a rhythmic connective web allows a better fusion of inner and outer events and ideas than linguistic connectives which do not allow the same degree of fusion. Whatever the poetic function of these sounds, their evocation of our childlike nature ties in with our previous findings concerning the dynamism and the playfulness of the imagery in Rumi's lyric. Perhaps, in this way, he wishes to acknowledge the babbling of the child within and its purpose. Before further speculation, let us look for other findings that may confirm our reading of these sound patterns.

Now Rumi's poetry opens to us like the door to a newly discovered edifice: the rich and explorable edifice of our own childhood, certain to offer many unexplored nooks and crannies. If the organizing impulse within his poetry shows trends parallel to the rhythm of the moments of childhood, so much more may be evoked using this model. It allows us to discover dungeons, attics, or gardens we would have not otherwise believed existed. Above all, it bridges the gap between depth, seriousness, and erudition (qualities that we tend to attach to learned persons from centuries past) and freshness, playfulness, mischief, desire for exploration, and many other characteristics that are easily overlooked when examining the works of an established—for some critics sacred—figure such as Rumi.

Playfulness

Let us enter the edifice from the gate of playfulness, the universal mark of childhood.[13] In addition to being a normative feature in the rhythm of childhood, playfulness is the quality that, as we have seen, is most characteristic of rhythm in Rumi's *ghazals*.[14] Shafīʿī Kadkanī refers to this quality in relation to the metrical rhythm in the *Dīvān* when he describes it as *awzān-i khīzābī*. *Khīzābs* are little waves created on the surface of a stream when the monotonous flow of water is blocked by an object in its way. *Khīzābs* are busy and noisy. Movement is the most visible part of their existence. Indeed it is their entire existence. This metrical peculiarity in Rumi's lyric is what Dashtī describes as *ẓarbī* and Heny terms "the strong tendency for a recurring insistent musical beat."[15] This phenomenon may be formally expressed through bracketing and phrasal grouping. The following example gives us a concrete musical face to put to the above theoretical speculation:

Jān-e jān'hā'ī, tu jān rā bar shekan
Kas tu'ī, dīgar kasān rā bar shekan
Gawhar-i bāqī! darā dar dīd'hā!
Sang bestān! bāqiyān rā bar shekan.
(D, 2011:1–2)

The sound of "tam, tatam tam, tam, tatam tam, tam tatam" which enlivens the whole *ghazal,* fits nicely with the mischievous theme of breaking every useless object, which is the verbal message of the poem:

You are the life of lives, break my life into pieces;
You are my relative, make me turn away from others.
O everlasting jewel, make yourself manifest!
Take a stone and shatter all else into pieces.

Playfulness in the *Dīvān* has other manifestations besides the above "recurring insistant musical beat." For example, it is manifested in the previously mentioned changing length of the *ghazals,* which plays with our expectations by fluctuating between lengths of three to over fifty lines. In a more discreet manner, a gamelike effect on the semantic level is created by rhyming words from completely divergent semantic spheres such as "queens" and "screens" or "elope" and "pope" in English.[16] In *ghazal* 2007, for instance, the words *jahān* and *āsmān,* meaning "the world" and "the sky," conventionally considered proper rhyming partners, are rhymed with the word *nardebān* (the colloquial for *nardebām,* or ladder). Still more of a mismatch in the same *ghazal* is the adverb *keshkeshān,* meaning to drag something on the ground with a good deal of struggle. Not only is the term from a different lexical family (adverb as opposed to adjective or noun like the rest of the rhymes) and notoriously close to spoken language, but it mocks the serious atmosphere of the *ghazal* by introducing an informal and trivial activity.

Freshness and Naturalness

A trend similar to playfulness in the *Dīvān* is the childlike rhythm of freshness and naturalness. Not only does the reader of the lyrics quickly become aware of the ease with which the phrases fit into normal speech patterns, the poet foregrounds his lack of interest in artificially ornamented language as a major theme. Heny's study offers a way to describe this quality in technical and tangible terms. Using samples from the *Dīvān,* she shows that in Rumi's poetry not only is the correlation between the sentence boundary and the metrical foot boundary upheld, it is reinforced by interior rhyming and syntactic parallelism.[17] The following is one of the examples quoted by Heny, typical of many *ghazals* in the *Dīvān*:

Khunuk ān kas ke chu mā shud, hame taslīm u reẓā shud
Geruv-e ʿishq u junūn shud, guhar-e baḥr-e ṣafā shud.

(D, 760:1)

(Happy the one who has become like us; who has become all surrender and contentment;
Who has become the pledge of love and madness; who has become a jewel in the sea of purity.)

The metrical foot in the above verse is a *faʿalātun*, four of which constitute one hemistich. Not only does each pair of *faʿalātun* contain one complete sentence, but the interior rhyme reinforces the natural rhythm of the sentences. It should be emphasized that although the above example and many more in the *Dīvān* are "elaborate contrapuntal pattern between the super-imposed meter and the ordinary rhythm of speech," the violation to which the syntactic rhythm is subjected is absolutely minimal.[18] It is a sign of Rumi's tendency to remain natural that instead of injuring the natural syntactic makeup of the language to achieve rhythm and harmony, he often makes use of expected phrasal and stress-patterns to enliven the music of his poetry.[19]

Patterns of Exploration

Another affinity one may detect between the fundamental organizing impulse within the *Dīvān* and the rhythm of childhood are the patterns of exploration and the sense that the momentum of search must be upheld.[20] This rhythm of exploration is maintained in numerous ways. We observed previously that imagery plays a dynamic part in keeping the sensation of movement and change alive: we explored our feelings as we fell with the raindrops from cracks in the ceiling, travelled to the ocean on the shoulders of currents, and wafted to unknown gardens with the breeze. Thematically speaking as well, there is much emphasis on encouragement to explore. In the example quoted in the previous chapter in which lovers are encouraged to soar into the sky and visit the next world, not only does the search not end there, but in fact the real exploration only begins in the world beyond the next (D, 1713:1–2). Elsewhere, Rumi is clear concerning this topic: "The function of the eye," he says, "is but to see wondrous things" (D, 716:1). In the chapter on imagery, we also noted that the variety of images he poetically explored are much wider than his classical counterparts.

On a formal level, Rumi exhibits the same curiosity to explore Persian metrical schemes. Shafīʿī Kadkanī's comparison of the first one hundred *ghazals* in the *Dīvāns* of Ḥāfiẓ, Saʿdī, and Rumi reveal that while our poet's enthusiasm to test new metrical patterns was almost twenty five-percent higher than Saʿdī's, his capacity to explore this area was nearly twice as much as Ḥāfiẓ's. On a similar note, Rumi's experimentation with the poetic use of rhyme resulted in an unusually wide spectrum of examples. The poet's exploration of the possibilities of rhymes was so persistent that it leads Shafīʿī Kadkanī to the following speculation: Rumi's constant complaints about the poet's obsession with rhyme is but an indication of his fascination with the device.[21] Finally, speaking of the rhythm of exploration, what deserves to be highlighted most is Rumi's prominent role in remapping the generic horizons of the *ghazal*. As we shall see in the next chapter, due to our poet's tendency to explore untrodden lands, this highly conservative genre began to function in ways that it had not done prior to Rumi's time.

Opening Questions

The flow of the rhythm of childhood is often punctuated with questions that are perhaps unanswerable. It has been claimed that children ask questions more to "engage another person" than to elicit an answer.[22] This suggests a striking parallel between the childlike act of posing questions in order to interact with others and the poetic use of the interrogative mode to get the reader involved. Hollander has observed in his "questions of poetry" that poems often pose questions they can barely answer.[23] What they do, instead, is to make us ask questions concerning their questions. Leaving unanswered things "hanging in a final question" is, from Hollander's point of view, more serious than actually providing answers.

Rumi is a master of such unanswerable questions or "conversational acts," to use the psychological term.[24] The *Dīvān* is punctuated with the pain and the pleasure of asking. Rumi's favorite questions are opening questions which often begin a *ghazal* and become the propelling force that sustains its momentum. Out of one hundred randomly chosen *ghazals* (523–623) twenty-two, almost one fourth of the total, open with questions. A small portion of these questions are answered. The rest serve to involve the reader through stimulating a search for solutions. In the interactive process that follows, the poem succeeds in getting the reader more and more involved as it unfolds towards an answer:

> Why should I dance in the rays of his Sun?
> So that each dancing particle remembers me.
> Each particle is pregnant with the irradiation of his face;
> The smallest joys of that union give birth to a hundred more particles!
> (D, 621:1–2)

More often than not, however, the questions are not expected to lead to an answer. These include questions such as whether the "radiance" in the "lightning" is the beloved (D, 577:1) or why "human nature changes color from moment to moment" (D, 554:1). Such questions underscore their own unanswerability; nevertheless, to adopt an interrogative mode is in itself opting for a certain poetic device, like employing a trope or playing with certain images. It sets a rhythm, in this case a paradoxical one. As the emphasis on complete surrender and unquestioning acceptance permeates the poems, so the questions with their mischievous tone punctuate them. In Rumi's customary fashion, these questions disrupt the flow of the poems and create stumbling blocks that keep the reader engaged.

Mischief

In tracing the rhythm of childhood in the *Dīvān*, mischief itself should not be overlooked. As another universal mark of childhood, mischief may be seen as a way of breaking the monotony and introducing an element of unpredictability. One can say with certainty that, as far as abiding by literary conventions are concerned, in the history of Persian classical literature no poet was so inclined to "mischief" as Rumi. The *Dīvān* has remained open to "unpoetic" images and ideas, simultaneously light and playful meters have been employed to bring a genre as stern as the *ghazal* to give expression to ecstasy. Moreover, all sorts of other canonic boundaries have been crossed to breathe the childlike sense of freshness and play into this body of literature. Since we are in the present chapter particularly concerned with the sonic games for which poetry provides the best playground, let us look at our poet's mischievous breach of the conventions in some of these games. Although in Persian poetry the number of short and long syllables and the order in which they appear is precisely specified, a poetic licence known as "coalescence" allows a long syllable to be replaced by two short metrical positions if necessary. Study shows that whereas poets known for attention to meter such as Saʿdī demonstrated reluctance to make use of this allowed exception, Rumi used it frequently, bending metrical patterns to preserve the fresh and natural rhythm of speech.[25] The same lack of concern for maintaining flawless metrical practice in favor of preserving the word structure may be observed in Rumi's reluctance to make use of liaisons, a term applied to a restructuring of the final consonant of a word to make it the first consonant of a following vowel-initiated word, maintaining metrical rhythm to the full. An example is to pronounce the verb *bar/āram* (I raise, I bring up) as *ba/rāram,* which breaks morphological boundaries but enhances the smooth flow of the verse. Again, this convention, ignored by Rumi, was popular with poets concerned with producing "diamond-like" *ghazals.*[26]

Food and Drink

Finally, no childhood is complete, or has a truly playful rhythm, without food and drink. It would seem that it is not the food itself but the care and attention of the one who offers it that the child finds most nourishing. Whatever the secret, Rumi must have known it. In order to revive our memories of utter delight at the sight of a lollypop (or its medieval equivalent), he spreads on the table of his poetry a colorful collection of food and drink. In a randomly chosen series of one hundred *ghazals* (D, 2119–2219) seventeen kinds of food and drink are repeatedly mentioned. These include the more conventional ones such as milk, honey, and wine as well as foods not usually mentioned in *ghazals* such as cheese, *dūgh,* meat, and bread.[27] Generally one might observe that the occurrence of cooked food such as soup, rice, and kebab is less frequent in the sample than that of honey, sweetmeats, and other sweets. His list of fruits, including apples, peaches, plums, grapes, pomegranates, and more, is equally mouthwatering.

Rhythm of Childhood and a Better Understanding of Rumi's Poetry

The time is now ripe to ask the fundamental question: Where do we go from here? That is to say, we have examined the ways in which the organizing impulse, the ingrained rhythm within Rumi's lyric, reveals patterns astonishingly similar to those we can identify in the tapestry of our childhood. What does this new insight add to our understanding of his poetry?

Since the term *childhood* is loaded with psychoanalytic nuances, it seems necessary to explain at the outset that this discussion does not intend to lead to any such investigation of the lyrics. The reason for this is the desire to let the poems, and not specific psychological findings, be our guide. This should help us work with a broader and more flexible vision of childhood through avoiding preshaped ideas, specifically molded concepts, and overused terminology. Let us bring to this study something of the flavor of the exploration and adventure that colored our own childhood. We may follow any of the poems, images, or concepts which we feel to be significant or relevant; the roads that lie ahead are as numerous as the verses or ideas in the *Dīvān*. Admittedly, different roads will lead to different destinations, but unpredictability is itself part of the poetic effect. It is by now clear that when it comes to the *Dīvān*, settling for final solutions and fixed "correct" interpretations will only obscure the inherent dynamism and diminish the poetic performance.

Before attending to our general concern—namely, a consideration of what our reading does for an understanding of these lyrics—let us test our childhood idea by applying it to a master trope that resonates in the memory of the entire *Dīvān*: the tale of the reed cut off from the reed bed. This is the recurring account of the separation of humankind from its divine origin, one of the most fundamental of Rumi's concerns[28]

Where there is the fragrance of God,
The masses come in throngs.
Because the souls are thirsty for Him;
The thirsy hears the call of the water-bearer.
They are the suckler of His generosity and searching
For the direction from which mother may arrive.
They are in separation, waiting
For the union to draw near.
From Muslim, Jew, and Christian
Every dawn rise the sound of prayer.

(D, 837:1–5)

By playing the tune of our childhood, the inner rhythm of the lyrics gives expression to our cry of separation from the origin. It makes us protagonists in a brief allegorical tale: the tale of children separated from their mother. As such, we are in greater need of love than the blame and punishment offered by so many tales of morality. In this way are we redeemed of our chronic ignorance. After all, who can punish a child for not knowing the way out of a maze in which he happens to be lost? As a result, we can afford to be kind to ourselves and hold on to our sense of humor. As for curing the disorder, we may graciously accept the love potion cooked in the crucible of the poet's lyrics and extended to us by his healing words. It is more effective than hatred or hiding the problem under the cover of arrogance. There is hope that dancing to the ever-playful tune of his poetry will truly revive the child within us and the lost innocence along with it. This is the stubborn, persistent, tireless child who can pursue the object of his search, untouched by doubt and despite the hardship of the quest, the child we may gently admonish but also love and nourish so that it may grow to be a divine person.

The above remarks are centered around one specific example. They can, however, serve as clues to other allegorical tales to be recovered from the memory of the *Dīvān*. The poetic implications of the reading suggested in these observations are profound.

The major fruit of this mode of continuous access to childhood is to be able to keep the door to the world of make-believe always open. How much more magical can the fictive game of poetry become than when played by the child within who can truly believe in magic? In this simple and delightful way, we cease to be the poet's devoted disciples, hard-working pupils, readers in search of wisdom, or simply lovers seeking an incantation to tame the heart of the beloved. And yet, we become all of those things by turning into playmates for the poet. Like children, we babble our most inexpressible inner feelings to one another. We play and tirelessly explore. We ask unanswerable questions and get into mischief. At times, we soothe our inner restlessness with nourishing words. At other times, we keep spinning around without even asking to what end. However, at all times we are aware of one important thing. We are not passive recipients of the poet's words of wisdom. We interact with him, because we are playing this game together. We can trust one another and believe in the magic of make-believe. And we know one more thing: As long as we turn together, and the magic of poetry lasts, we will be able to turn funerals into whirling dances.

CHAPTER 8

Turning the Funeral into a Whirling Dance
Remapping the Generic Horizons

A Diamond or a Dance?

As the present critical inquiry progressed and eventually highlighted the rhythm of childhood as the main organizing impulse in the *Dīvān*, the metaphor of dancing was frequently used to shed light on intricacies difficult for the descriptive mode to capture. It is time to note that the extensive use of this motif in the work has reasons besides Rumi's own dedication to the practice of whirling.

The biggest advantage of drawing a parallel between the poetic act and a dance (or even a funeral) is to underscore that both participants in the analogy are actions. In the place of the metaphoric "diamond" that once described the perfection and brilliance of a *ghazal*, there is now need for metaphors that can free us from the notion of literature as a flawless but passive object.[1] There is need for metaphors that make us aware of literary works not as permanently shaped "things," but as records of subjective encounters by varying individuals exposed to the transitory values of changing societies.[2] True, there will be a wider range of literary acts than it is ever possible to convey by a single metaphor (including dancing). But that only gives us cause for celebration, because it means that our personal encounters with the complexity and intricacy of the individual work are manifold. These encounters, therefore, cannot be contained within the descriptive range of a single metaphor. As critics we may happily echo Murray Krieger's words of wisdom that "there is no danger of theory or criticism explaining away literature or eliminating our need to experience it." It would not then be so hard "to feel," as he suggests, "like the forthright but simple and unimaginative Horatio when he is advised—in well-known words—by brooding Hamlet . . . 'there are more things in heaven and earth, Horatio/ than are dreamt of in your philosophy.' "[3] Our consolation is knowing that literary creation is an act continuously unfolding on the stage of our evolving imagination. Therefore, there is always more to explore, more to uncover, and more to understand.

Instability of the Generic Structure

There is not even agreement as to the limits of the territory to be explored. Is literature a vast curriculum of learning that includes almost anything? Or is it what fits in the more limited demarcation that keeps certain genres separate from the extended notion of literature? More importantly, how do we come to terms with the fact that even within the smaller and more selective repertoire of genres, those considered to be dominant and pivotal change with the passage of time? In other words, how do we cope with the mutability of literature, the source of its flexibility, richness, and power, which is also responsible for the "instability of the generic structure" and much difficulty in comprehending literary evolution and change? Here, too, there is a consolation. As has been pointed out, in literature there is no *ex nihilo*. This is a domain in which one constantly runs into familiar concepts and structures, a domain in which change only masks forms of continuity. In this continuum, segments of older genres are used as building blocks for the new ones.[4] If not assembled versions of earlier generic material, new kinds are often less easily recognizable transformations of existing genres. These latter are changes that have survived the passage of time and have followed a gradual and less visible pace of evolution. In the final analysis, they are all the same thing: variations on the theme of continuity.

As critics in this alluring and illusive environment charged with pregnant silences and paradoxical emotions, whose uncertainties and weaknesses form its strength, we have cause for both joy and apprehension. Joy because the delights of our journey are many and varied, apprehension because we can develop rigid control mechanisms that blind us to the most charming. And joy again, because if we learn to interact with the poems as opposed to applying our critical tools from a distance, the charm of poetry will disable our control mechanisms.

We have come a long way from the world of timelessly immutable genres and narrowly defined canonic models. There is an equally long distance between the traditional worship of generic regulations in dominant genres as unbreakable rules made in heaven and the later view that these conventions are hostile shackles that suffocate creative abilities. An even bigger leap was required to the notion of genres not as mere tools to classify literature, but as constantly changing entities, fundamental instruments of literary communication. We now appreciate that the relation of the literary work to its genre is not a passive membership of some sort, but in fact involves active modulation. We even admit that much of this communicative modulation affects us in ways not readily comprehensible to our analytical faculty.

Medieval Persian Literature and Genre Studies

Many of the changes of perspective mentioned here have evolved on the Western scene, have been primarily available to the Western critic, and have been applied for the most part to literature produced in the West. Not surprisingly, there has been reluctance, even apprehension, in applying new views to the literature of the Muslim world, particularly that of the medieval period. Philological studies of this literature have been seen as relevant and permissible—after all *logos* is holy in almost any belief—but subjecting the works of such mystical and remote figures as Saʿdī and Rumi to a phenomenological analysis or to the latest theory of genres is still viewed with suspicion.[5]

And so modern generic understanding is still not readily applied to the genre of *ghazal,* for example. The binding conventions of the genre are still viewed as suffocating the creative abilities of medieval Persian poets. The period in which Saʿdī and Ḥāfiẓ produced their perfectly polished, "unchangeable" *ghazals* is still idealized as the golden age of the genre in Persian literature. The problem, of course, does not rest in acknowledging the skills of such poets, but rather in the fact that any approaches of a different kind are simply overlooked. Rumi, for instance, whose efforts clearly furthered the horizons of the genre but whose work does not fit in the above description, is treated as a lesser poet who merely failed to emulate ideal models, Sanāʾī and ʿAṭṭār. In this case, there is an "explanation," too: as a sincere mystic he was not primarily interested in writing good poetry. In short, it has not been possible for us to appreciate that modernization and change are not the prerogatives of the modern era and that in Rumi we are dealing with a poet whose revolutionary poetic vision necessitated a great deal of modulation, even departure, when it came to negotiating with the generic conventions.

Of course, the study of medieval literature poses its own specific problems. For instance, no matter how hard we try, we cannot "unknow," as it were, the knowledge that we have accumulated over time, separating us from the period we study in order to arrive at the earlier states of genres. We can and must, however, treat that literature as literature in its general sense and the people who produced it, despite possible differences in taste, as ordinary poets with similar aims and aspirations. No doubt their intended horizons of meaning will not always precisely correspond to the one we attempt to reconstruct in our readings. But in the same way that we often have to recover meaning from culturally or linguistically alien contexts, here, too, we must strive to bridge the gap and reach a reasonably close understanding. Many general evaluative criteria will remain the same. Originality, elegance in variation, clarity, generic competence, and generic height are among these. Needless to say, a writer may demonstrate relative weakness in a certain area and compensate for it in another. It is the critic who should remain aware of what tools to use when and what to emphasize most.[6] Most importantly it should be remembered that although writers differ with regard to their degrees of interest in innovation, any artistically significant creation necessarily involves some degree of departure from its generic model. In the absence of such a departure from convention the work would not show any distinctive characteristic of its own. This is an important point, for it tells us that each significant work of art, Eastern or Western, automatically alters and expands the genre in which it has been created. The same point shows why genres must not be regarded as fixed systems of coding but as constantly changing coded systems of literary expression. Indirectly, it tells us that the distinctive mark or personal signature of an artist should be sought not so much in how he upholds the conventions (although this forms an important element in his work), but in the distinctive ways he chooses to alter or subvert tradition. This is a point to bear in mind when dealing with Rumi, whose major contribution rests frequently in his departures from tradition to extend the generic borderlines of the *ghazal*. I shall say more on this in the pages to come.

Rumi and the "Fragmented" Genre of *Ghazal*

Discussions of Persian *ghazal* traditionally concentrate on a number of areas: the origins of the genre, its formalistic features, and the much-discussed questions of fragmentation and unity. The latter issue will be dealt with in a more detailed manner in the present chapter. The question of origins has not presented any overwhelming problems, whether the *ghazal* has been seen as a later development of the Persian *tarānah*, a permutation of the *taghazzul*, or the *nasīb* which has declared itself independent of the *qaṣīdah*. All the views acknowledge to different degrees the continuity of the pre-Islamic traits and the impact of exposure to non-Iranian, particularly Arabic, literature.[7]

The process, of course, should not be seen as leading to the extinction of the older kinds from which the modal transformation of the *ghazal* emerged. The old and the new continue to exist side by side.[8] This is true of many norms and conventions that generally characterize the poetry of Rumi's time. His own poetry, despite a distinctive tendency toward innovation, provides us with a wide spectrum of these norms and conventions. Furthermore, verses composed in the exact rhyme and meters used by earlier poets, and often expressing similar ideas, illustrate his adherence to the widespread tradition of imitating authoritative models. This tradition enhanced the poetic resonance through incorporation of verses already well-known to the reader. At times, it was used to demonstrate the poet's ability to revive old subjects and use them in new and effective ways. The following is an example of Rumi's imitation of Khāqānī (d. 1199):[9]

> The four walls of the house turned into windows;
> The ceiling collapsed and the threshold disappeared.
> (Khāqānī)[10]

> Behold the damage done to the house of existence by love;
> The ceiling collapsed and the threshold disappeared.
> (D, 2363:6)

Similarly, the idea of adapting the *ghazal* for mystical purposes was by no means peculiar to Rumi. Rather his work was the continuation of an already well-established tradition.[11] On the sonic level, Rumi, despite his constant complaints concerning the limits of discourse, did not seem to be bothered by the exact metrical tradition and the formalistic challenges posed by the genre. As the previous discussion of rhythm has demonstrated, Rumi's use of the metrical patterns covered a comparatively wide range, and his adoption of the *radīf* was characteristically broad and innovative. This gives us reason to believe that rather than dismissing the challenge of the formal generic conventions, he responded to them seriously and creatively. His direct comments on these regulations, however, show an ironic awareness that he was regarding or disregarding them at will. This is to be expected, though in his case it was a little exaggerated, for provoking a poet to transcend the limitations of previous examples is one of the constructive challenges a genre poses to the artist.

Not only did the challenges of *ghazal*-writing make it an attractive choice for Rumi; there were other equally compelling reasons why he should produce in this genre. With Sanā'ī (d. 1130–1), ʿAṭṭār (d. 1220), Anvarī (d. 1189–90), Khāqānī (d. 1199), Ẓahīr (d. 1201), and Jamāl al-Dīn

Iṣfahānī (d. 1192) in the background, the genre had acquired canonic status by Rumi's time. Employing a wider repertoire of subjects than the merely homiletic and panegyric ensured for the *ghazal* a wider readership and the possibility of carrying the mystical message outside the court to the unknown, even uneducated masses. Not to mention that the shortness of the poems, in comparison to the *qaṣīdah,* made them suitable for memorization and recitation (with or without music) in Sufi gatherings. On the whole the genre, despite the modern view of its rigid conventionality, presented an extremely flexible option.[12]

No doubt, the *ghazal* owes part of this flexibility to the syntactic and topical autonomy afforded by each verse. That is to say, the so-called fragmentation and lack of unity that have dominated premodern and modern discussions of this genre were, in fact, the source of its flexibility and strength. On this, I would like to add a few words.

As Hillmann has summarized in his study of unity in the *ghazals* of Ḥāfiẓ, the objection to the disparity of the verses in this genre goes back a long way.[13] The debate, however, has changed course dramatically over the past few decades. Earlier critical appraisals typically accepted the exceptional place the genre occupied as the agency for lyric expression in Persian literature while in the same breath condemning its fragmentary nature. These accounts never tackled, never even asked, the question why such a seriously defective genre had maintained its supreme literary position for so long. Modern critical appraisals, on the other hand, have concentrated on proving that the *ghazal* did not in fact lack unity, pointing out that well-produced examples of the genre do indeed show signs of organic wholeness. Hillmann, for example, in search of unity in the *ghazals* of Ḥāfiẓ, presents readings that underscore the intrinsic wholeness in some of the better-known works of this poet. Those *ghazals* in which Hillmann is unable to detect thematic unity he rates as unsuccessful examples of the genre. In so doing, he has no choice but to recognize as failures poems that have been regarded by millions of readers for centuries as unquestioned masterpieces. Hence, he evaluates "the Turk of Shīrāz" as "a composition totally devoid of a distinct character and poetic effect." Elsewhere, he judges the same poem to be "not even a poem" due to its "disunity and incoherence."[14] While no critic may claim that everything Ḥāfiẓ wrote was flawless, the critical procedure that reduces a poem admired by many generations of readers as a highly effective work into a non-poem has to be examined carefully. Hillmann himself is baffled by the widespread success of this poem. In the end, he attributes its success to such extrinsic factors as the accessibility of the poem caused by its place at the beginning of the *Dīvān,* as well as to the apocryphal anecdotes that have, ever since its creation, surrounded it.[15]

Curiously, in all the debates concerning unity in the *ghazal* and the seemingly unresolvable problem presented by fragmentation, no attention has been paid to the fact that the strength of this genre and its suitability for lyric expression may indeed stem from this supposed weakness. That is to say, the syntactic autonomy of the verses which has led to the possibility of thematic autonomy provides the *ghazal* with the potential to progress beyond thematic coherence to become a series of disjointed echoes, momentary glimmers of ideas, flashes of emotions, and contrasting or even conflicting images. A modern analogy may be an abstract painting that does not offer its viewer a single coherent story but rather the colorful, albeit seemingly disconnected, pieces of many. In this way it can produce a powerful lyrical effect missing in paintings based on lucid stories. Another good modern analogy is the art of photography. What is the point of capturing a small fragment of an instant? Why should photographic exhibitions attempt to bring isolated visual moments together when motion pictures can provide us with the most coherent narrative sequence of such moments? One might think this an imperfect analogy, for after all, even photographic exhibitions often have a unifying theme. This is a legitimate concern. But the sequence of the apparently disconnected elements of the *ghazal* do in fact have their unifying themes: the universe of the gradually formed and widely known poetic norms and conventions that resonate in the memory of each single *ghazal*. In this solid and familiar traditional ground are rooted all the roses which stand for a host of conflicting concepts, from beauty, aroma, youth, and fragility to coquetry, lack of sophistication, neglect of the lover, friendship with worthless thornlike people, the shortness of life, and more. Lesser characters carry their own bag of familiar stories, as well. Indeed, when reading a *ghazal*, there is little danger of running into strangers. We know the good and the bad personalities even before we have read our first line. There will always, for example, be the *dūst* (friend, beloved, patron) and the *muddaʿī* (the hypocrite claiming to be the lover). The plot, the struggle for unattainable love, may show variations, but it will rarely be a complete surprise, and the ending will in a majority of cases be the imminent death of the suffering lover. As readers we supply the unwritten text that frames the brief glimpses of images and momentary flashes of ideas to lend coherence to this seemingly fragmented world. Our reservoir of tradition, our literary memories, are the catalyst for much of the meaning generated by the text. In the meantime, the *ghazal* can afford to be fractured, disjointed, broken into pieces, but vivid and effective like a collection of photographs of striking moments. By becoming a reader we have joined the dramatis personae with the distinct responsibility of supplying and preserving the storyline. In effect, we have freed the poet to roam from subject to subject with no fear of losing track of the story. By so doing, we have empowered him to be as brief and as allusive as he chooses. He can come up with single, apparently disconnected, statements as striking as the flashes of light in the dark or as clear and continuous as broad daylight. This contract between poet and reader has helped many "structurally confused compositions" orient themselves and resonate for centuries in the memory of a literary tradition.[16]

The heavy presence of norms and conventions, however, does not mean that once fully developed the genre of *ghazal* remained fixed in time. Indeed, as mentioned before, genres are subject to constant change. With their powerful and imposing codes, they are there partially to challenge the creative writer to conform, make variations, innovate, or even violate them.[17] A successful artist will achieve any combination of these without altering the genre beyond recognition. Rumi may easily be placed in such a category. To evoke the central metaphor, the funeral that Rumi transformed into a whirling dance remains an occasion to bid farewell to a departed friend, albeit not with sadness at eternal separation but joy of reunion.

Rumi and Alterations in the Genre of *Ghazal*

Rumi's poetic vision altered the *ghazal* but not beyond recognition. Until his time, the *ghazal* had either been a vehicle for personal, worldly, sensual love, as in the works of such poets as Anvarī and Ẓahīr, or in comparison to their approach, a more abstract and elevated medium in the hands of poets such as ʿAṭṭār who sought mystical expression. True, the borderlines were obscure, and the ambiguity itself provided the genre with further effectivity, but the main trait in each group was fairly distinct.[18] Rumi adopted the genre, as have many other poets, for the purpose of mystical expression. In so doing he benefited not only from such widely known *ghazal*-writers as ʿAṭṭār and Sanāʾī but had less critically recognized models such as Aḥmad-i Jām.[19] In practice, however, he expanded the generic horizons of *ghazal* to accommodate much that it traditionally had not. Such major impositions of personal vision by a single artist upon a genre are rare but not without precedent. De Bruijn observes, for instance, that Sanāʾī used the prosodic structure of a *qaṣīdah* but without including in it most constituent elements of a laudatory poem. The composition was wholly adopted to homiletic purposes.[20] What Rumi did with the formal structure of the *ghazal* did not involve such a visibly dramatic change. It did, however, expand the horizons of the genre in the specific areas discussed below.

Juxtaposing the Spiritual and the Carnal

Rumi's brand of mysticism was a multifaceted one. It involved a great deal of personal and tangible feeling, a tendency toward action, and a specific interest in evoking carnal and sensual experience. Instead of promoting the view that one has to transcend the human level to experience the mystical, Rumi tended to see the mystical as just an aspect of the human experience. With characteristic boldness he crossed the borderline between the spiritual and the carnal to emphasize that the two were indeed one and the same, a view he expressed directly in his didactic *Maṣnavī*:

> Love whether of this kind or that kind,
> Shall ultimately guide us to the king.[21]

Contrary to the *Maṣnavī*, in the *Dīvān* the analytical orientation loses ground to the personal and experiential. Here, the mode of communication becomes descriptive and distinctly sensual. In this tangible human ambience, with a persuasive visual clarity that transcends intellectual clarification, Rumi molds the carnal and the spiritual beloved into one:

> If anyone asks you about the *ḥūrīs*, show your face, say: like this!
> If anyone asks you about the moon, climb up on the roof, say: like this!
> If anyone seeks a fairy, let them see your countenance,
> If anyone talks about the aroma of musk, untie your hair [and] say: like this!
> If anyone asks: " How do the clouds uncover the moon?" untie the front of your robe, knot by knot, say: like this!
> If anyone asks: "How did Jesus raise the dead?" kiss me on the lips, say: like this!
> If anyone asks: "What are those killed by love like?" direct him to me, say: like this!
> If anyone kindly asks you how tall I am, show him your arched eyebrows, say: like this!
>
> (D, 1826:1–6)

It is, of course, not uncommon for mystical verse to make use of love imagery, but often the tone is vague and vividly erotic details are avoided. Rumi is aware of this tradition. In his poem, he preserves sensuality precisely because he wishes it to be understood in ordinary human terms rather than in a vague and generalized fashion. The kind of love with which he is concerned does not exclude the human level of sensual expression. To appreciate Rumi, it is important to understand that in his poetry these two manifestations of love are not opposites that cancel each other out. Nor is it the case that he uses carnal love reluctantly as a mere allegorical representation for spiritual love. Rather the love to which he alludes is vast and multifaceted. It embraces a wide panorama of human experience, spiritual and carnal. Indeed the carnal is tangible, strong, and familiar, if ultimately impermanent and less developed than the spiritual; thus it offers the reader a taste of love to encourage and initiate him or her into the sequence of experiences which could lead to the higher spiritual stage. On a poetic level, too, it is important to read the passages with erotic allusions as evoking sensual love not as a masked summoning of the spiritual. The line that draws a parallel between the disrobing of the beloved and the appearance of the moon from behind the clouds derives its poetic force from the tension between celestial gravity and human physical attraction. If all the elements in the verse represented only the heavenly, the tension would be completely lost. Rumi, however, does specify that the spiritual is the ultimate goal, although the former is not its opposite or essentially of a base nature. The beloved mentioned in the above poem is also transformed into the Divine by the time we get to the eleventh line of the *ghazal*:

> To blind [with envy] the one who says: "How can a human being reach God?"
> give us each a candle of purity, say: like this!
>
> (D, 1826:11)

Again the generic potential of the *ghazal* to maintain an ambiguous double face through selective thematic discontinuity is what makes this transition smooth. The fact that individual lines within the overall context can preserve varied identities helps them to swing between the sacred and the profane or remain indeterminant, as the poem demands. Through sharpening the sensual edge and then giving it a distinct share in the spiritual cosmos, Rumi abolishes the imaginary boundary between the two and creates his specific brand of mystical lyricism. It is no surprise that in real life he was dedicated to dance and music, turning a spiritual event into a festive and a public occasion. On the poetic level too, he avoids abstraction, transcendence, and elitism. Instead, he marks his mysticism with a sensual color that makes the experience accessible and worldly.

Extended Commentary in the *Ghazal*

As Rumi's brand of mysticism is not remote and transcendental but related to daily experience, it demands a poetic expression with equal generic flexibility to accommodate this practical dimension. It requires a genre with complex and multiple functions. Genres do not acquire complexity overnight. They need time to expand their horizons and become capable of tackling the central issues with which they need to deal. Meisami observes, for instance, that "the central problem in the development of romance is the need for a style that can convey the inner experience of its protagonists: a style at once expressive of emotion and capable of commenting on the significance of the actions and events depicted."[22] The *ghazal*, due to its preoccupation with the general and the abstract and the independence of single verses, usually does not have the interest or the space in which to deal with detailed emotional expression. Similarly, extensive commentary on any topic requires a didactic mode and thematic continuity which, in the proper sense of the term, are not found in the *ghazal*. Rumi departs from this general tradition and expands the functions of the genre by making it a vehicle of direct and specific commentary when required. On such occasions, not only does he expand the repertoire of authorized subjects for the genre, but he also preserves thematic unity and disregards the conventional limitation on the length of the *ghazal*. A perfect example is *ghazal* 1734, which comprises a detailed commentary on the activity of the spiritual dance or *samā*ʿ. This poem provides a carefully argued recommendation, supported with scriptural citations, to let the inner self come to life with music as the dead do on the day of judgment (D, 1734:10). At the outset one might question the poetic wisdom of not giving this piece a formalistic expression more conducive to narration and commentary, such as the *Maṣnavī*. Further investigation of the poem, however, makes clear that the formalistic signature is not accidental. If, through the choice of form, the poet signals us to be prepared for lyrical effects, it is because we are dealing with an emotionally poignant commentary studded with lyrical moments. In other words, it is not that the lyrical quality of the *ghazal* has been sacrificed to become a suitable vehicle for commentary. It is, rather, that the commentary has been elevated to a poetic status so as to be able to express itself in a lyrical mode:

> What is *samā*ʾ? A message from the fairies hidden in your heart;
> With their letter comes serenity to the estranged heart.
> The tree of wisdom comes to bloom with this breeze;
> The inner pores of existence open to this tune.
> When the spiritual cock crows, the dawn arrives;
> When Mars beats his drum, victory is ours.
> The essence of the soul was fighting the barrel of the body;
> When it hears the sound of the *daf*, it matures and calms down.[23]

A wondrous sweetness is sensed in the body;
It is the sugar that the flute and the flute-player bring to the listener.
(D, 1734:1–5)[24]

The piece contains the traditional ingredients of ethical and religious commentaries. A direct quotation from the Qur'ān (15:29) appears in the poems (D, 1734:9), as do allusions to the *ḥadīth* and to prophetic anecdotes and miracles. The ecstasy of the dancers, for instance, who spring from their corners is compared to the enthusiasm of Jacob, restless with the scent of the Joseph's shirt:

From each corner springs a restless Jacob
For his senses have recieved the scent of Joseph's shirt.
Because the soul came to life with: "I breathed of My spirit into him."[25]
The divine spirit is its best food and drink.
Because the resurrection of the dead comes with blowing the trumpet,
The joy of hearing music brings the dead to life.
(D, 1734:8–10)

Looking from our historical vantage point, we now know that in later stages of the development of the *ghazal*, specifically with Ḥāfiẓ, such Qur'ānic allusions become a commonplace of the genre. But even then, passing references are more typical than extended quotes as in the above.

Narrative Expression

Rumi adds yet more to the traditional function of the *ghazal* by frequently making it a vehicle for narrative expression, although in most of these cases the narrative element is not foregrounded. In other words, we have often already absorbed part of the story before we realize that a related sequence of events is being presented to us. There are few *ghazals* which open as a traditional story would. We encounter a person or an event, accidentally it seems, but having done so, we do not abandon it abruptly as would be the case with most traditional *ghazals*. Instead, we follow the person or the object in question for most, at times the whole, of the poem. A good example is *Ghazal* 2388, analyzed in chapter 7. This eighteen-line poem, which explores a mysterious hidden presence, is made up of a description of this being, his relation to the poet and to the rest of the world, and finally an encounter between him and the poet. The poem departs from its traditional generic model not only in its tendency to narrate and preserve thematic unity, but in that it uses concrete description and benefits from a minimum of generalization and abstraction.

For instance, the being is not hovering somewhere in an imaginary heaven or in the poet's mind but is actually "holding on to the front of the poet's robe" (D, 2388:1). Neither is he so mysterious as to have no counterparts in the material world. He is like a merchant (*saudā'garī*) and a sweet sweet-seller (*shīrīn shikar'furūshī*) (D, 2388:4–5). The reality of the poem does not wholly correspond to our immediate and objective daily reality. The familiar dramatis personae and the concrete descriptive style of the poem, however, bring the two close together.

A second group of narrative *ghazals,* which exist in proportionally smaller numbers than the group just mentioned, conform even more closely to the traditional patterns of storytelling:

> I heard that a Kurd lost his camel in a desert;
> He searched for his camel in the desert at length.
> Unable to find it, he sadly went to sleep by the roadside
> His heart ravished with the longing for the camel.
> (D, 2544:1–2)

At first, it seems that this poem has nothing in common with a *ghazal* but the rhyme patterns. As the Kurd goes to sleep, however, a lyrical moon soars into the sky like a "polo ball" (D, 2544:3). Not only does this moon reveal the whereabouts of the lost camel causing the Kurd to weep with joy like "fresh spring clouds" (D, 2544:4,) but it transforms itself into a candle of divine wisdom that irradiates the darkness of the human body and changes it into *shab-i Qadr,* the night in which the first verse of the Qur'ān was revealed to the Prophet (D, 2544:6–7). The moon then undergoes yet another transformation, abandoning the Kurd and the camel altogether to become the agent of love, the concurrent cause and cure for madness (D, 2544:8). Our lyrical journey is interrupted as we are transformed into the river bed in which the moon has been bathing. The moon itself has turned into water (D, 2544:9).

Alteration of Finer Features of the Genre

In addition to the above general areas, Rumi's poetic innovations had an impact on some finer generic features of the *ghazal.* We shall here proceed to look at the more significant among such altered features. First, a clarification is in order. Some characteristics, singled out in the present work as specifically associated with Rumi's work, may, whether singly or in groups, be present in the works of other poets, too. This is to be expected. Literary change is rarely the result of monogenesis. Often similar departures from the tradition, with varying degrees of emphasis, surface in the works of different authors under different circumstances. What makes them significant here is the consistent, deliberate, and prominent manner in which they occur throughout the *Dīvān* to form a distinct poetic vision and attain specific literary objectives. The following overview of such key generic features in the *Dīvān* demonstrates Rumi's consistency in promoting his overall vision. It also confirms his general tendency to steer clear of the perspective that associates lyricism with a remote, abstract, and unreal world. These features all demonstrate his aptitude for an action-oriented poetry, willing to play a participatory role and form an interactive dimension of experience.

The New Dramatis Personae

In the *Dīvān,* we have seen the thematic conventions of the *ghazal* breached to let the least "significant" creatures and the least "poetic" activities into the lyric domain. As a result, the *ghazals* have become stages on which to act out more than the abstract and generalized story of the ungovernable and irrational passion of love for the cruel and capricious beloved.[26]

We have also seen Rumi's departure, when there is need for extended metaphors, from the tradition that kept the *ghazal*-writer within the single line syntactically and prosodically. Indeed, the example quoted earlier of the beloved portrayed as the tailor of the lovers illustrates both these features: it elevates a lowly tailor to a stature worthy of participation in the love and poetry, and it unfolds the metaphor over the course of five lines (D, 216:1–5).[27]

More significantly, the unconventional part the tailor plays in this *ghazal* is representative of a wider subversive attempt through which Rumi dismantles the apparatus of the conventional dramatis personae that peoples the *ghazal* of the period. This faceless crowd includes such figures as the *muddaʿī* (the one who falsely claims to be in love), the *raqīb* (the opponent of the lover/poet), the *muḥtasib* (the prosecutor), the *malāmat'gar* (the blamer), and the *ḥājib* (the watchman who never allows the lover a glimpse of the beloved's face). These characters, who are more personifications of bad traits in the human personality than real individuals, disappear almost completely in the *Dīvān.*[28] Rumi's brand of mystical lyricism has little use for these stock characters whose main function, as adversaries to the poet, is to convert threats into remote and empty menace by means of abstraction and conventionalization. No reader could be expected to be seriously frightened by the poet's complaint that the beloved has conspired with the *muddaʿī* to take his life. But Rumi wishes his reader to feel real fear. The kind of action-generating poetry that he aimed to create would fail if it relied on the antagonistic power of such stock characters as its source of threat. Dangers removed and vitiated by convention would fail to convey the poignance that he wishes to convey in the experience of love as action. The *mudda'ī* is an empty threat, so Rumi chooses the sharp blade of the saw, for example, hacking a dead tree to demonstrate what death will do to an stagnant existence:

> If the tree was able to move from place to place,
> It would not suffer from the saw and the harshly inflicted wounds.
> Neither the sun nor the moon could be light-giving;
> If they remained stagnant like a hard piece of rock.
> How bitter would be the Euphrates, the Tigris and the Oxus;
> If they remained in one place like the sea!
>
> (D, 214:1–3)

The *Dīvān*'s reliance on such stock characters in positive support is also minimal. Rumi refrains, for example, from appearing as the nightingale or other varieties of singing birds who conventionally represent the poet. Rather, he chooses from a wide range of highly unconventional personae such as the blood in the lover's veins.[29] Many of these personae have triumphal and happy characters which stand in sharp contrast to the conventionally poor (*bīchārah*), the outcast (*gharīb* or *āvārah*), the helpless (*ẕa'īf*), or the deprived (*maḥrūm*) lover. The fundamental assumption of the lover's helplessness in the face of the beauty and glory of the beloved still holds. The weakness, however, is not intrinsic to the character of the lover, which can be drastically transformed through union with the beloved. Not only is the union attainable, but it is the ultimate goal that makes the suffering meaningful. The attainability of the union itself is a departure from the lyric's general convention, on which I shall say more.

First, let me point out that in the *Dīvān* the new dramatis personae are frequently drawn from the natural world. We have seen, in the section on imagery, that in his poetic universe Rumi builds dancing trees, playful little waves, whirling planets, and chattering birds as significant constituents. Nature is prominently present in the works of classical Persian poets before and after Rumi, too. More frequently, though, as Clinton observes in his analysis of the poetry of Manūchihrī, these portrayals of nature are carried out from a distance. Where elaborate details are provided, they are a combination of the real and the fantastic, much as in Persian miniature paintings.[30] Rumi has little interest in a realistic portrayal of nature, either. He does, however, considerably reduce the distance at which he portrays nature. In fact, Rumi does not so much describe nature as interact with it. Often, he becomes a part of it by endowing nature with a voice, passion, and wisdom of its own. When he speaks to us as the sky, the tree, or the wave, we are no longer passively admiring the natural beauty of these elements. Rather, we are running, rolling, or singing with them.[31] This bringing of nature within reach is indicative of a general tendency to change poetry from exotic and remote into accessible. It is part of Rumi's overall transformation of an enchanted castle fit for royalty into a playground the reader can imagine him- or herself playing on. The stars, for example, are no longer diamonds that adorn the royal crown of the night but companions whom the poet employs to take his "prostration" to the beloved as they bend to listen to Rumi's grievance:

I sent a message to you last night through a star:
I said: "Give my greetings to that moon-faced one."
I prostrated myself and said "Take this prostration to that sun
Who turns rough stones into gold with his rays."
I opened my breast and showed it [the star] the wounds;
I said: "Give the news of my state to that heart ravisher, that blood thirsty one!"

(D, 143:1–3)

In this now fascinating, now confusing tale of life, we and nature are in the same boat, hence our cooperation. The main protagonists in this fable are not mighty kings, noble viziers, or exalted beloveds. We are the main protagonists. Even God, when He joins in, is somehow personalized. This is in part achieved by assigning Him the nurturing, motherly role discussed in the previous chapter:

I moved from place to place to soothe the baby of my heart;
Babies calm down when one rocks the cradle.
Feed the baby of our heart, free us from the need to wander about,
O you who cure in each instant a hundred incurables like me.

(D, 143:4–5)

The potential closeness of the beloved/God, the personalized character of nature, plus the familiar and worldly dimensions of love create an atmosphere of hope in Rumi's poetry which leaves no excuses for inaction. This is in marked contrast with the usual frame of mind that dominates the *ghazal* both in Arabic and Persian. Indeed, one of the main generic features of this poetry has been described as a general mood of hopelessness and passionate inaction in the face of unfulfilled love.[32]

Attainability of Love

Rumi does not portray love as unattainable, nor does he endorse inaction as desirable or even possible. On the contrary, the more animated, hopeful, and active the lover, the greater the possibility of union, just as the tree would have escaped the ax if it had not been condemned by its nature to inaction. This, of course, should not be read as an endorsement of human free will. Nor is the humanity, shackled by its limiting nature, considered to be more free than the earthbound tree. Freedom is understood as ultimately resulting from divine intercession rather than from human efforts. Yet here, specific factors are at work to incorporate the vision of the attainability of love into the lyrics without detracting from the supreme authority of the beloved or subverting the overall value system of the genre. In most traditional lyric poetry, the principle of the unattainability of love generally rests on the belief that only under this circumstance can the lover prove his worthiness. That is, the lover is worthy only if he/she is prepared to continue his/her devoted service in the absence of any hope for reward. Secondly, uniting with the beloved seriously diminishes the value of the lover, whose nobility increases through suffering and devotion.[33] In Rumi's vision of mystical love, however, while devoted service is essential, yearning for the reward of union does not vitiate the lover's devotion. Indeed, it is a legitimate desire and a catalyst to add to the momentum of the journey. More importantly, far from diminishing the value of the lover, union with the beloved elevates him to divine status. That is why the lover has to have hope in the attainability of love and is expected to take action to realize that union. Hence the high proportion of poems in the *Dīvān* which celebrate the dream of union, even the realization of it in the here and now:

> The Spring of the souls has arrived, O new branch begin to dance!
> Since Joseph has arrived, O land of Egypt, O the sugar begin to dance!
> The war has come to an end, the song of the harp can be heard;
> Joseph has emerged from the well, O one with no artistic aptitude! begin to dance!
>
> (D, 189:1, 8)

Note that the dance of union is open to, even in need of, more participants. Furthermore, it is not taking place on a remote celestial plane but beneath the newly sprouted branches of a tree a few steps away.

It is also remarkable that the sentence *bi-raqṣ ā* (begin to dance) or (come dancing), which forms the refrain in the *ghazal*, is a verb in the singular imperative, the most informal and intimate fashion of address.

In other words, not only is the dance of union taking place nearby, but our poet is not preaching to us about it from a pulpit. He is at our doorstep inviting us to join in:

> O drunken one who has come to life, nothingness is written all over you!
> The invitation to annihilation has arrived. Start the journey, begin to dance!
> (D, 189:6)

In this fashion, in a vast majority of *ghazals* in the *Dīvān*, hopelessness is converted to hope and presented to us by the poet in the guise of a friend or a companion. This accessibility presents the *ghazal*-poet in a new light. In place of the aloof and indifferent lover who is humble only before the beloved and detached from all else, we meet a different personality in the poet of the *Dīvān*. This is a charming person, at times outspoken and harsh but always informal, loving, and intimate. Often we feel we know him well. At times he hides behind the mask of unfamiliar personae so as to arouse curiosity, produce playful effects, or create the need for seeking. By and large, however, we are able to recognize him and be certain that he has the same sense of familiarity with us. Standing in our path, eager to help, he breaches yet another lyrical convention: that of the aloofness of the poet.

The Dramatic Representational Aspect

This informal relationship with the reader, in Rumi's poetry, has other poetic implications. The Persian court poet, as Meisami has pointed out, was often forced to resort to oblique expression to protect his position, even his life, in the face of possible offense taken by royalty or courtiers.[34] Rumi, due to the informality he has bestowed on the genre, could afford to be direct if need be, even harsh:

> If you do not plan to rescue your heart from this turmoil and introduce it to the business of love,
> What are you going to do with the heart? Come, sit down and talk to me about it!
> If you do not enter the circle of men for fear of unmanliness,
> [at least] Stay at the men's door like the door knob and keep knocking.
> (D, 1850:6–7)

Here, the intimacy of the relationship has eliminated the need for oblique expression. The informality sharpens the contrast between the tenderness and the candor in the tone. While the contrast operates as a source for poetic tension, the openness of the reproach displays the poet's sincerity. The absense of court decorum is prominent. As readers, we know that his love and anger are heartfelt and free of such conventions. The freedom from courtly etiquette, however, does not mean that the need for allegorical expression is entirely eliminated. The difficulty in verbalizing the experience of love will remain a problem not only for Rumi but for poets of all time. Rumi, as I have argued in the previous chapters, does not solve this problem so much by adopting allegorical modes of expression but by letting his manner of poetic expression become an allegory for the unruliness of love. Through watching him grapple with the intricacies and inadequacies of expression, we see the paradox of love unfold to the extent that it can ever be unfolded.

A further implication of this directness in addressing the reader is that it gives the representational aspect of Rumi's poetry a distinctly dramatic color. This is a feature generally minimized or absent in lyric poetry. Whether or not we approve of Frye's metaphor for the lyric poet as a speaker who has turned his back to his listeners, there is no question that lyricism benefits greatly from the mode of communication with the self. Whereas drama has preserved the flavor of ritual, lyric poetry has universally demonstrated a dreamlike quality in which the emphasis is on communing with the self.[35] The audience is taken into consideration, but only as the one who will benefit from the poet's communication with the self rather than as the primary addressee. Rumi's *ghazal* poetry presents a clear departure from this norm by frequently assuming the presence of an audience that is there to be directly addressed. Further elaboration may help to place distinctive and unorthodox representational aspects of Rumi's lyric in the context of medieval Persian poetry.

It may be argued that medieval Persian lyric poetry has, in general, a more dramatic ambience than its Western counterparts. This is true insofar as the entertaining nuance and the existence of a nom de plume in the majority of the examples presuppose an audience and a sense of performance on the poet's part. From a wider perspective, however, this argument can apply to any poem regardless of its generic, historical, or cultural context. That is, the assumption of some form of an audience is corollary to the composition of any poem. Perhaps the more critical point here is to be aware of the specific way in which the poet relates to the audience in the *ghazal* as opposed to other genres. In a *qaṣīdah,* for instance, the poet normally uses his pen name to remind the audience of the identity of the artist to be credited for the fineness of the poetic craft presented to them. The *qaṣīdahs* of Khāqānī (b. 1121–2) are typical in this respect. The following example shows how Khāqānī's nom de plume appears in a ninety-line *qaṣīdah* in praise of Muḥammad:

> The slave Khāqānī takes refuge in the threshold of the Messenger of God,
> For slaves are treated with respect in this exalted threshold.[36]

The next twelve lines which end this *qaṣīdah* are in praise of Khāqānī, whose poetic excellence is compared to that of the Arab poet Ḥassān and his poetry to a mirror in which the face of Muḥammad is reflected best:[37]

> His [Khāqānī's] poetry is the miracle of all time;
> By God, the Persians will never hear or see words more excellent than his.[38]

The *ghazal* poet may, on occasion, boast of poetic excellence, but he frequently uses his pen name to address *himself*. As in the following verse by Ḥāfiẓ, these instances are often used to contemplate emotional or philosophical issues:

> Silence! O Ḥāfiẓ! no one knows the divine secret:
> Who do you ask "What has happened to the bygone times?"[39]

The dramatic representational aspect in Rumi's lyric is a distinct generic feature of his *ghazals*. It occurs consistently and exhibits a number of clear features. To begin with, the communication is not directed to an audience affiliated with a certain social circle such as the court or even a broader social class. Second, the nature of the relationship is normally not that of entertaining, impressing the audience with artistic skills, or offering the poetic product in expectation of material or ethical reward. It is a relationship that remains, within the context of a dramatic encounter, remarkably personal, private, and intimate. It can, therefore, create in each reader the sense that he/she is not a part of the crowd but a single individual that the poet is addressing. Ḥāfiẓ, to use a different example, addresses the collective community of Muslims as a general, one might say faceless, audience: "O, Muslims! I once had a heart."[40] Furthermore, the conventional and generalized nature of the topics presented in the address rules out any desire on the poet's part to establish a more personal relationship. Rumi, as we have seen, frequently adopts a personal attitude, even a rebuking one, as the case requires. His addresses deal with specific issues and are often expressed in the singular which lends them an air of intimacy:

> Come! Join us! We are lovers!
> [Come] so that we may let you into the garden of love!
> [Come] live in our house, like a shadow;
> For we are neighbors with the Sun!

> You are water, but you are a whirlpool, [you are] imprisoned;
> Come! Join us! for we are the flowing flood.
>
> (D, 1536:1–2, 6)

While the spiritual message is present in the background, it is translated into an immediate and specific concern, much like a personal conversation:

> You do not see the light, how do you know what it is? You are blind.
> How does the one who has not seen black recognize white?
>
> (D, 350:2)

The well-known *ghazal* addressed to pilgrims travelling to Mecca is an example of how this relationship is made personal even when relating to wider audiences:

> O pilgrims to the Ka'bah! Where are you? Where are you?
> The beloved is right here, come back!
> Your beloved is residing next door;
> What are you searching, confused, in the desert?
> If you see the formless manifestation of the beloved's form
> You will be the master, the House, and the Ka'bah yourself.
> Ten times you reached that house [Ka'bah] through the same route;
> Just once climb up the roof of this house [your soul].
>
> (D, 648:1–4)

This direct and intimate relationship with the reader transforms the formal limitation and traditional repetitiveness of the genre and breathes an air of spontaneity into the *Dīvān*.[41] Once more, Rumi's vision of poetic communication with the reader moves the genre away from convention and distance in the direction of closeness and personal contact. Favoring the dynamism of direct contact, it modulates a rigid, age-old feature into a lively and fresh one.

A Panorama of Continuity and Change

We are reaching the end of this monograph. Looking back at our exploration of the *Dīvān*, we have witnessed a vast panorama of liveliness and change. We have witnessed the transgression of syntactic, morphological, and prosodical boundaries. We have seen how the didactic nature of commentary, the magic of storytelling, and the intensity of lyricism can be effectively combined. We have sensed the wisdom of the old fused and invigorated with the playfulness and dynamism of the child. In short, we have seen a poetics of aloofness and seclusion behind the walls of convention transformed into a poetics of warmth and interaction.

It is time to overcome the resistance to the idea that "modernism is not a modern invention" and acknowledge that our poet was a reformer. Equally significantly, it is time to realize that modern criticism of Near Eastern literatures has, generally, not been attentive to this urge in premodern development of Persian poetry to go beyond its existing boundaries. If, as critics, we had looked in the right place or asked the right questions, this urge and the zeal with which it is reflected in medieval figures such as Rumi would have emerged.

There is, at the same time, no sense in portraying Rumi as an iconoclast, a nonconformist, and a misfit who cared nothing about time-honored tradition. Such a portrayal would be as misleading as the view which attributes all his subversive attempts against the less-favored aspects of the tradition to a lack of poetic interest or skill. It has been rightly observed that "only by knowing the beaten track, after all, can he [an artist] be sure of leaving it." Neither is it hard to imagine that, as Fowler observes, in order to decide which rule to break, you need to know them all.[42] Often, knowing the rules is not enough, either. A transgression of traditional boundaries requires not only a knowledge of relevant generic models as yardsticks to measure the plausibility of the new product but also a deep attachment to the tradition. Only the one who genuinely cares about a tradition can consciously or unwittingly subject it to the upheaval of change (though each individual's share usually constitutes a small step in a complex process). Rumi did not dislike or disrespect the poetic tradition in which he was trained, indeed immersed. The chapters of this book have demonstrated how thoroughly and lovingly he had absorbed this tradition and continued to do so even after his meeting with Shams. He allowed his poetic vision to be stimulated and challenged by tradition but not limited or completely shaped by it. It is important not to dismiss the old as irrelevant or worship the new as entirely novel or independent. Rumi's contribution should be viewed as a loud and lively echo, but one which would have been meaningless without the old resonances.

The present work has also demonstrated the continuity in the social function of Persian poetry. We have seen how poetry was used to entertain and morally guide in the early centuries after Islam, primarily through the *qaṣīdah*. We have also witnessed how, with the subsequent development of the courtly romance it took on the more complex function of expressing the emotion of the protagonists as well as commenting on the significance of actions and events.[43] With Rumi, we observe mystical lyricism embedded in the realm of experience, interacting with the world as Rumi visualizes it and serving as a forceful catalyst for action. Now a playful song, now an awakening tale, now a silent whisper, it contains the world in itself, the world turned into an echo:

> I silently moaned so that for a hundred centuries to come,
> The world will echo in the sound of my *hayhā*,
> It will turn on the axis of my *hayhāt*.[44]
>
> (D, 562:7)

NOTES

Chapter 1—Rumi: The Person and the Poet

1. Often known as *Masnavī-i ma'navī,* this work was edited by Reynold A. Nicholson in the early decades of this century. This edition, in eight volumes, contains the text, English translation, and commentary. The title of the present section, "I wonder which me is me?," is a quotation from the *Dīvān: Zīn du hizār man u mā 'ay 'ajabā man chi manam?* (D, 1397:1).

2. See the brief introduction by Furūzān'far to the Tehran edition: Rumi, *Fīhi mā fīh,* ix. The first English translation, by A. J. Arberry appeared as *The Discourses of Rumi* (London: Murray, 1961). A recent translation under the same title, by Thackston Wheeler, Jr., attempts to make the text more accessible in English—see *Discourses of Rumi* (Atlantic Highlands, N.J.: Humanities Press International, 1993).

3. Mu'īn al-Dīn Sulaymān ibn 'Alī, known as Parvānah, governed Asia Minor on behalf of the Saljuks during Rumi's life and was killed at the hand of the Mongols in 1276 A.D. shortly after Rumi's death. For Persian historical sources on him, see Badī' al-Zamān Furūzān'far, *Risālah dar taḥqīq-i aḥvāl va zindigānī-i Maulana Jalāl al-Dīn Muḥammad,* 137–40; also the full-scale study by Nejat Kaymaz, *Pervane Muinuddin Süleyman*. In one instance, Rumi prays that God may grant the amir's wish as well as the wishes that he is incapable of making! For if the latter were made known to him, our poet observes, the amir would be ashamed of his earlier wishes. See *Fīhi mā fīh,* 130–31.

4. Rumi, *Fīhi mā fīh,* 168.

5. Ibid, 148.

6. I shall henceforth refer to this work as the *Dīvān*. I have used the edition edited and prefaced by Badī' al-Zamān Furūzān'far, entitled *Kullīyāt-i Shams yā Dīvān-i kabīr*. The collection was named after Rumi's spiritual master Shams al-dīn of Tabrīz whose name "Shams" Rumi adopted as pen name. See Shams al-Dīn Aḥmad Aflākī, *Manāqib al-'ārifīn,* 2: 614; Dawlat'shāh Samarqandī, *Tazkirat al-shu'arā',* 147. Shams will be further discussed in this chapter.

7. Shamīsā considers seven the average number of lines in a *ghazal*—see *Sayr-i ghazal dar shi'r-i fārsī, az āghāz tā imrūz,* 2.

8. The earliest existing biographical source on Rumi is the *Valad'nāmah* compiled by his eldest son Bahā' al-Dīn Valad. The text, with an introduction by Jalāl Humā'ī, was published in Tehran 1936. Another significant classical biographer of Rumi is Farīdūn ibn Aḥmad, known as Sipahsālār, Rumi's disciple of forty years. Also known as *Risālah-'i Sipahsālār* or *Manāqib-i khudāvandgār,* this text was edited by Badī' al-Zamān Furūzān'far and published as *Risālah dar aḥvāl-i Maulānā Jalāluddīn Rūmī* (1946). The *Manāqib al-'ārifīn* of Aflākī, noted above, should also be mentioned. Aflāki, who died eighty years after Rumi, included much detail on

the poet and his companions in his biography. Besides these sources, Rumi's *Fīhi mā fīh*, as well as the discourses of his master Shams, known as the *Maqālāt-i Shams*, contain valuable biographical hints.

9. Furūzān'far, with his *Risālah dar taḥqīq-i aḥvāl,* is one of the earliest modern biographers of Rumi in Iran. Abdülbaki Gölpınarlı's biography, through full exploration also of the Turkish sources, adds to the wealth of existing information on Rumi—see *Mevlānā Celaleddin: Hayatı, Felsefesi, Eserlerinden Seçmeler*. The most prominent biographer of Rumi in the West is Annemarie Schimmel, whose latest study of Rumi, *I Am Wind, You Are Fire,* should be mentioned. William Chittick, though more interested in the spiritual teachings of Rumi, has included biographical remarks in his work *The Sufi Path of Love: The Spiritual Teachings of Rumi.*

10. Aflākī, *Manāqib al-ʿārifīn,* 2: 709–11.

11. Ibid, 2: 731.

12. The unconventional length of the *ghazals,* mentioned earlier, is an example.

13. For signs of awareness of this danger in the poetry of the period, see Furūzānfar, *Risālah dar taḥqīq-i aḥvāl,* 14–15.

14. For details of the journey as reflected in Persian historical sources, see Furūzānfar, *Risālah dar taḥqīq-i aḥvāl,* 14–32.

15. Rumi's father Bahā' al-Dīn Valad describes the incentive for the journey as a general dissatisfaction caused by the antagonistic attitude of the people of Balkh (*Valad'nāmah,* 190–91; cf. Fritz Meier, *Bahā'-i Walad*).

16. Not only was Rumi too young to be affected by this, as recent biographers have observed, the commonly accepted view that the family emigration was a result of this hostility is no longer acceptable. See Schimmel, *I Am Wind, You Are Fire,* 12.

17. Bahā' al-Dīn Valad, *Valad'nāmah,* 193. For Furūzānfar's comments and citations, see *Risālah dar taḥqīq-i aḥvāl,* 34.

18. For Rumi's allusions to Sanā'ī and ʿAṭṭār, see Jan Rypka, *History of Iranian Literature,* 236. Rumi's possible encounter with the great mystic Ibn al-ʿArabī is accepted by Furūzānfar on the authority of Khvārazmī in the *Javāhir al-asrār.* He further speculates that it would be unusual for an inquisitive soul such as Rumi to live in Damascus and show no interest in meeting a figure of Ibn al-ʿArabī's reputation—see *Risālah dar taḥqīq-i aḥvāl,* 43. For information on Ibn al-ʿArabī, see A. Ateş, "Ibn al-ʿArabī," *The Encyclopaedia of Islam,* 3: 707–11; his most recent biographer, Claude Addas, in *Quest for the Red Sulphur: The Life of Ibn ʿArabī,* is silent on the possible encounter of Rumi and Ibn al-ʿArabī.

19. It is possible that the meeting in Konya was not the first encounter between Shams and Rumi, as Aflākī states that they had met before in Damascus—see *Manāqib al-ʿārifīn,* 2: 618.

20. For references to grasshoppers and other animals in the *Dīvān,* see chapter 5. On the topic of Rumi's first poetic experiences, Gölpınarlı rightly observes that

he had written poetry before his encounter with Shams, though in insignificant quantity—see Gölpınarlı, *Mawlānā Jalāl al-Dīn*, 402–406.

21. For more on Rumi's generic choice and his modifications of it, see chapter 8.

22. Shamīsā, *Sayr-i ghazal dar shi'r-i fārsī*, 168.

23. Aflākī, *Manāqib al-'ārifīn*, 1: 185.

24. Willis Barnstone, *The Poetics of Ecstasy: Varieties of Ekstasis from Sappho to Borges*, 7; cf. Ninian Smart "Interpretation and Mystical Experience," 78–91. Smart argues that the distinction between an experience and its interpretation is not easy to make for the reason that "the concepts used in describing and explaining an experience vary in their degree of ramification," 82.

25. John Hollander, *Melodious Guile: Fictive Pattern in Poetic Language* (New Haven and London: Yale University Press, 1988), 6.

26. Much has been written on the limitations of hermeneutic interpretation. For a fresh approach, where poetic interpretation has been suggested as a contrasting technique, see the preface to Christopher Collins's *The Poetics of the Mind's Eye: Literature and the Psychology of Imagination*, ix–xxviii.

27. For an imaginative and insightful discussion of mystical poetry, see Menocal's comments concerning Ibn al-'Arabī's and Roman Llull's poetry entitled "Love and Mercy," in Maria Rosa Menocal, *Shards of Love: Exile and the Origins of Lyric*, 57–90.

28. Welch D. Everman, *Who Says This? The Authority of the Author, the Discourse, and the Reader*, 3–33.

29. These poems are interactive not only insofar as they engage the reader in their active poetic game, but in an intratextual sense as well. They display a constant awareness on the part of the poet of his previously written works. In other words, once created, they encourage further mystical experience and affect the creation of other works to be. Numerous examples of poetry recitation included in Sufi rituals confirm this crucial role of poetry. For a recent account, see Tadayyun's observations of a 1992 *Samā'* in Tehran in which *ghazals* of Rumi 'Aṭṭār and 'Irāqī were sung to music, in *Maulanā va ṭūfān-i Shams*, 195.

30. Of these *ghazals* a small percentage is in Arabic. Furthermore, most printed editions of the *Dīvān* contain a number of quatrains and *tarjī'bands* attributed to Rumi. The poems in Arabic and those in generic forms other than *ghazal* have been excluded from the present study.

31. Of these more than 500 verses, 174 appear in partial or indirect quotation wheras the rest are fully cited. In all cases, they are followed by a reference to the specific *ghazal* and hemistich in the *Dīvān*.

32. The translations of the poems from Persian into English are mine. To my knowledge, there is presently no complete and satisfactory translation of the *Dīvān* into English.

Chapter 2—Rumi's Lyrical Output: Historiography and Analysis

1. A desire echoed by many mystics and reminiscent of the Wittgensteinian leap into silence. See Ludwig Wittgenstein, *Tractatus Logico-Philosophicus*, 6.51–6.522. I deal with the literary and philosophical manipulation of the concept of silence fully in chapter 4, where I argue that Rumi's grappling with silence is more of a literary exercise to enhance poetic expression than any sign of hatred for poetry.

2. Indeed, we are free to ignore the entire range of Rumi's self-evaluative remarks by way of subscribing to the view that in literary assessment, an author may have a "peculiar interest" in analyzing his own work. Nevertheless, in so doing, he does not necessarily have a "peculiar authority"—see Northrop Frye, *Anatomy of Criticism*, 5. For more on the authority of the author, see Welch D. Everman, *Who Says This?: The Authority of the Author, the Discourse, and the Reader*, 65; cf. W. K. Wimsatt on the authorial intention in *The Verbal Icon: Studies in the Meaning of Poetry*, 3–39.

3. Rumi, *Fīhi mā fīh*, 74.

4. J. T. P. De Bruijn, *Of Piety and Poetry: the Interaction of Religion and Literature in the Life and Works of Ḥakīm Sanā'ī of Ghazna*, 155–60. To consider poetry from the viewpoint of pious medieval Muslims as inherently "immoral," as Schimmel states, however, is an overstatement—see *I Am Wind, You Are Fire*, 34. As De Bruijn points out, poetry had elicited the approval of mainstream religious scholars long before Rumi's time (*Of Piety and Poetry*, 166). Besides, poetry as the major cultural product of the medieval Muslim world could not have been in such an open conflict with ethical and religious belief, not to mention that some poets of the same period such as Niẓāmī of Ganjah (d. 1211) considered poetic inspiration as related to prophetic revelation: *pardah- 'i rāzī kih sukhan parvarīst//sāyah-'ī az pardah-'i payghambarīst*—see *Kullīyāt-i Khamsah-'i Niẓāmī-i Ganjavī*, ed. Bāqir Mu'īn'far, 20; cf. the chapter entitled "The Licit Magic of Poetry" in Johann Christoph Bürgel, *The Feather of Simurgh: The "Licit Magic" of the Arts in Medieval Islam*, 53–84.

5. The sixteenth-century biographer Dawlat'shāh describes how Rumi whirled around a pillar in his house in complete ecstasy reciting poetry that others took down. His sole comment about the entire *Dīvān* is that most of it expressed Rumi's pain of separation from Shams—see *Tadhkirat al-shu'arā'*, 149. Rumi's contemporary biographers have not been more attentive to his poetry in terms of acknowleding its merits or carrying out deailed studies. Earlier this century, R. A. Nicholson declared "Jalalu'ddin lacks the colour and perfume of Hāfiz . . . his music is rich and full, but for the most part he plays on one string; he has no sense of humour; his allegory is often grotesque and his execution careless" (*Selected Poems from the Dīvāni Shamsi Tabriz*, xlvi). Furūzān'far draws attention to the lack of evenness in Rumi's verse—see Furūzān'far, *Risālah dar taḥqīq-i aḥvāl*, 93, 156. Schimmel describes his verse as "technically correct" but certainly different from "the refined, diamondlike *ghazals* of poets like Ḥāfiẓ or Jāmī"—see Schimmel, *I Am Wind, You Are Fire*, 45. Chittick tells us "Rumi had no respect for poetry as such. If poetry has any value, it is found in the meaning and message it

conveys. In any case Rumi had no choice in his own versifying"—see *The Sufi Path of Love,* 270. Meisami attributes a "general lack of originality" to Rumi's treatment of conventional figures. However, her analysis of the poet's use of allegorical imagery in" depiction of spiritual invisibilia" is insightful—see "Allegorical Gardens in the Persian Poetic Tradition: Nizami, Rumi, Hafez," 242. For further comments on this latter paper, see chapter 5 on Rumi's use of imagery in the present work. Gölpınarlı, the Turkish commentator and scholar of Rumi, does acknowledge Rumi's interest in poetry; yet he, too, subscribes to the view that poetry consists of meaning poured into metrical patterns and ornamented with rhymes. We are therefore told that "even though Rumi likes poetry, he certainly is not fond of rhyme and metrical rhythm,"—see *Mawlānā Jalāl al-Dīn,* 406.

6. There are signs that this view is changing, even though extensive studies have not been carried out. In a volume on the relationship between poetry and Islamic mysticism that has recently come to my attention, Amīn Banānī observes the connection between "the source and structure" of Rumi's "mystical thought" and "the nature and the process of his poetic creativity." In this respect the lone voice of Banānī stands out as a sign of recognition of the superficiality of the division discussed—see "Rūmī the Poet," 28. In the same volume, Johann Christoph Bürgel focuses on Rumi's poetic artistry in a detailed discussion of the "interrelations connecting form and meaning" in the *Dīvān*—see " 'Speech is a Ship and Meaning the Sea': Some Formal Aspects in the Ghazal Poetry of Rūmī," 44–69.

7. In his eight-page account of Rumi, Dawlat'shāh mentions his poems only twice. The first is a short reference to the fact that he expressed the mysteries of the hidden world through poetry. The second refers to the significance of separation from Shams for Rumi's lyrics to which I alluded in a previous note. He also gives the number of verses in the *Dīvān* and in the *Maṯnavī*—see *Tadhkirat al-shuʿarāʾ,* 144–51.

8. Aflākī, *Manāqib al-ʿārifīn,* 1:86–89.

9. Ibid, 2:623–24.

10. Gölpınarlı, *Mawlānā Jalāl al-Dīn,* 402–6.

11. We have already pointed to historical inquiry which shows that poetry had elicited the approval of religion by Rumi's time—see De Bruijn, *Of Piety and Poetry,* 155–60.

12. Jacques Derrida, *Writing and Difference,* 278–93. For theories of poetry based on this concept, see Roman Jakobson, "Concluding Statement: Linguistics and Poetics," 350–77.

13. This, I would like to re-emphasize, is not the case with the general Persian-speaking readership. Rumi's *ghazals* easily rank among the most popular examples of Persian lyric poetry.

14. On a more practical note, factual evidence indicates that listening to music, dancing, and producing poetry often took place simultaneously.

15. Aflākī, *Manāqib al-ʿārifīn,* 1:185.

16. *Marā burrīd u khūn āmad, ghazal pur khūn burūn āmad//Burīd az man Ṣalāḥ al-Dīn, bi-sū-yi ān diyār āmad.*

17. One such example is the work of the German philosopher Edmund Gustave Albert Husserl (1859–1938)—see *A Dictionary of Philosophy*, 157.

18. Robert R. Magliola, *Phenomenology and Literature: An Introduction*, 4.

19. Ibid., 5. For discussion of the German philosopher Martin Heidegger, see *A Dictionary of Philosophy*, 43.

20. Emil Staiger, *Basic Concepts of Poetics (Grundbegriffe der Poetik)*, 17–18.

21. Magliola, *Phenomenology and Literature*, 6–7.

22. Ibid., 63.

23. A good example is Emil Staiger, who suggested under Heideggerian influence a fundamental reorientation of study of genres—see *Basic Concepts of Poetics.*

24. Ibid., 27.

25. David A. White, *Heidegger and the Language of Poetry*, 76.

26. Magliola, *Phenomenology and Literature*, 83.

27. Martin Heidegger, *Being and Time*, 199.

28. Ibid., 193.

29. David A. White, *Heidegger and Language of Poetry*, 143.

30. Heidegger, *Being and Time*, 204.

31. Ibid., 205.

32. Magliola, *Phenomenology and Literature*, 66–67. The concept of poetic contribution playing a major originative role is neither peculiar to Heidegger nor is it a modern invention. For example, Ibn Sīnā (d. 1037), in his discussion of continuous intellectual emanation speaks, of the peculiar abilities of the *poetic logic* benefiting from *ramz* (symbolic speech) and *īmā'* (hints). According to him, it is this logic that renders possible the concurrent communication of the divine message on a variety of levels. See Peter Heath, *Allegory and Philosophy in Avicenna (Ibn Sīnā) with a Translation of the Book of the Prophet Muḥammad's Ascent to Heaven*, 150–51.

33. Staiger, *Basic Concepts of Poetics*, 7.

34. Magliola, *Phenomenology and Literature*, 58–59.

35. Veronique M. Foti, *Heidegger and the Poets: Poiesis, Sophia, Techne*, xv.

36. Magliola addresses these and similar issues that phenomenology does not resolve in the work that has been frequently cited in the present chapter, *Phenomenology and Literature*, 61.

37. Staiger, *The Basic Concepts of Poetics*, 7.

38. Ibid., 9, 20, 30.

39. This is certainly true of Persian philosophy and mysticism in which the Illuminationist philosophers, most notably Shihāb al-Dīn Suhrawardī (d.1191),

based philosophical investigation on *ʿilm-i ḥuẓūrī* (presential knowledge), which can take the form of mystical intuition. See Hossein Ziai, *Knowledge and Illumination: A Study of Suhrawardī's Ḥikmat al-Ishrāq*.

40. Heidegger, *Frühe Schriften*, 352. The quotation here is taken from John D. Caputo, *The Mystical Element in Heidegger's Thought*, 7.

41. Caputo, *The Mystical Element*, 6.

42. Ibid., 7.

43. The above paraphrase of Heidegger's approach to poetic creativity is from Luanne T. Frank's introduction to Staiger's *Basic Concept of Poetics*, 27.

44. On the authority of the author to criticize his own work, see note 2 above.

45. On the divine nature of poetic inspiration, see notes 32 and 39 above.

Chapter 3—The "Footless" Journey in "Nothingness": The Power of Illogical Tropes

1. The title of this chapter alludes to the following verse from the *Dīvān: Mī shudam dar fanā chu mah bī-pā* ("I was journeying footless in nothingness like the moon" [D, 1759:10]).The inexpressibility of the mystical is the focus of a monograph by Michael A. Sells to which I shall return, *Mystical Languages of Unsaying*.

2. Elizabeth B. Davis, "The Power of Paradox in the 'Cantico espiritual,'" 206.

3. For a standard logical argument on the unacceptability of contradiction, see R. M. Sainsbury, *Paradoxes*, 141–44.

4. An allusion to the verse *Pā-yi istidlāliyān chūbīn buvad//pā-yi chūbīn sakht bī tamkīn buvad* (the legs of the logicians are made of wood//wooden legs are immensely hard to control)—see Rumi, *Maṯnavī*, 1:2128.

5. One of the rare places where this is mentioned is the opening chapter of Sainsbury's creative attempt to breathe soul into paradoxes—see *Paradoxes*, 1.

6. An allusion to the verse *Āb kam jū tishnigī āvar bi-dast//tā bijūshad ābat az bālā u past* (Do not search for water, search for thirst//so that water may gush forth for you from high and low)—see Rumi, *Maṯnavī*, 3:3212.

7. Michael Sells has used the phrase in relation to Ibn ʿArabī's paradoxical writings, see p. 36 below.

8. For the use of paradox in other formal genres such as *rubāʿī*, see the following section.

9. Rashīd al-Dīn Muḥammad Vaṭvāṭ, *Ḥadāʾiq al-siḥr fī daqāʾiq al-shiʿr*, 24–25.

10. Shams al-Dīn Muḥammad b. Qays al-Rāzī, *al- Muʿjam fī maʿāʾīr ashʿār al-ʿajam*, 344.

11. Annemarie Schimmel, *A Two-Colored Brocade: The Imagery of Persian Poetry*, 40.

12. For an overview of Persian lyric, see Heshmat Moayyad, "Lyric Poetry,"

120–46. Shamīsā's monograph *Sayr-i ghazal dar shiʿr-i fārsī* on the development of *ghazal* comprehensively documents the traditional views of Persian scholars on the subject. Invaluable as this only work of its kind is, it remains loyal to the commonly accepted views and patterns of literary analysis. It acknowledges the contribution of a small number of master lyricists who furthered *ghazal* within conventionally legitimate boundaries and overlooks the contribution of the less conventional figures. For instance, Ḥāfiẓ is declared as the *ghazal*-writer with whom the *ʿIrāqī* style reaches the end of its development—see Shamīsā, *Sayr-i ghazal dar shiʿr-i fārsī,* 130. Julie Scott Meisami, in *Medieval Persian Court Poetry,* devotes a chapter to the genre entitled "Ghazal: The Ideals of Love" (237–98). Interesting as the chapter is, in line with the overall focus of Meisami's monograph, it concentrates on the "courtly" subgenre instead of the *ghazal* in general. Other works with significant references to Persian *ghazal* will be discussed in the concluding chapter of the present work.

13. Rypka, *History of Iranian Literature,* 207.

14. Khāqānī Shīrvānī, Afẓal al-Dīn Badīl b. ʿAlī, *Dīvān-i Khāqānī-i Shīrvānī,* 548–52.

15. Rypka, *History of Iranian Literature,* 197–99.

16. Anvarī, Awḥad al-Dīn ʿAlī, *Dīvān-i Anvarī,* 765–70.

17. Jan Rypka, *History of Iranian Literature,* 210–13. Niẓāmī is also considered to be an influential figure in the development of the form *maṣnavī.* De Bruijn describes his contribution as "systematization of technical principles which were used by earlier *maṣnavī* writers"—see J. T. P. De Bruijn, *Of Piety and Poetry,* 189.

18. Niẓāmī Ganjavī, Ilyās b. Yūsuf, *Dīvān-i qaṣā'id va ghazalīyāt-i Niẓāmī-i Ganjavī,* 259–64.

19. Jan Rypka, *History of Iranian Literature,* 252.

20. Musharrif al-Dīn b. Muṣliḥ al-Dīn Saʿdī, *Kullīyāt-i Saʿdī,* 411.

21. Saʿdī, *Kullīyāt,* 415.

22. *Īn kuzah'gar-i dahr chinīn jām-i laṭīf // mī-sāzad u bāz bar zamīn mī-zanadash* (such a fine goblet, the potter of fate // makes only to break on the ground again) (ʿUmar Khayyām, *Tarānah'hā-yi Khayyām,* 83). For more on Khayyām, see Rypka, *History of Persian Literature,* 189–93.

23. Khayyām, *Tarānah'hā-yi Khayyām,* 84.

24. Pūrjavādī, Naṣr Allāh, *Zindagī va āṣār-i Shaykh Abū al-Ḥasan Bustī,* 55–58. Sufi manuals such as Najm Dāyah's *Mirṣād al-ʿibād min al-mabda' ilā al-maʿād* contain wide selections of such mystical *rubāʿīs*—see *The Path of God's Bondsmen from Origin to Return.*

25. Abū Saʿīd Abū al-Khayr, *Sukhanān-i manẓūm-i Abū Saʿīd-i Abū al-Khayr,* 14.

26. Aḥmad-i Jām, *Dīvān-i Shaykh Aḥmad-i Jām (Zhindah'Pīl),* 454. For Aḥmad-i Jām and his order the Jāmīs, see Ahmet Karamustafa, *God's Unruly Friends: Dervish Groups in the Islamic Later Middle Period, 1200–1500,* 78–81.

27. Rumi himself composed *rubāʿīs*, as well. Furūzān'far includes 1,983 in his edition of the *Dīvān*. Many of these contain paradoxical expressions such as *bīzāram az ān āb kih ātash nashavad* (I hate the water that does not become fire) *Dīvān-i Shams*, 8:135.

28. The definition of *shaṭḥ* given here is attributed to Ibn al-Khafīf in an anonymous manuscript quoted in Carl Ernst, *Words of Ecstasy in Sufism*, 21. For the whole range of topics in the *shaṭḥīyāt*, see pages 25–45 of the same work.

29. ʿAyn al-Quḍāt Hamadānī, *Tamhīdāt*, quoted in Ernst, *Words of Ecstasy in Sufism*, 77.

30. ʿAṭṭār, Farīd al-Dīn Muḥammad, *Tadhkirat al-auliyāʾ*, 114.

31. Sells, *The Mystical Languages of Unsaying*, 84–88.

32. A. E. Malloch, "The Technique and Function of the Renaissance Paradox," 193.

33. Rumi, *Masnavī*, 1:113.

34. Rosalie L. Colie, *Paradoxia Epidemica: The Renaissance Tradition of Paradox*, 7.

35. Sometimes the collection is called *Dīvān-i Kabīr*. The name of Shams, however, will appear on the cover or the title page.

36. Dawlat'shāh, *Tadhkirat al-shuʿarāʾ*, 148–49. Ẕabīh Allāh Ṣafā considers Rumi's adoption of "Shams" as his pen name responsible for the reputation of the collection as the *Dīvān-i Shams*—see *Tārīkh-i adabīyāt dar Iran*, 469.

37. Since some *ghazals* contain the word *khāmūsh* (silent) in their closing lines, the term has been mentioned as Rumi's possible nom de plume prior to adopting the name of his master Shams for this purpose. However, the number of such *ghazals* is considerably less than those that contain Shams's name—see Furūzān'far, *Risālah dar taḥqīq-i aḥvāl*, 148.

38. *khud gharībī dar jahān chūn Shams nīst*, the *Masnavī*, I: 119.

39. A reference to the frequently cited Sufi concept *ʿilm-i ladunni* (a knowledge from the divine presence) alluding specifically to chapter 18, verse 65 in the Qur'ān: . . . *wa-ʿallamnāhu min ladunna ʿilman*, (. . . and we endowed him with knowledge of our own)—see *The Qurʾān With Parallel Arabic Text*, 300.

40. The flexibility of the *ghazal* as a genre, despite its supreme conventionality, has been commented upon—see Meisami, *Medieval Persian Court Poetry*, 239–40.

41. Howard A. Slaatte, *The Pertinence of The Paradox: The Dialectics of Reason-In-Existence*, 241.

42. Quoted here is a parallel in Christian mysticism. See Nicholas of Cusa, *Of Learned Ignorance*, 17.

43. Despair in the face of the ineffable is not by any means unique to Rumi. Augustine's confessions are a good example: "What can anyman say when he speaks of thee? But woe to them that keep silence . . ." (Augustine, *Confessions*, I.iv.); the Muslim mystical tradition has numerous parallels. The tenth- and eleventh-century mystic of Herat, ʿAbd Allāh Anṣārī, for example, puts it this way: "I

have a pain for which there is no cure. My eyes fell upon something no tongue can describe." (ʿAbd Allāh Anṣārī, *Sukhanān-i Pīr-i Herāt*, 109).

44. In the *Fīhi mā fīh* (213), Rumi is explicit about his powerlessness in the face of the autonomy of the words: *Sukhan-i man bi-dast-i man nīst va az īn rū mī- ranjam. Zīrā kih mī-khvāham kih dūstān rā mawʿiẓah gūyam va sukhan munqād-i man namīshavad* . . . (My words are not under my control. For this reason I suffer. Because I intend to give advice to the friends, but the words do not obey me.) Rumi, using his paradoxical method of expression again, turns the weakness into strength. The autonomy of these words, he tells us, is a result of their divine nature. By the same virtue, he concludes, their reviving effect is of a far-reaching divine quality.

45. A metaphor borrowed from J. Hillis Miller, *The Linguistic Moment: From Wordsworth to Stevens*, 55.

46. Frye, *Anatomy of Criticism*, 250; for a fuller discussion of the dramatic quality in the Persian lyric poetry see the concluding chapter.

47. Colie, *Paradoxia Epidemica*, 35.

48. Andras Hamori, *On the Art of Medieval Arabic Literature*, 36.

Chapter 4—"How Sweetly with a Kiss Is the Speech Interrupted": Rumi's Poetics of Silence

1. The quotation in the title of this chapter is a translation of the following verse from the *Dīvān: Bi-zakhm-i būsih sukhan rā hamī chih khush shikanand!* (D, 218:6).

2. The concept of silence has been thoroughly explored in the second half of this century. Some of the major contributors are Max Picard, *The World of Silence;* Fernando Poyatos, *Man Beyond Words: Theory and Methodology of Non-verbal Communication*; Stephen A. Tyler, *The Said and the Unsaid: Mind, Meaning, and Culture;* Bernard P. Dauenhauer, *Silence: The Phenomenon and its Ontological Significance.*

3. Bruce Kawin, "On Not Having the Last Word: Beckett, Wittgenstein, and the Limits of Language," 196–97.

4. Wittgenstein, *Tractatus Logico-Philosophicus*, 6.51–6.522.

5. The tenth- and eleventh-century mystic of Herat ʿAbd Allāh Anṣārī (d. 1088) underscored the significance of silence during the advanced stages on the spiritual path in the phrase: "The true mystic is not revealed to the world. The tongue that can articulate divine knowledge is lifeless (it will not move to utter a word)"—see Anṣārī, *Sukhanān-i Pīr-i Herāt*, 6. Almost two centuries later, Saʿdī (d. 1292) echoed the same views in his *dībāchah* to the *Gulistān*: *ʿĀshiqān kushtigān-i maʿshūqand / barnayāyad zi-kushtigān āvāz* (The lovers have been slain by the beloved / No voice can come from the slain)—see Saʿdī, *Kullīyāt-i Saʿdī*, 29. For the English translation, see *The Gulistan or Rose Garden of Sa'di*, 59. For a discussion of the three responses to the dilemma of transcendence, including silence, see Michael A. Sells, *Mystical Languages of Unsaying*, 1–13.

6. Peggy Sue McCracken, *The Poetics of Silence in the French Middle Ages*, 3.

7. Jan Svartvik and Anna-Brita Stenstrom, "Words, Words, Words: The Rest is Silence?," 342–43, 352.

8. Kathleen Mullaney, "A Poetics of Silence: Derek Mahon 'At One Remove,' " 45–46.

9. Mark C. Taylor, "Sounds of Silence," 179–82.

10. Susan Sontag, "The Aesthetics of Silence," 196.

11. The term here rendered "silencing wine" in the original Persian is *khāmūshānah,* which emphasizes the silencing effect but is vague about the exact nature of the drink. The term wine has been chosen on the basis that the drink is supposed to have been served in a *paymānah* or wine cup.

12. On the intentionality of silence, see Dauenhauer, *Silence: The Phenomenon and its Ontological Significance.*

13. Cf. Kawin, "On Not Having the Last Word."

14. We shall return to Beckett's silence and its absurdist emphasis later in this section.

15. *Iḥrām* is the seamless clothing worn by the pilgrims to Mecca—see A. J. Wensinck and J. Jomier, "Iḥrām," *Encyclopaedia of Islam,* new ed., 3:1052–1053.

16. A reference to chapter 3, verse 97 in the Qur'ān concerning the house of *Ka'bah,* to which Muslims make an annual pilgrimage: *fīhi āyātun bayyinātun maqāmu Ibrāhīm wa-man dakhalahu kāna āminan* (In it there are veritable signs at the spot where Abraham stood. Whoever enters it is safe) (*The Qur'ān,* 61).

17. Sontag, "Aesthetics of Silence," 187.

18. The terms used for writing poetry are *guftan* or *surūdan,* which denote oral narration or singing as well. The implied oral nature of the act reinforces its revealing quality.

19. Although some of the images mentioned here in relation to silence (e.g., the green-robed preachers of the spring) are fairly original, some images, such as that of the many-tongued lily who despite its many tongues observes silence, have been frequently used before and after Rumi—see Shams al-Dīn Muḥammad Ḥāfiẓ Shīrāzī, *Dīvān,* 109.

20. Taylor, "Sounds of Silence," 178.

21. Ibid., 184, 186.

22. David J. Wren, "Abraham's Silence and the Logic of Faith," 159.

23. Renee Riese Hubert, "The Paradox of Silence: Samuel Beckett's Plays," 83.

24. Ibid., 83–84.

25. Alfred Corn, "Wallace Stevens and the Poetics of Ineffability," 180.

26. The phrase "project of spirituality" is used by Susan Sontag, "Aesthetics of Silence," 181.

27. The position of the Holocaust survivors vis-a-vis silence should not be reduced to the reaction of someone who has been through an extremely fearful

experience. These people witnessed a use of language to make Hitler's campaign possible and even deceive victims into cooperating in their own destruction. Using the same medium to express to the incredulous reader the true dimensions of the tragedy seemed out of the question. Most of these witnesses, therefore, opted for silence. For a literary analysis of stunned silence, see Marie Meisel Cedars, *Speaking Through Silence: The Art of Elie Wiesel*, 2.

28. Janice Sanders Moreno, "Silence in the Poetry of Leopoldo Lugones," 761.

29. McCracken, *The Poetics of Silence*, 8.

30. Ibid., 10.

31. The expression "interpretive opening" was suggested by McCracken, *Poetics of Silence*, 11.

32. *Gar chih tafsīr-i zabān raushan'gar ast/ Līk ʿishq-i bī-zabān raushan'tar ast*—see Rumi, *Maṯnavī*, 1:113.

33. The statement cited here was made about the significance of silence in the poetry of the twentieth-century Irish poet Derek Mahon—see Mullaney, "Poetics of Silence," 45.

34. Sontag uses the expression "participating in the ideal of silence" to point to the seriousness and commitment inherent in the message that this intentional silence sends—see "Aesthetics of Silence," 184.

35. For a discussion of this tension in Hindu literature, see Grazia Marchinana, "Beyond Poetry: Metaphysical Silence," 41–52.

36. D, 328:4; see the heading in the following chapter.

Chapter 5—"Wondrous Birds Grow from the Palm of My Hand": The Dynamism of Imagery in the *Dīvān*

1. The quotation in the title of this chapter is a translation of the following verse from the *Dīvān*: *Khud az kaf-i-dast-i man murghān-i ʿajab rūyand* (D, 328:4).

2. More comprehensive treatments will be found in the works of Annemarie Schimmel in chronological order: *The Triumphal Sun: A Study of the Works of Jalāloddin Rumi*; *As Through A Veil: Mystical Poetry in Islam*; and *Two-Colored Brocade*. Works that cover shorter time spans and more limited imagery will be cited as we progress.

3. "Rumi's Imagery," chapter 2 in Schimmel, *The Triumphal Sun*, and Ghulam M. Fayez, "Motion Imagery in Rumi and Whitman," are only two examples.

4. For example, an allusion Rumi made in *Fīhi mā fīh* to the contempt felt for the poet in his homeland has led to the generalization concerning Rumi's dislike for poetry—see chapter 2, note 3.

5. On the rigidity of Sufi idiom, see Schimmel's comments on the conventionality and predictability of the imagery (*As Through a Veil*, 58).

6. Ibid., 95.

7. Rosemond Tuve, *Elizabethan and Metaphysical Imagery: Renaissance Poetic and Twentieth-Century Critic*, 6.

8. For a standard definition of imagery at the turn of this century, particularly those applied to Elizabethan literature, see Henry W. Wells, *Poetic Imagery Illustrated From Elizabethan Literature*, 34.

9. Angus Fletcher, *Allegory: The Theory of a Symbolic Mode*, 2.

10. Ibid., 73.

11. The Persian for "if you sit face to face with me" reads *rukh bar rukh-i man nihī*, which could literally be translated as "if you put your face upon mine." The general message is "show you are close to me" so that I may reveal a secret. The term *rukh*, meaning the face, also refers to the rook in the game of chess. While this makes a nice pun, the idea of moving the rook on the chessboard corresponds to the concept of being checkmated in the next verse.

12. Rumi's habit of ending a *ghazal* with thematic allusions to beginning, and in particular his frequent suggestion that the readers compose the closing lines, is discussed in chapter 4 in detail.

13. Bakhtin uses this concept in relation to the primacy of context over text in what he terms "utterances" in a novel. It may be seen as a "condition governing the operation of meaning" in any text, according to Michael Holquist. He maintains that "all utterances are heteroglot in that they are functions of a matrix of forces practically impossible to recoup and therefore impossible to resolve." See Mikhail Mikhailovich Bakhtin, *The Dialogic Imagination: Four Essays by M.M. Bakhtin*, 428.

14. Collins, *Poetics of the Mind's Eye*, xii.

15. John Hollander, "The Footing of His Feet: On a Line of Milton's," 21–29.

16. Meisami, "Allegorical Gardens," 241.

17. Robert M. Rehder, "The Style of Jalāl al-Dīn Rumi," 276.

18. Ibid., 278.

19. This lack of attention in Persian traditional *ghazal* to the world at large is described by Shamīsā as *maḥdūdīyat-i lughāt va maẕāmīn* (the limited nature of words and concepts) permitted for use in the genre—see Shamīsā, *Sayr-i ghazal dar shiʿr-i fārsī*, 255–61.

20. Rehder, "Style of Jalāl al-Dīn Rumi," 281. Rehder's study contains brief insightful remarks on Rumi's attention to the concept of change. Unfortunately, his insightful comments on the poems are flawed by an urge to find concrete and conclusive explanations where uncertainty may be more helpful. He tells us, for instance, that the *Masnavī* has been preferred to the lyrics because of the belief that a longer poem is superior to a short one (283). This preference for the *Masnavī* is open to question; but even if it was not the case, Rehder's explanation would not have sufficed. One might remember, in this respect, that the *Rubāʿīyāt* of ʿUmar Khayyām are among the shortest and also the most popular poems.

21. For example, Fayez provides a long list of flight and bird imagery in "Motion Imagery in Rumi and Whitman," 40–45.

22. Some poets such as Naṣir-i Khusraw (d. 1072–1077) go as far as to equate laughter with lack of wisdom: *Khandah az bī- khiradī khīzad, chūn khandam man? kih khirad sakht giriftah ast garībānam* (Laughter is a sign of folly, how can I laugh?/ For I am firmly in the grip of wisdom). For more on the poet Nāṣir-i Khusraw, see Rypka, *History of Iranian Literature,* 185–89.

23. The difference in the personality should not be attributed to any difference in characterization of the sun and the moon. Elsewhere the moon exhibits the same warriorlike quality when its rise threatens to melt the sky (D, 164:10).

24. Fletcher is here referring to Aristotle—see Fletcher, *Allegory,* 76–77. Techniques that utilize surprise are common to the *Dīvān.* One of Rumi's favorites is what is today known to us as the inversion of the trope. The moon, for instance, acquires new metaphorical roles. Conventionally, it always represents the beloved. If the lover is ever likened to this heavenly figure, it is the pale and sickly lover wasting away, like the disappearing moon, with the desire for one glimpse of the full moon of the face of the beloved. In contradistinction to this cliché, in the *Dīvān* the lovers often thrive on love. They shine among a hundred people, as does "the shimmering moon among the stars" (D, 232:4).

25. For a study of *samāʿ* in Rumi, see Schimmel, *The Triumphal Sun,* 217–22.

26. "Our world" is the rendering for *dar u dīvār-i mā,* which, literally translated, means "our door and wall." This expression is often used to mean "everywhere," as in the following example in the celebrated *tarjīʿband* by Hātif Isfahānī (d. 1783–4): *yār bī-pardah az dar u dīvār// bi-tajallīst yā ūl al-abṣār* (Unveiled, the beloved has manifested himself from *the door and the wall* // behold! O the people blessed with eyesight)—see *Tarjīʿband-i Hātif,* 16.

27. I would refrain from calling this general characteristic an "iconographic method of personification," a phrase which Meisami uses in relation to garden imagery in Rumi. Her observation, however, makes sense with regard to the specific *ghazal* she quotes. See Meisami, "Allegorical Gardens," 242.

28. In the chapters to come, we shall look at the semantic, syntactic, and formalistic implications of reading the *Dīvān* as a manifestation of change.

29. The quality of indirectness of the speech, in which the poet does not directly address the readers, is not peculiar to the Persian lyric. Frye describes it as the poet "turning his back on his audience." It may be seen as a generic feature of the lyric. See Frye, *Anatomy of Criticism,* 271.

30. This well-known *ghazal* begins with the description of the beloved as follows: *zulf āshuftah u khuy kardah u khandān lab u mast.* See Ḥāfiẓ, *Dīvān,* 17.

31. *Sar farā gūsh-i man āvard* (she put her head close to my ear) is the expression used in the poem—see Ḥāfīẓ, *Dīvān,* 17.

32. It has been pointed out to me that the concept of the "reader" used here should be expanded beyond the reader of the page to include the participant in the *samāʾ* circle. After all, many of Rumi's *ghazals* were composed in such circles,

where the audience responded to the singing and interacted with the singer. This is an intriguing point for further investigation into the Persian mystical *ghazal*. The works of many *ghazal*-writers who showed affinity with *samāʿ* and live music, e.g. Aḥmad-i Jām, exhibit dramatic patterns similar to those of Rumi. At the same time, there is no question that Rumi maintained an authorial relation with the readers of the written text. Not only did he compose the *Masnavī* to be read and study other authors' written texts, but he addressed many of the *ghazals* in the *Dīvān* to generations to come.

33. Cf. an interesting discussion on search for symbolic meaning by Edwin Honig in his *Dark Conceit: The Making of Allegory*, 183.

34. The question of the role that generic conventions play is a fundamental concern of criticism. The view that these conventions should be seen as tools for communication and positive challenges to the artist rather than as hindrances to creativity is also a legitimate one. The concluding section of the present work will return to this issue in some detail.

35. Schimmel, *I Am Wind, You Are Fire*, 45.

36. Paradoxically, along with the need for defying control, there is praise for complete surrender. But this is not surprising in mystical love, which is fraught with paradoxes of all kind—see chapter 3 above.

37. What is translated in the first part of the verse as "physical needs" is in the original a specific allusion to the senses of smell and vision: *tu asīr-i bū u rangī*. *Bū u rang* (more often in the reverse order *rang u bū*) commonly denote the general physical characteristics of things.

38. A dove in Persian utters the words *kū, kū*, which literally mean "where is." Here Rumi makes a playful pun by repeating the word *kū* three times in the first hemistich.

39. Schimmel, *Two-Colored Brocade*, 192–200.

40. The Persian is as follows: *Ay magas ʿarṣah-'i Sīmurgh nah jawlān'gah-i tust // ʿIrz-i khud mī-barī u zaḥmat-i mā mīdārī* (O fly! the arena in which a *sīmurgh* flies is not suited to you // you are making a show of your incompetence and giving us unnecessary trouble [by trying to imitate *Sīmurgh*]) (Ḥāfiẓ, *Dīvān*, 281).

41. Rumi, *Dīvān*, *ghazals* 1623–1723.

42. Ḥāfiẓ, *Dīvān*, 3, 17.

43. Ibid., *ghazals* 1–100.

44. Fletcher, *Allegory*, 105.

45. Meisami, "Allegorical Gardens," 242.

Chapter 6—"A Hundred Drums Are Being Played in My Heart": The Intricacies of the Sonic Game

1. Among contemporary critics, ʿAlī Dashtī refers to this phenomenon as the dominance of the *awzān-i ẓarbī* or meters with a distinct beat and considers it a result of Rumi's affinity with music and the composition of the *ghazals* during

*samā*ʿ sessions. See ʿAlī Dashtī, 23. Two other contemporary critics, Shafīʿī Kadkanī and Furūzān'far, express similar views. Their comments on the *Dīvān*, due to their extent and significance, will be discussed in detail later in the present chapter. The quotation used in the title of this chapter is a translation of the following verse from the *Dīvān: Ṣad duhul mīzanand dar dil-i mā* (D, 246:1).

2. For an interesting discussion of the Darwinian view that humans retain the tidal rhythms of the sea from which they come, the significance of harmony between the two, and its reflection in poetry, see Emilie Sobel "Rhythm, Sound and Imagery in the Poetry of Gerard Manley Hopkins," 431. For examples of Rumi's relationship with nature, see the section in chapter 5 titled "The Enactment of Freedom in the *Dīvān*."

3. George Lansing Raymond, *Rhythm and Harmony in Poetry and Music together with Music as a Representative Art*, 2.

4. Peter Levi, *The Noise Made by Poems*, 78.

5. The term was used by Hollander in *Melodious Guile*.

6. Walter Bernhart, in "The Iconic Quality of Poetic Rhythm," 209, speaks in detail of the two aspects of poetic rhythm mentioned here.

7. Louis L. Martz, *The Poetry of Meditation*, 39.

8. Rene Wellek and Austin Warren, "Euphony, Rhythm, and Meter," 63–75.

9. For a discussion of meter in different languages, see Wellek and Warren, "Euphony, Rhythm, and Meter," 74. A strong proponent of the irrelevance of stress in Persian meter is Laurence Paul Elwell-Sutton, *The Persian Meters*, 220–22. Jeannine Marie Heny, in her meticulous study *Rhythmic Elements in Persian Poetry*, devotes a whole chapter to "Stress Patterns in Persian Poetry." This detailed and comprehensive doctoral dissertation is the most exhaustive investigation so far into the Persian prosodic system. The results of this inquiry (281–337) show that stress patterns are in fact fairly significant in certain Persian meters.

10. Bernhart, "Iconic Quality," 209.

11. George Raymond, for instance, conducted long and laborious research to demonstrate that central elements of poetic rhythm such as accent and pause are physiologically embedded in our speech habits and as such are inseparable from the art of poetry—see Raymond, *Rhythm and Harmony in Poetry and Music*, 2.

12. In this respect, Wellek and Warren observe "each stress has its own peculiarities according to its position in the verse"—see "Euphony, Rhythm and Meter," 72.

13. Luigi Ronga, *The Meeting of Poetry and Music*, 156.

14. Hollander, *Melodious Guile*, 6.

15. Levi, *Noise Made by Poems*, 76, 82.

16. Marina Tarlinskaja, "Rhythm-Morphology-Syntax-Rhythm," 23.

17. For Abrams's four categories of literary theories based on the communication model, see *The Mirror and the Lamp: Romantic Theory and the Critical Tradition*, 3–29.

18. These, in the case of the *ghazal*, are supposed to be derivatives of twenty to twenty-four main meters. For an overview of different approaches, see the section on *ʿarẓ-i ghazal* in Shamīsā, *Sayr-i ghazal dar shiʿr-i fārsī*, 214–30.

19. Elwell-Sutton, *Persian Meters*, 83–85.

20. Heny, *Rhythmic Elements in Persian Poetry*, 16.

21. Furūzān'far, *Risālah dar taḥqīq-i aḥvāl*, 34–46.

22. Shafīʿī Kadkanī, *Mūsīqī-i Shiʿr*, 389. He uses the term *Manẓūmah-'i Shamsī*, which refers to the solar system, as a pun for the *Dīvān*, which is *manẓūmah* because it is versified and is *Shamsī* insofar as it contains the name of Shams in its commonly known title.

23. Shafīʿī Kadkanī, *Musīqī-i Shiʿr*, 403.

24. Schimmel, *I Am Wind, You Are Fire*, 197–200.

25. Darlene D. Mettler, *Sound and Sense: Musical Allusions and Imagery in the Novels of Iris Murdoch*, 45–59.

26. Shafīʿī Kadkanī, *Mūsīqī-i Shiʿr*, 403.

27. Aflākī, *Manāqib al-ʿārifīn*, 2: 709–11.

28. A reference to chapters 36 and 110 in the Qurʾān, known as *Yā'sīn* and *al-Naṣr*, respectively.

29. This is in line with the findings of Marie Heny in *Rhythmic Elements in Persian Poetry*.

30. The "cave" and the "beloved" are associated through a reference to Muḥammad and his companion Abū Bakr staying in a cave. Together they hid from the pursuing Meccans during their migration from Mecca to Medina, the event that marked the beginning of the Islamic calendar: "The two of them stayed in the cave for three days" (Ibn Ishaq, *The Life of Muhammad: A Translation of Ibn Ishaq's Sirat Rasul Allah*, 224).

31. This explicitly shows that Elwell-Sutton's observation concerning the haphazard stress patterns in quantitative prosodic systems and their variable number per line does not accurately assess their significance for the rhythm of the verse—see Elwell-Sutton, *Persian Meters*, 222.

32. A most interesting discussion of repetition in Persian *qaṣīdah* in general, and in the poetry of Manūchihrī in particular, may be found in Jerome W. Clinton's critical study of this poet's *Dīvān*. On a different but equally significant note, Clinton points out for the first time that "the permutations of repetition" are a usual way to preserve a sense of unity in these poems—see *The Dīvān of Manūchihrī Dāmghānī: A Critical Study*, 57–58.

33. The question of unity in the medieval Persian *ghazal* will be discussed in some detail in the concluding chapter.

Chapter 7—"The Rhyme and the Sophistry, Let the Flood Take Them All": The Rhythm of Childhood in the Quest for Love

1. The quotation in the title of this chapter is a translation of the following verse from the *Dīvān: Qāfiyah u maghlaṭah rā gū hamah saylāb bibar!* (D, 38:3).

2. Bernhart, "The Iconic Quality of Poetic Rhythm," 211.

3. The evolution of this idea is analysed by John Hollander in *The Untuning of the Sky: Ideas of Music in English Poetry 1500–1700.*

4. Hollander, *The Melodious Guile*, 13.

5. For the association of the beloved, friend, or companion and the cave, see chapter 6, note 31.

6. This idea is by no means exclusive to Rumi. A classical example of such a view in relation to English poetry is that of George Herbert, apparent in his reaction to those who criticized his constant revision of his old poems:

> The friends that have it I do wrong,
> Whenever I remake a song,
> Should know what issue is at stake;
> It is myself that I remake

(Quoted in Louis L. Martz, *The Poetry of Meditation*, 321).

7. Ibid., 25–43.

8. Not surprisingly, the practice of whirling as a "parallel" to his poetry has caught the imagination of scholars of Rumi. See the section on "Rumi's Ghazal as Dance" in "Ecstasy and Order: Two Structural Principles in the Ghazal Poetry of Jalāl al-Dīn Rumi," J. C. Bürgel's contribution in *The Legacy of Mediaeval Persian Sufism*, 72.

9. Beth Bjorklund, "Elements of Poetic Rhythm: Stress, Syllabicity, Sound, and Sense," 351.

10. Hollander, *Melodious Guile*, 133–35.

11. The refrain, which is called *radīf* in Persian, consists of a word or words which come after the rhyme and get repeated throughout the *ghazal*. Shafīʿī Kadkanī, *Mūsqī-i Shiʿr* (409–11), observes that refrains used in the *Dīvān* are longer and more varied in comparison than those in the lyrics of Saʿdī and Ḥāfiẓ.

12. Sobel, "Rhythm, Sound, and Imagery."

13. Certain commonly known childlike qualities, such as mischief, do not require documentation, whereas some, like playfulness or exploration, might. The literature on childhood behavior is extensive. Michael Cole and Sheila R. Cole, *The Development of Children*, 2d ed. (New York; Oxford: Scientific American Books, 1993), is noteworthy for its encyclopedic inclusion of divergent early and recent

views; see p. 139 for the latest research that considers playfulness in babies as the major sign of regularity in their biological functions.

14. In chapter 5, based on my findings concerning Rumi's use of imagery, I concluded that playfulness is the most suitable general rubric to characterize these images.

15. For Dashtī's comment see the present chapter, note 1. Cf. Heny's study, *Rhythmic Elements in Persian Poetry*, 260.

16. For W. K. Wimsatt's theories of such effects, see Wellek and Warren, "Euphony, Rhythm, and Meter," 65.

17. Heny, *Rhythmic Elements in Persian Poetry*, 208–21. The English translation of the example quoted above is also by Heny.

18. The phrases in inverted commas comprise a definition of versified language that Wellek and Warren offer based on the Russian Formalist view ("Euphony, Rhythm and Meter," 73).

19. Rumi's rhythmic utilization of stress-patterns is also substantiated by Heny's study. Incidentally, this is another reason why Elwell-Sutton's insistence on the irrelevance of stress-patterns for Persian poetry should be re-examined. See Heny, *Rhythmic Elements in Persian Poetry*, 323. For more on Elwell-Sutton, see chapter 6, note 9.

20. "Pre-reaching," or the attempt to reach out and explore, has been recognized as one of the first reflexes that does not disappear but instead continues to develop in human beings—see Michael Cole and Shiela R. Cole, *The Development of Children*, 181.

21. Safīʿī Kadkanī, *Musīqī-i Shiʿr*, 401, 406.

22. This is part of a complex phenomenon known in the literature on the development of verbal skills in children as *conversational acts*—see Michael Cole and Sheila R. Cole, *The Development of Children*, 292.

23. Hollander, *The Melodious Guile*, 40.

24. Cole and Cole, *The Development of Children*, 292.

25. Heny, *Rhythmic Elements in Persian Poetry*, 116, 141.

26. Ibid., 82–93.

27. *Dūgh* is churned sour milk, whey, buttermilk (F. Steingass, *A Comprehensive Persian-English Dictionary*, 2nd ed. [New Delhi: Oriental Reprint], 545).

28. The best-known version of this trope appears in the two highly lyrical lines which open the *Mas̱navī*, a primarily didactic work. See Jalāl al-Dīn Rumi, *The Mas̱navī*, 1:1–2. The idea of separation from the origin finds numerous echoes in the *Dīvān*, too. Our souls rush like running floods to reunite with the ocean of souls (D, 7:13), and the rose receives the poet's message to find a remedy for its separation from the rose garden (D, 13:1). Elsewhere, the pain of separation from the origin is compared to pain felt in a limb which is severed from the body (D, 43:11).

Chapter 8—Turning the Funeral into a Whirling Dance: Remapping the Generic Horizons

1. Although Schimmel, in *I Am Wind, You Are Fire,* has described fine examples of classical Persian *ghazal* as diamondlike (45), the view of poetry as a valuable *object* has been around for some time. Cf. the use of the noun *naqd* (money, valuables) and the verb *naqd* (separating true from false coins) in the expression *naqd-i adabī* (literary criticism)—see Dihkhudā, *Lughat'nāmah,* s.v. *naqd.*

2. Alastair Fowler, *Kinds of Literature: An Introduction to the Theory of Genres and Modes,* 1.

3. Murray Krieger, *Words About Words About Words,* 17–18.

4. Fowler, *Kinds of Literature,* 11, 143, 156.

5. Using appropriate theoretical models to avoid superficial and arbitrary application across cultures is, of course, an added difficulty.

6. Fowler, *Kinds of Literature,* 259, 261, 275.

7. For a summary of the various theories of the origin of the *ghazal,* see A. Bausani, "Ghazal, ii. In Persian Literature," 3:1033–36. Some Iranian scholars have shown interest in monogenesis and searched for individual writers who may be seen as the "inventor" of the genre. For an overview of works of the first *ghazal*-writers and for the so-called first surviving *ghazal,* see Shamīsā, *Sayr-i ghazal dar shiʿr-i fārsī,* 43–44.

8. Meisami points to the survival of the *qaṣīdah* regardless of the popularity of the *ghazal*—see *Medieval Persian Court Poetry,* 237–98.

9. On the tradition of demonstrating the ability to treat old subjects in a novel way, see Meisami, "Norms and Conventions of the Classical Persian Lyric," 203–07.

10. Khāqānī, *Dīvān,* 60; for more examples of Rumi's imitation of Khāqānī, see Shamīsā, *Sayr-i ghazal dar shiʿr-i fārsī,* 90.

11. For a comprehensive and meticulous study of this tradition, see De Bruijn, *Of Piety and Poetry.*

12. This flexibility has been commented upon by Meisami, *Medieval Persian Court Poetry,* 239–40.

13. Michael C. Hillmann, *Unity in the Ghazals of Hafez,* 8–9, 47–49.

14. The *ghazal* opens with the verse *agar ān Turk-i Shīrāzī bi-dast ārad dil-i mā rā / bi-khāl-i Hinduyash baskhsham Samarqand u Bukhārā rā* (If that Turkish beloved of Shīrāz returns my love // I shall give away [the cities] of Samarqand and Bokhara for her / his Indian mole)—see Ḥāfiẓ, *Dīvān,* 2. For Hillmann's comments, see *Unity in the Ghazals of Hafez,* 141–42.

15. Hillmann, *Unity in the Ghazals of Hafez,* 156 (no. 9). One may of course suggest that the *ghazal* had to be well known for any stories to be created around it.

16. The phrase has been used by Hillmann in relation to a *ghazal* he considers

incoherent (*Unity in the Ghazals of Hafez,* 141). In relation to the shared literary memory that supplies the storyline for the *ghazal,* my attention has been drawn to a fascinating practice which continues to this day. In Persian musical performances in *samāʿ* often the singer weaves into the song recitation of verses from other poets to enhance performance or provide a commentary on the original poem he sang. Here the audience is presupposed to be able to participate in the literary memory which makes the allusiveness and referentiality of these quotations meaningful. In this case, the audience is the community sustained by *samāʿ*. There are other parallels, such as the exegetical procedure applied by many Sufi writers to the Qurʾānic text. Here the author weaves freely into his text brief excerpts from the Qurʾān to provide personal commentary. The fragmented quality of the quotations is compensated by the fact that they resonate in the literary/spiritual memory of a presupposed audience.

17. Fowler, *Kinds of Literature,* 23.

18. Some scholars clearly speak of the development of two distinct currents among the *ghazal*-writers, namely the *ghazal-i ʿāshiqānah* (the *amorous ghazals*) and the *ghazal-i ʿārifānah* (the mystical *ghazals*), see Shamīsā, *Sayr-i ghazal dar shiʿr-i fārsī,* 130.

19. The thematic similarity and metrical parallels between the *ghazals* of Aḥmad-i Jām and some of Rumi's compositions are astonishing. On occasions, Rumi borrowed verbatim phrases and ideas from Aḥmad and left no doubt about his familiarity with the works of the former poet and his dedication to him. Cf. the following three *ghazals* beginning with *mā zindah bi-nūr-i kibriyāʾīm, ʿāshiqī bar man parīshānat kunam,* and *mā zi-bālāʾīm u bālā mī-ravīm* in the *Dīvān-i Shams* (D: 1665, 1756, and 1674) to the *ghazals* of Aḥmad-i Jām: *mā maẓhar-i dhāt-i kibriyāʾīm* and *āmadam tā bāz ḥayrānat kunam//az vujūd-i khud parīshānat kunam,* as well as *mā bi-pā-yi ʿishq bālā mī-ravīm* in the *Dīvān-i Shaykh Aḥmad-i Jām (Zindah Pīl)* (311, 313). Furthermore, Ahmad's participation in *samāʿ* sessions points to his belief in the affinity of poetry and music and their utilization for spiritual development, something else he shared with Rumi. The corpus of his colorful poetry, which numbers around two thousand verses, remains critically unstudied.

20. De Bruijn, *Of Piety and Poetry,* 180.

21. Rumi, *Masnavī,* 1:111.

22. Meisami, *Medieval Persian Court Poetry,* 81–82.

23. *Daf* is a Persian percussion instrument made with animal skin.

24. Using the word *zakhmah* in the sense of a plectrum, here Rumi creates a pun with the word *zakhm* (wound), evoking the medical practice of bloodletting and therefore referring allegorically to the curative effects of the *samā*ʾ.

25. A reference to the Qurʾanic verse (15:29) addressed to the angels concerning the creation of the first human being, *Fa idhā sawwaytuhu wa-nafakhtu fīhi min ruḥī faqaʿū lahu sājidīn* (when I have fashioned him and breathed of My spirit into him, kneel down and prostrate yourselves before him) (*The Qurʾān,* 262).

26. Meisami accurately lists the above as the main conventional topic of lyric—see "Norms and Conventions of the Classical Persian Lyric," 203–04.

27. See chapter 3 on paradox.

28. On these stock characters in Persian lyric poetry, see Meisami, *Medieval Persian Court Poetry*, 264–66.

29. See the discussion on the versatility of the poetic voice in chapter 5.

30. For an elaborate discussion of Manūchirī's approach to describing nature, see Clinton, *Dīvān of Manūchirī*, 100–10.

31. For an example of the poetic voice heard from natural elements, see chapter 5.

32. Shamīsā describes mystical lyricism of post-Mongol Iran as marked with passivity, hopelessness, and defeat—see *Sayr-i ghazal dar shiʿr-i fārsī*, 83–84. The emotion at the heart of the Arabic *ghazal* has also been characterized as pernicious, debilitating, and antisocial—see Hamori, *On the Art of Medieval Arabic Literature*, 38.

33. Meisami, *Medieval Persian Court Poetry*, 253–55.

34. On court poet and the need for oblique expression, see Meisami, *Medieval Persian Court Poetry*, 14–18.

35. Frye, *Anatomy of Criticism*, 250.

36. Khāqānī, *Dīvān*, 99.

37. For more on the Arab poet Ḥassān ibn Thābit, see W. ʿArafat, "Ḥassān b. Thābit," *The Encyclopaedia of Islam*, 3:271–73.

38. Khāqānī, *Dīvān*, 100.

39. Ḥāfiẓ, *Dīvān*, 106.

40. Besides this indirect confession to love, there are other examples, such as the plea for help: " What is the cure? help me O Muslims!"—see Ḥāfiẓ, *Dīvān*, 136, 61. Even when the tone is more personal and the audience is narrowed to "friends," the message, despite its higher degree of intimacy, remains general and emotionally distant: "O friends! do not blame Ḥāfiẓ for looking at beauty" (224).

41. Concerning the courtly *ghazal*, Meisami observes: "The initial impression of spontaneity, or of 'sincerity,' produced by its ostensible status as a love lyric that expresses personal emotion gives way, on reading many such poems, to a conviction of its repetitiveness and extreme conventionality" (*Medieval Persian Court Poetry*, 239). While this does not apply to all *ghazals*, not even to all courtly *ghazal*, it gives an accurate reflection of how in the vast majority of the cases repetitiveness and conventionality have obscured the finer qualities of the genre.

42. Fowler, *Kinds of Literature*, 32.

43. Meisami, *Medieval Persian Court Poetry*, 82.

44. *Hayhāt* and *hayhā*, a corruption of the same term, in Persian means "alas" or "woe to me!"—see F. Steingass, *A Comprehensive Persian-English Dictionary*.

BIBLIOGRAPHY

Abrams, M. H. *The Mirror and the Lamp: Romantic Theory and the Critical Tradition.* New York: Oxford University Press, 1953.

Abū Saʿīd Abū al-Khayr. *Sukhanān-i Manẓūm- i Abū Saʿīd Abū al-Khayr* [1356], ed. Saʿīd Nafīsī. Tehran: Kitābkhānah-ʾi Sanāʾī, 1977.

Addas, Claude. *Quest for the Red Sulphur: The Life of Ibn ʿArabī.* Cambridge, U.K.: Islamic Texts Society, 1993.

Aflākī, Shams al-Dīn Aḥmad. *Manāqib al-ʿārifīn*, ed. Tahsin Yazıcı. 2 vols. Ankara: Türk Tarih Kurumu Yayınları, 1980.

Aḥmad-i Jām. *Dīvān-i Shaykh Aḥmad-i Jām (Zhindah Pīl)* [1365], ed. Aḥmad Karamī. Tehran: Nashrīyāt-i Mā, 1989.

Anṣārī, ʿAbd Allāh. *Sukhanān-i Pīr-i Herāt* [1361], ed. Muḥammad Javād Sharīʿat. Tehran: Shirkat-i Sihāmī-i Kitāb'hā-yi Jībī, 1982.

Anvarī, Awḥad al-Dīn ʿAlī. *Dīvān-i Anvarī* [1364], vol. 2, ed. Muḥammad Taqī Mudarris Raḍavī. [Tehran]: Shirkat-i Intishārāt-i ʿIlmī va Farhangī, 1985.

ʿArafat, W. "Ḥassān b. Thābit." *The Encyclopaedia of Islam*, new ed., 3: 271–73.

Ateş, A. "Ibn al- ʿArabī." *The Encyclopaedia of Islam*, new ed., Leiden: E. J. Brill, 1960– . 3: 707–11.

ʿAṭṭār, Farīd al-Dīn Muḥammad. *Tadhkirat al-auliyāʾ* [1361], ed. Nāṣir Hayyirī. Tehran: Intishārāt-i Chikāmah, 1982.

Augustine. *Confessions and Enchiridion*, trans. Albert C. Outler. Philadelphia: The Westminster Press, 1955.

Bahāʾ al-Dīn Valad. *Valad'nāmah* [1315], ed. Jalāl Humāʾī. Tehran: Kitāb'furūshī va Chāp'khānah-ʾi Iqbāl, 1936.

Bakhtin, Mikhail Mikhailovich. *The Dialogic Imagination: Four Essays by M.M. Bakhtin*, ed. Michael Holquist. Trans. Caryl Emerson and Michael Holquist. Austin: University of Texas Press, 1981.

Banānī, Amīn. "Rūmī the Poet." In *Poetry and Mysticism in Islam: the Heritage of Rūmī*, ed. Amīn Banānī, Richard Hovannisian, and Georges Sabagh. Cambridge: Cambridge University Press, 1994. 28–43.

Barnstone, Willis. *The Poetics of Ecstasy: Varieties of Ekstasis from Sappho to Borges.* New York & London: Holmes & Meier, 1983.

Bausani, A. "Ghazal, ii. In Persian Literature." *The Encyclopaedia of Islam*, new ed., Leiden: E.J. Brill, 1960– . 2:1033–36.

Bernhart, Walter. "The Iconic Quality of Poetic Rhythm," *Word & Image* 2, no. 3 (1986): 209–217.

Bjorklund, Beth. "Elements of Poetic Rhythm: Stress, Syllabicity, Sound, and Sense," *Poetics* 8 (1979): 351–65.

Bürgel, Johann Christoph. "Ecstasy and Order: Two Structural Principles in the Ghazal Poetry of Jalāl al-Dīn Rumi." In *The Legacy of Mediaeval Persian Sufism*, ed. Leonard Lewisohn. New York & London: Khaniqahi Nimatullahi Publications, 1992. 61–74.

———. *The Feather of Simurgh: The "Licit Magic" of the Arts in Medieval Islam*. New York & London: New York University Press, 1988.

———. "'Speech is a Ship and Meaning the Sea': Some Formal Aspects of the Ghazal Poetry of Rūmī." In *Poetry and Mysticism in Islam: The Heritage of Rūmī*, ed. Amin Banani, Richard Hovannisian, and Georges Sabagh. Cambridge: Cambridge University Press, 1994. 44–69.

Caputo, John D. *The Mystical Element in Heidegger's Thought*. Athens: Ohio University Press, 1978.

Cedars, Marie Meisel. *Speaking Through Silence: The Art of Elie Wiesel*. Ph.D. dissertation, University of Texas at Arlington, 1984.

Chittick, William. *The Sufi Path of Love: The Spiritual Teachings of Rumi*. Albany: State University of New York Press, 1983.

Clinton, Jerome W. *The Dīvān of Manūchihrī Dāmghānī: A Critical Study*. Minneapolis: Bibliotheca Islamica, 1972.

Colie, Rosalie L. *Paradoxia Epidemica: The Renaissance Tradition of Paradox*. Princeton, N.J.: Princeton University Press, 1966.

Collins, Christopher. *The Poetics of the Mind's Eye: Literature and the Psychology of Imagination*. Philadelphia: University of Pennsylvania Press, 1991.

Corn, Alfred. "Wallace Stevens and the Poetics of Ineffability." In *Ineffability: Naming the Unnamable from Dante to Beckett*, ed. Peter S. Hawkins and Anne Howland Schotter. New York: AMS Press, 1984. 179–87.

Dashtī, ʿAlī. *Sayrī dar Dīvān-i Shams* [1362]. [Tehran]: Intishārāt-i Jāvīdān, 1983.

Dauenhauer, Bernard P. *Silence: The Phenomenon and Its Ontological Significance*. Bloomington: Indiana University Press, 1980.

Davis, Elizabeth B. "The Power of Paradox in the 'Cantico espiritual,'" *Revista de Estudios Hispanicos* 2 (1993): 204–23.

Dawlat'shāh Samarqandī. *Tazkirat al-shuʿarāʾ* [1338]. Tehran: Khāvar, 1959.

De Bruijn, J. T. P. *Of Piety and Poetry: The Interaction of Religion and Literature in the Life and Works of Ḥakīm Sanāʾī of Ghazna*. Leiden: E. J. Brill, 1983.

Derrida, Jacques. *Writing and Difference*, trans. Allan Bass. Chicago: University of Chicago Press, 1978.

Dihkhudā, ʿAlī Akbar. *Lughat'nāmah* [1348]. Tehran: Tehran University Press, 1969.

Elwell-Sutton, Laurence Paul. *The Persian Meters*. Cambridge: Cambridge University Press, 1976.

Ernst, Carl W. *Words of Ecstasy in Sufism*. Albany: State University of New York Press, 1985.

Everman, Welch D. *Who Says This?: The Authority of the Author, the Discourse, and the Reader*. Carbondale & Edwardsville: Southern Illinois University Press, 1988.

Fayez, Ghulam M. "Motion Imagery in Rumi and Whitman," *Walt Whitman Review* 25 (1979): 39–51.

Fletcher, Angus. *Allegory: The Theory of a Symbolic Mode*. Ithaca, N.Y.: Cornell University Press, 1964.

Flew, Antony, ed. *A Dictionary of Philosophy*. 2d rev. ed. New York: St. Martin's Press, 1984.

Foti, Veronique M. *Heidegger and the Poets: Poiesis, Sophia, Techne*. Atlantic Highlands, N.J. & London: Humanities Press, 1992.

Fowler, Alastair. *Kinds of Literature: An Introduction to the Theory of Genres and Modes*. Cambridge, Mass.: Harvard University Press, 1982.

Frye, Northrop. *Anatomy of Criticism: Four Essays*. Princeton, N.J.: Princeton University Press, 1971.

Furūzān'far, Badīʿ al-Zamān. *Risālah dar taḥqīq-i aḥvāl va zindigānī-i Maulana Jalāl al-Dīn Muḥammad* [1333]. Tehran: Kitāb'furūshī-i Zavvār, 1954.

Gölpınarlı, Abdülbaki. *Mevlānā Celāleddin: Hayatı, Felsefesi, Eserlerinden Seçmeler*. Istanbul: Varlık, 1952. (Persian translation: *Mawlānā Jalāl al-Dīn: zindagānī, falsafah, āthār va guzīdah-'ī az ānhā* [1363], trans. and notes by Tawfiq Subhani. Tehran: Muʿassasah-'i Muṭālaʿāt va Taḥqīqāt-i Farhangī, 1984.

Ḥāfiẓ Shīrāzī, Shams al-Dīn Muḥammad. *Dīvān* [1365], ed. Muḥammad Qazvīnī and Qāsim Ghanī. Tehran: Eqbal, 1986.

Hamori, Andras. *On the Art of Medieval Arabic Literature*. Princeton, N.J.: Princeton University Press, 1974.

Hātif Isfahānī. *Tarjīʿband-i Hātif*. Oakland, Cal.: Iranzamin, [n.d.].

Heath, Peter. *Allegory and Philosophy in Avicenna (Ibn Sīnā) with a Translation of the Book of the Prophet Muḥammad's Ascent to Heaven*. Philadelphia: University of Pennsylvania Press, 1992.

Heidegger, Martin. *Being and Time*, trans. John Macquarrie and Edward Robinson. London: SCM Press, 1962.

———. *Frühe Schriften*. Frankfurt: Vittorio Klostermann, 1972.

Heny, Jeannine Marie. *Rhythmic Elements in Persian Poetry*. Ph.D. Dissertation, University of Pennsylvania, 1981.

Hillmann, Michael C. *Unity in the Ghazals of Hafez*. Minneapolis & Chicago: Bibliotheca Islamica, 1976.

Hollander, John. "The Footing of His Feet: On a Line of Milton's." In *On Poetry and Poetics, Swiss Papers in English Language and Literature* 2, ed. Richard Waswo. Tübingen: Bunter Narr, 1985. 21–29.

———. *Melodious Guile: Fictive Pattern in Poetic Language*. New Haven & London: Yale University Press, 1988.

———. *The Untuning of the Sky: Ideas of Music in English Poetry 1500–1700* (Princeton, N.J.: Princeton University Press, 1961).

Honig, Edwin. *Dark Conceit: The Making of Allegory*. Evanston: Northwestern University Press, 1959.

Hubert, Renee Riese. "The Paradox of Silence: Samuel Beckett's Plays," *Mundus Artium: A Journal of International Literature and the Arts* 2, no. 3 (1969): 82–90.

Ibn Ishāq. *The Life of Muhammad: A Translation of Ibn Ishaq's Sirat Rasul Allah*, trans. A. Guillaume. Oxford & New York: Oxford University Press, 1982.

Jakobson, Roman. "Concluding Statement: Linguistics and Poetics." In *Style in Language*, ed. Thomas A. Seboek. Cambridge, Mass.: MIT Press, 1960. 350–77.

Karamustafa, Ahmet T. *God's Unruly Friends: Dervish Groups in the Islamic Later Middle Period, 1200–1550*. Salt Lake City: University of Utah Press, 1994.

Kawin, Bruce. "On Not Having the Last Word: Beckett, Wittgenstein, and the

Limits of Language." In *Ineffability: Naming the Unnamable from Dante to Beckett*, ed. Peter S. Hawkins and Anne Howland Schotter. New York: AMS Press, 1984. 189–202.

Kaymaz, Nejat. *Pervane Muinuddin Süleyman*. Ankara: Ankara Üniversitesi Basımevi, 1970.

Khāqānī Shīrvānī, Afẓal al-Dīn Badīl b. ʿAlī. *Dīvān-i Khāqānī-i Shirvānī* [1357], ed. Ẓiyā' al-Dīn Sajjādī. Tehran: Intishārāt-i Zavvār, 1978.

Krieger, Murray. *Words About Words About Words: Theory, Criticism, and the Literary Text*. Baltimore & London: Johns Hopkins University Press, 1988.

Levi, Peter. *The Noise Made by Poems*. London: Anvil Press Poetry, 1977.

Magliola, Robert R. *Phenomenology and Literature: An Introduction*. West Lafayette, Ind.: Purdue University Press, 1977.

Malloch, A. E. "The Technique and Function of the Renaissance Paradox," SP, LIII (1956): 193.

Marchinana, Grazia. "Beyond Poetry: Methaphysical Silence." In *Studies in Mystical Literature*. Taichung: English Department of Tunghai University, 1980. 41–52.

Martz, Louis L. *The Poetry of Meditation: A Study of English Religious Literature of the Seventeenth Century*, rev. ed. New Haven & London: Yale University Press, 1962.

McCracken, Peggy Sue. *The Poetics of Silence in the French Middle Ages*. Ph.D. Dissertation, Yale University, 1989.

Meier, Fritz. *Bahā'-i Walad*. Acta Iranica, vol. 14. Leiden: E. J. Brill, 1989.

Meisami, Julie Scott. "Allegorical Gardens in the Persian Poetic Tradition: Nizami, Rumi, Hafez," *International Journal of Middle East Studies* 17 (1985): 229–60.

———. *Medieval Persian Court Poetry*. Princeton: Princeton University Press, 1987.

———. "Norms and Conventions of the Classical Persian Lyric: A Comparative Approach to the Ghazal." In *Proceedings of the Nineteenth Congress of the International Comparative Literature Association, Innsbruck 1979, I: Classical Models in Literature*. Innsbruck: Innsbrucker Beiträge zur Kulturwissenschaft, 1981. 203–7.

Menocal, Maria Rosa. *Shards of Love: Exile and the Origins of Lyric*. Durham, N.C. & London: Duke University Press, 1994.

Mettler, Darlene D. *Sound and Sense: Musical Allusions and Imagery in the Novels of Iris Murdoch*. New York: Peter Lang, 1991.

Miller, J. Hillis. *The Linguistic Moment: From Wordsworth to Steven*. Princeton, N.J.: Princeton University Press, 1985.

Moayyad, Heshmat. "Lyric Poetry." In *Persian Literature*, ed. Ehsan Yarshater. [New York]: Bibliotheca Persica, 1988. 120–46.

Moreno, Janice Sanders. "Silence in the Poetry of Leopoldo Lugones." *Hispania* 4 (December 1963): 760–63.

Mullaney, Kathleen. "A Poetics of Silence: Derek Mahon 'At One Remove.'" *The Journal of Irish Literature* 18, no. 3 (1989): 45–54.

Najm al-Dīn ʿAbd Allāh Muḥammad Rāzī "Dāyah." *The Path of God's Bondsmen from Origin to Return*, trans. Hamid Algar. Delmar, N.Y.: Caravan Books, 1982.

Nicholas of Cusa. *Of Learned Ignorance*, trans. Fr. Germaine Heron. New Haven: Yale University Press, 1954.

Niẓāmī-i Ganjavī, Ilyās b. Yūsuf. *Kullīyāt-i Khamsah-'i Niẓāmī-i Ganjavī* [1362], ed. Bāqir Mu'īn'far. Tehran: Intishārāt-i Zarrīn, 1983.

———. *Dīvān-i qaṣā'id va ghazalīyāt-i Niẓāmī Ganjavī* [1362], ed. Sa'īd Nafīsī [Tehran]: Intishārāt-i Furūghī, 1983.

Picard, Max. *The World of Silence*, trans. Stanley Godman. Chicago: Regnery, 1952.

Poyatos, Fernando. *Man Beyond Words: Theory and Methodology of Non-verbal Communication*. Oswego, N.Y.: The New York State English Council, 1976.

Pūrjavādī, Naṣr Allāh. *Zindagī va ās̱r-i Shaykh Abū al-Ḥasan Bustī* [1364]. Tehran: Mu'assasah-'i Muṭāla'āt-i Taḥqīqī va Farhangī, 1985.

The Qur'ān With Parallel Arabic Text, trans. N. J. Dawood. London: Penguin, 1990.

Raymond, George Lansing. *Rhythm and Harmony in Poetry and Music together with Music as a Representative Art: Two Essays in Comparative Aesthetics*, 2nd rev. ed. New York & London: Putnam, 1904.

al-Rāzī, Shams al-Dīn Muḥammad b. Qays. *al- Mu'jam fī ma'ā'īr ash'ār al-'ajam* [1338], ed. Muḥammad 'Alī Furūghī. Tehran: Kitābfurūshī-i Tehran, 1959.

Rehder, Robert M. "The Style of Jalāl al-Dīn Rumi." In *The Scholar and The Saint: Studies in Commemoration of Abu'l-Rayhan al-Bīrūnī and Jalal al-Din al-Rumi*, ed. Peter J. Chelkowski. New York: New York University Press, 1975. 275–85.

Ronga, Luigi. *The Meeting of Poetry and Music*, trans. Elio Gianturco and Cara Rosanti. New York: Merlin Press, 1957.

Rūmī, Jalāl al-Dīn. *Fīhi mā fīh* [1362], ed. Badī' al-Zamān Furūzān'far. Tehran: Amīr Kabīr, 1983. (English translations: *The Discourses of Rumi*, trans. A. J. Arberry. London: J. Murray, 1961; *Discourses of Rumi*, trans. Wheeler Thackston, Jr. Atlantic Highlands, N.J.; Humanities Press International, 1993.)

———. *Kullīyāt-i Shams yā Dīvān-i kabīr*, ed. Badī' al-Zamān Furūzān'far. Tehran: Amīr Kabīr, 1976.

———. *Mas̱navī-i ma'navī*, ed. and trans. Reynold A. Nicholson. 8 vols. London: Luzac, 1925–40.

Rypka, Jan. *History of Iranian Literature*, ed. Karl Jahn. Trans. P. van Popeta-Hope. Dordrecht, Holland: Reidel, 1968.

Sa'dī, Musharrif al-Dīn b. Muṣliḥ al-Dīn. *Kullīyāt-i Sa'dī* [1366], ed. Muḥammad 'Alī Furūghī. Tehran: Amīr Kabīr, 1987.

———. *The Gulistan or Rose Garden of Sa'di*, trans. Edward Rehatsek. New York: Putnam, 1964.

Ṣafā, Ẕabīh Allah. *Tārīkh-i adabīyāt dar Iran* [1369], vol. 3, part 1. Tehran: Intishārāt-i Firdawsī, 1990.

Sainsbury, R. M. *Paradoxes*. Cambridge & New York: Cambridge University Press, 1988.

Schimmel, Annemarie. *A Two-Colored Brocade: The Imagery of Persian Poetry*. Chapel Hill & London: University of North Carolina Press, 1992.

———. *As Through a Veil: Mystical Poetry in Islam*. New York: Columbia University Press, 1982.

———. *I Am Wind, You Are Fire: The Life and Work of Rumi*. Boston & London: Shambhala, 1992.

———. *The Triumphal Sun: A Study of the Works of Jalāloddin Rumi*. London: Fine Books, 1978.

Sells, Michael A. *Mystical Languages of Unsaying*. Chicago & London: University of Chicago Press, 1994.

Shafīʿī Kadkanī, Muḥammad Riẕā. *Mūsīqī-i Shiʿr* [1368]. 2nd rev. ed. Tehran: Intishārāt-i Āgāh, 1989.

Shamīsā, Sīrūs. *Sayr-i ghazal dar shiʿr-i fārsī, az āghāz tā imrūz* [1362]. Tehran: Intishārāt-i Firdawsi, 1984.

Shams-i Tabrīzī. *Maqālāt-i Shams* [1358], ed. Muḥammad ʿAlī Muvaḥḥid. Tehran: Intishārāt-i ʿIlmī, 1979.

Sipahsālār, Farīdūn ibn Aḥmad. *Risālah dar aḥwāl-i Maulānā Jalāluddīn Rūmī [Risālah-'i Sipahsālār/Manāqib-i Khudavandgār]* [1325], ed. Badiʿ al-Zamān Furūzan'far. Tehran, 1946.

Slaatte, Howard A. *The Pertinence of The Paradox: The Dialectics of Reason-In-Existence*. New York: Humanities Press, 1968.

Smart, Ninian. "Interpretation and Mystical Experience." In *Understanding Mysticism*, ed. Richard Woods. New York: Image Books, 1980. 78–91.

Sobel, Emilie. "Rhythm, Sound and Imagery in the Poetry of Gerard Manley Hopkins." In *Between Reality and Fantasy*, ed. Simon A. Gronlick and Leonard Barkin. New York & London: Jason Aronson, n.d. 427–45.

Sontag, Susan. "The Aesthetics of Silence." In *A Susan Sontag Reader*. New York: Farrar Straus Giroux, 1982. 181–204.

Staiger, Emil. *Basic Concepts of Poetics (Grundbegriffe der Poetik)*, ed. Marianne Burkhard and Luanne T. Frank. Trans. Janette C. Hudson and Luanne T. Frank. University Park: Pennsylvania State University Press, 1991.

Steingass, F. *A Comprehensive Persian-English Dictionary*. New Delhi: Oriental Reprint, 1981.

Svartvik, Jan and Stenstrom, Anna-Brita. "Words, Words, Words: The Rest is Silence?" In *Papers on Language and Literature: Presented to Alvar Ellegard*, ed. Erik Frykman. Göteborg, Sweden: Acta Universitatis Gothoburgensis, 1985. 342–53.

Tadayyun, ʿAṭā' Allāh. *Maulānā va ṭūfān-i Shams* [1372]. Tehran: Intishārāt-i Tihrān, 1993.

Tarlinskaja, Marina. "Rhythm-Morphology-Syntax-Rhythm." *Style* 18, no. 1 (1984): 1–26.

Taylor, Mark C. "Sounds of Silence." In *Kierkegaard's Fear and Trembling: Critical Appraisals*, ed. Robert L. Perkins. University, Ala.: University of Alabama Press, 1981. 165–88.

Tuve, Rosemond. *Elizabethan and Metaphysical Imagery: Renaissance Poetic and Twentieth-Century Critic*. Chicago: University of Chicago Press, 1974.

Tyler, Stephen A. *The Said and the Unsaid: Mind, Meaning, and Culture*. New York: Academic Press, 1978.

ʿUmar Kayyām. *Tarānah'hā-yi Khayyām* [1342], ed. Ṣādiq Hidāyat. Tehran: Amīr Kabīr, 1963.

Vaṭvāṭ, Rashīd al-Dīn Muḥammad. *Ḥadā'iq al-sihr fī daqā'iq al-shiʿr* [1362], ed. *ʿAbbās* Iqbāl. [Tehran]: Kitābkhānah-yi *Sanā'ī* and Kitābkhānah-yi Ṭahūrī, 1983.

Wellek, Rene, and Austin Warren. "Euphony, Rhythm, and Meter." In *Discussions of Poetry: Rhythm and Sound,* ed. George Hemphill. Boston: Heath, 1961. 63–75.

Wells, Henry W. *Poetic Imagery Illustrated From Elizabethan Literature.* New York: Columbia University Press, 1924.

Wensinck, A. J., and J. Jomier. "Iḥrām." *The Encyclopaedia of Islam,* new ed., Leiden: E.J. Brill, 1960– . 3: 1052–53.

White, David A. *Heidegger and the Language of Poetry.* Lincoln & London: University of Nebraska Press, 1978.

Wimsatt, W. K. *The Verbal Icon: Studies in the Meaning of Poetry.* New York: Noonday Press, 1953.

Wittgenstein, Ludwig. *Tractatus Logico-Philosophicus,* trans. D. F. Pears and B. F. McGuiness. London: Routledge & Kegan Paul, 1961.

Wren, David J. "Abraham's Silence and the Logic of Faith." In *Kierkegaard's Fear and Trembling* ed. Robert L. Perkins. University, Ala.: University of Alabama Press, 1981. 152–64.

Ziai, Hossein. *Knowledge and Illumination: A Study of Suhrawardī's Ḥikmat al-Ishrāq.* Atlanta: Scholars Press, 1990.

INDEX

Printed in the United States
24955LVS00001B/283-294